PETE SEEGER
WITH DAVID BERNZ

CHOPPING WOOD

THOUGHTS & STORIES OF A LEGENDARY AMERICAN FOLKSINGER

JAW BONE

CHOPPING WOOD
Thoughts & Stories Of A
Legendary American Folksinger
Pete Seeger *with* **David Bernz**

A Jawbone book
First edition 2024
Published in the UK and the USA by
Jawbone Press
Office G1
141–157 Acre Lane
London SW2 5UA
England
www.jawbonepress.com

ISBN 978-1-916829-02-2

Printed by Short Run Press, Exeter

1 2 3 4 5 28 27 26 25 24

TABLE OF CONTENTS

FOREWORD
BY ARLO GUTHRIE

In August of 1990, I was in Denmark with Pete and Toshi. We were scheduled to perform together at the Tønder Folk Festival, and we'd arrived a few days early. We traveled around, visiting different ports taking in the sights and chatting with people who shared a similar love for wooden ships. We were invited to sail on the Fulton, a three-masted schooner built in 1915 and restored to her original condition. During the voyage a sudden fierce storm came up. We took shelter in the galley while most of the young people who were also aboard went below. But not Pete.

Pete stood at the helm as gigantic waves rocked the ship. The gale-force winds were blowing across the Baltic Sea, wreaking havoc. As I looked out from the galley, I saw Pete at the helm. He stood there like a statue, untroubled by the circumstance. I saw the mythic man, and I loved him all the more. I witnessed the mythic Pete, more true to himself than any version of reality. I knew and saw him as he truly was.

Pete enjoyed playing, innovating, being social, and loving solitude—but he was more than any one thing. The myth that lived in Pete lives in us all. But his true self was closer to the surface than most. I, for one, am a witness to it.

Pete also loved chocolate. While he was in a New York hospital, with little time left, I was in communication with his family. They told me that although Pete wanted a chocolate cake, his doctors had restricted his diet and said that a chocolate cake wasn't good for him. I immediately called members of my family and sent Pete a chocolate cake. He passed away a few days later.

ARLO GUTHRIE
NOVEMBER 2023

PREFACE
BY DAVID BERNZ

Many people know Pete Seeger as one of the world's great folksingers and songwriters, an icon whose contribution to peace through culture brought us all closer together as we vied, against history, for a saner, cleaner, safer world. But I also view Pete Seeger as one of America's greatest minds. Pete was a gifted conversationalist and storyteller, and he possessed an encyclopedic memory and an innate skill for synthesizing complex ideas into a few choice phrases. His combination of accessible music and captivating storytelling is why Pete, well into his nineties, remained one of the world's most effective communicators.

As the strength of his singing voice wavered with age, Pete relied more and more upon his abilities with spoken word. He honed his skills in this area further, not only by performing concert after concert but also through the process of answering question after question in literally thousands of interviews.

Pete was generous to a fault. I like to say that he'd give you the rocks off his own hill if you needed them, and I know that to be true because that's exactly what he once did for me when I was building a stone wall in my garden. Like Shel Silverstein's famous 'giving tree,' Pete didn't stop giving until there was nothing left of him, and while that worried his family, they largely came to accept it. Day in and day out, year after year, people asked Pete to speak into their microphones in support of one good cause after another, and most often Pete said yes. Requests came from radio stations and television outlets, newspapers and magazines from large publishers and tiny organizations; from peace activists, environmentalists, labor unions, authors, historians, and documentary filmmakers. Some made the trek up the mountain to his home in Beacon, New York; others brought Pete down to their studios. Some interviews were arranged months in advance; others occurred off the cuff, backstage at a concert or festival. Pete answered questions in person, over the telephone, over the internet, and even via a cellphone held up to the microphone on a concert stage.

All of this amounted to a heck of a lot of practice. Certain subjects tended to come up again and again, and many of Pete's answers developed into stories that he sharpened over time, focusing in on important details and excising the extraneous. I feel very fortunate to have been in a position to witness this evolution in a way that few others have.

Perhaps I should start at the beginning.

I came to Pete's music and his politics somewhat genetically—that is, I was born into them. My father, Harold Bernz, was one of seven kids in a not-so-well-to-do Jewish family in east New York. As a young man, he worked in tanning cellars in the garment district on the Lower West Side. The conditions were brutal, and talk of labor unions and workers' rights got his attention. Like many others, he became radicalized by the Great Depression, and soon he was helping to organize meetings. After serving in World War II, he developed an interest in folk music via labor songs, and by 1948 he was volunteering at the *People's Songs Bulletin*, where he was soon on the editorial board. The country's first urban folk-song magazine, *People's Songs Bulletin* had been organized by Pete Seeger, Lee Hays, and others of the pre-McCarthy era who still believed that a singing labor movement could unite workers to achieve a better life.

Harold and my mother, Ruth, met at a holiday party at the apartment of Pete Seeger's mother that December. Ruth Levine had grown up in middle-class Brooklyn, the daughter of a poet and an insurance executive. She excelled at piano and classical singing, and while still in her teens she sang in the American People's Chorus and recorded the original version of Earl Robinson's famous 'Ballad For America' with Paul Robeson at Carnegie Hall.

A good many folksingers wandered in and out of the *People's Songs* office. Of all of them, my father became closest with Hays, the whiskey-throated bass singer from Arkansas who later became a member of The Weavers. The two shared an apartment for about a year, with my father being part friend to Lee and part enabler. Fred Hellerman, one of the other volunteers at the magazine and later a co-patriot of Lee in The Weavers, used to say, 'Harold and Lee had an arrangement: Harold would buy the groceries, and Lee would eat them.'

My parents married in 1954 and started having children. By the time I came along in 1958, I already had an older brother, Jon, and an older sister, Judith.

Meanwhile, Lee was spending his time touring with The Weavers. But when Ruth and Harold moved their young family to suburban Croton-on-Hudson in 1959, Lee followed us up there, staying many a weekend and often longer. My earliest childhood memories include listening to 'Uncle' Lee, both on Weavers records and snoring on the living room couch. We also listened to the records of Pete Seeger, and I especially liked the stories such as 'Abyoyo' and 'Sam The Whaler' and 'The Foolish Frog,' which I listened to over and over again. It was the early 1960s, and I was only four or five years old, but that potent combination of robust optimism that permeated those Weavers records and the empowering messages built into Pete's stories did more to set my lifelong musical and political sensibilities than anything else. That, and volunteering for the Hudson River Sloop Clearwater at their festivals and concerts.

Pete and others had founded the *Clearwater* to help fight pollution in the Hudson River. Their fundraising concerts began in 1966, and the boat was launched in 1969. Hearing Pete singing at the waterfront became a common occurrence from that point on.

In 1970, I took up the guitar. By then, Lee Hays had given up on our couch and bought the house next door.

• • •

The Weavers, and later Pete, were managed by another family friend, a true gentleman named Harold Leventhal. When Pete needed to be driven to a concert, Harold liked to keep it 'in the family,' so, not long after my brother and I could drive, Harold would call upon one of us to take Pete wherever he needed to go. I drove Pete to places such as Westbury Long Island; Ithaca, New York; and Allentown, Pennsylvania. These were long drives, and Pete would want to talk in the car. I was more than happy to listen.

As we drove along, Pete would cover a wide range of topics, from music to politics to history to science. One minute he'd tell me how to build a canoe, the next he'd explain the best way to boil maple syrup. He even shared some jokes and limericks that I dare not repeat. I didn't know it at the time, but throughout all of this, I was honing a sense of Pete's 'voice'—his lilt and his cadence. Pete on the records, Pete at the waterfront, Pete on the concert stage, Pete in the car— one thing that strikes me is that these were all essentially the same.

After returning home from college in 1980, I began singing with some of the musical groups that supported Clearwater, first in the Walkabout Clearwater Chorus and later with the Hudson River Sloop Singers. Pete joined us for many of our concerts, and although not everyone would admit it, it was always a bit of a thrill to be with him onstage. Our focus and energy were always sharper when he was around.

In the mid-1980s, Pete started having some trouble with his voice, and he began to shy away from solo performances and to rely more and more on others to help carry the programs. I suppose that's why he asked some of us to join him in 1990 at a well-publicized event in a large New York City nightclub in support of the *Daily News* strikers. The core of that group—myself, Caryl Towner, Dave Tarlo, and Terry Sullivan—formed a quartet we later named Stone Soup. Pete liked our sound and invited us to sing with him for the one-hundredth anniversary celebration at Carnegie Hall—a surreal experience, to say the least.

That same year, I married Mai Jacobs. Mai had been a childhood neighbor, and her family shared a similar political background to my own. Her grandfather, Walter Lowenfels, was a well-respected poet and a good friend of both Pete and Lee. He had co-written songs with each of them and shared credit on The Weavers' well-known anthem 'Wasn't That A Time.' It's long been family lore that Mai's mother, Judy, and her twin sister, Manna, were Lee's inspiration for the phrase, '*Oh Lord, I was the father of twins*' in the song 'Kisses Sweeter Than Wine.' Pete sang this song for us at our wedding, and it was not lost on me that he had also attended my parents' wedding, some thirty-six years earlier.

Shortly after getting married, Mai and I bought a home in Beacon, New York, coincidentally just a few miles north of Pete and Toshi. Hearing that I wanted to record some songs, my new father-in-law, Henry 'Stretch' Jacobs, bought me a Tascam 464 Portastudio, which was essentially a high-speed four-track cassette recording machine with a Dolby circuit to reduce the inevitable tape hiss.

This was around 1992, and digital home studios were not yet popular. When Pete found out that I had the machine, he asked me to record something for him, and then he asked again, and again, and again…

• • •

Pete always enjoyed being before a microphone, but it had little to do with ego and more to do with *mission*. Pete often said that a problem with many folklorists is that they discover things in a dusty book and put them in another book that

PREFACE BY DAVID BERNZ 9

sits on a shelf collecting dust. He was out instead to make a living breathing musical library of folk music that people could listen to and learn from—and for that, he needed a microphone.

In the 1950s and 60s, it was Moe Asch's microphone at Folkways Records down in New York City. I remember when Pete asked for help making learning CDs for the second edition of his songbook, *Where Have All The Flowers Gone.* We sent to the Smithsonian for his Folkways recordings and three boxes arrived containing almost eighty CDs. There were sea shanties and broadsides; farm songs and frontier songs; songs of immigrants and of black America; songs about civil rights, peace, and the environment; four volumes of American ballads; and much more—a truly dazzling array. I once asked Pete how he had learned all those lyrics, and he explained that if he felt a song was worth recording, he would just tape the words to the microphone stand and ask Moe to turn the machine on.

If Pete wanted to be in front of Moe Asch's microphone in the 50s and 60s, or on Columbia Records in the 70s, then at least for a time in the 1990s and 2000s, on a somewhat lesser scale, he was in front of mine. His recording requests ranged from mundane things to large-scale projects. In 1996, he came over to record a single song, a new take of 'Andorra,' at the request of the Andorran Consulate. Andorra is a small country in the Pyrenees, and Pete had been inspired to write the song when he found out their annual defense budget was less than five dollars. On the other side of the scale, in 1997, Pete had me bring the machine to Katonah, New York, to record an entire concert in front of four hundred people so that he could hear how he and his grandson, Tao Rodríguez, sounded with a big audience singing along.

In December of that year, Pete had me bring the Tascam to his barn, where we recorded a series of musical ideas. One of these, a song called 'Odds On Favorite,' ended up on a Smithsonian CD entitled *Headlines And Footnotes.* Another, an instrumental version of the old ballad 'The Water Is Wide,' appeared later on his Grammy-winning CD *Pete Seeger At 89.*

Most often, though, when Pete wanted to record something, he would come over to our house in Beacon. In 2001, we recorded a two-hour interview for the BBC for their special on the song 'We Shall Overcome.' In 2004, we recorded an interview about Woody Guthrie for researchers in Moscow, and in 2006 we recorded another lengthy interview for Ian Ruskin of the Harry Bridges Project.

(Bridges was the forward-thinking head of the Longshoreman's union out in San Francisco who during the 1930s and 40s brought the longshoremen into the middle class, and later, helped them deal with automation.)

One morning in July 2004, Pete came over to record some Hudson Valley stories for a project that a West Coast singer named Dana Lyons was working on. He walked over to my shelf and picked up my copy of Karl Karmer's well-known book, *The Hudson*. He turned, held the book with both hands and, without opening it, closed his eyes and began to speak slowly. An hour later, he had related an impressive series of tales of the early days of the Hudson Valley. One of them appears on *Pete Seeger At 89* under the title 'The First Settlers.'

It was after hearing the eloquence of this session that I first thought how some of the stories and interviews I had recorded might someday make a worthy book. I brought a copy of the tape to my office and had my secretary transcribe it so that I could see how it looked in print. After reading it, I started compiling the transcriptions of other tapes and interviews that resulted in this book.

• • •

I feel I should offer a few words about what this book is intended to be, largely by stating what it's not. This book is not intended to be a biography of Pete Seeger. For that, there are already some great choices, such as David Dunaway's revised *Pete Seeger: How Can I Keep From Singing* and Jim Brown's remarkable film *Pete Seeger: The Power Of Song*. Instead, this book is a collection of thoughts and stories that escaped from the different corners of Pete's mind, which, taken together, render a picture of how he felt and thought and spoke in a way that a biography could not.

Some of this material has appeared in other places and some has not, but I don't think any of it has ever been presented in quite the same way, because, among other things, this book is also not intended to be in perfect English. Pete was fond of saying that he liked a bit of grammatical imperfection every now and then. He often began sentences with the words *and* or *but* or *however*. In putting together this book, I have resisted the temptation to edit everything into perfect sentences and instead have opted, with minimal license, to leave Pete's speech pattern largely intact. It's my hope that those who knew Pete will be able to hear his voice in these words and once again feel his gentle lilt and familiar cadence, which, for lack of a better word, was downright musical.

For those who didn't get the chance to meet Pete or to hear him speak, I hope this book will offer a sense of the accessible manner in which he communicated. There was something in Pete's whimsical tone that appealed to our inner child and the innate sense of fairness that we all share—an informal familiarity that broke through barriers to reach into the hearts of his audience. Maybe this book can continue some of that work.

Chopping Wood is also not intended to be complete. As indicated by the use of the word *some* in many of the chapter headings, what is offered here is a mere sampling of Pete's thoughts and stories and favorite quotes and so forth. Hopefully, it does justice to Pete without too much distortion. It is also incomplete in another sense. Pete, like any creative person, tended to hone things over time. By definition, the material from which this book is culled is only a snapshot. It's how Pete told it that day.

This book is not intended to be one hundred percent historically accurate. Pete had a way of relating history with an emphasis on the *story* part of the word. He could place himself back in time, right into the room where events were taking place, and envision the words that were said and the thoughts resonating inside the heads of people now long gone. He often related stories in that manner, speaking on others' behalf. The content of such tales always contains a kernel of historical truth, but don't look for exact quotes or perfectly accurate historical facts, as you may not find them.

I'm reminded of the day Pete and I were singing the old song 'Peg And Awl,' which is about shoemakers displaced by automation. 'In the year eighteen and one,' the song goes, 'pegging shoes was all I done.' After we finished, Pete said to me, 'I hope you know that the automatic shoe pegging machine wasn't actually invented until the 1880s.' When I asked why we were singing 'in the year eighteen-and-one,' Pete said, 'Oh, it sings better.'

A word about the title. 'Chopping wood' is meant to be the same as some other old expressions like 'chewing the cud' or 'jawboning,' essentially when two friends get together and talk back and forth about various things. Here, Pete does most of the chopping with an occasional comment or story from me. But as Pete didn't like being lionized and rarely spoke of his own accomplishments, some of the material about how he put his values and beliefs into practice in his community are, of necessity, written by me. I include some of this material toward the end of the book along with some other asides, to round out the picture of Pete as he lived with 'local hero' status through his seventies, eighties, and nineties. So in the later chapters, I do a bit more of the chopping, but you will still occasionally hear from Pete.

Although I have put this volume together, I am likely just one of many people who could have done so. Pete's life was rich with relationships and correspondences and projects and organizations. There are thousands of people who harbor their own personal Pete stories. Under the circumstances, it felt odd to be the only other voice in this book, so I have tried where appropriate to intersperse the perspectives of others who also knew Pete. Some of these additional voices are well-known performers, while others are local citizens from here in the Hudson Valley; each shared their thoughts about Pete and his importance in their lives. And for each person who was included here, there are many others who could have been.

Finally, allow me to give a little advice on how to read this book. Nobody you meet tells their life story all at once; we get to know others more deeply over time. Likewise, placing all these stories one after the other is not how one should really get to know Pete Seeger. This book is not meant to be devoured cover-to-cover in a single sitting. I am hoping you will take some time to stop and let things settle in. Read a bit now and a bit later, in any order you please—slowly, if possible. If you do that, I think you'll find that you'll get to know Pete better.

This introduction ends largely where it began: with Pete's natural ability for communication. Most people meeting Pete for the first time were soon impressed by the breadth of his knowledge on a wide array of subjects, and by his ability to tell stories and recall important facts in great detail. But they were also equally impressed by the disarming and philosophical manner in which he spoke. What they were hearing was the voice of a man who loved this earth and the people in it, a man who loved nature, a man who would do no harm. Afterwards, almost all of them would make the same comment: *'If only I'd had a tape recorder with me.'*

Well, I am one of the fortunate ones who, for at least some of the time, had the microphone on.

DAVID BERNZ
BEACON, NEW YORK
FALL 2023

CHAPTER 01  SOME HISTORY

THE FIRST SETTLERS

I've often thought about the people who lived in the Hudson Valley long ago and what it must have been like for them, seeing Europeans for the first time. In my mind's eye, a native person from that time might tell it something like this:

I will tell you about the people who lived in this Hudson Valley a long time ago, and how one day we looked out and saw what seemed like a huge bird, the biggest bird anyone ever had seen, moving slowly across the water. When it got nearer, we could see it was not a bird. It was some kind of thing that had people on it. And then it came to rest and didn't move anymore. Who were they?

Our people had never seen anything like this in our lives. We only knew our own little part of the river. If you went too far away you could get in trouble, because each village protected its own hunting grounds. But living on the river we had food, oysters, and mussels, and we fished, and in the winter when the river was covered with ice we caught deer and other animals in the mountains.

But this strange, strange thing that we thought was a bird but now we know is not, let's go closer if we dare. When we came closer, we saw that they were people a little like us, but they had skin that was lighter than our skin was. Their faces were not brownish like our faces were, and most of them had some kind of covering on their bodies, not skins like we sometimes wear, but something which covered most of their body except their faces and hands. They shouted at us but we did not understand what they said, but we came closer, and they held out things they could give us, and we held out things that we could give them.

Well, this was the beginning of the end for us, and we didn't know it. After them, in other years came many, many more, they called them 'ships' and we used their words to describe them. They had lots of words that we did not know, but we learned some of their words, and they learned some of our words. And then more and more of them came, and they wanted to live on the shore like we did, but they wanted to live in what they called 'houses.' Instead of living with the cold of the winter, they had warm fires inside their houses. Pretty soon they were cutting down the trees and planting things in the ground. And then they seemed to take over. They were taking more and more land all the time.

We had a meeting with them. We had to use their language. And they said, 'We will give you this' and 'We will give you that.' It's true, they had things we wanted. When we had to cut down a tree, we used a stone tool, but they had a thing they called a hatchet and a bigger thing they called an axe, and they could cut down a tree so much quicker. And where we only had a stone tool, they had what they called a knife. And when we heated up sweet syrup, we could only heat it in big wooden trenches made of logs, but they had things they called iron pots. We wanted these things because they were very convenient, but what they wanted was more and more land.

At this conference, we were sitting on a bench near some of them, and one of us decided to move his seat a little closer to one of the settlers, and the man moved a little bit nearer the end of the bench. And then one of us moved still a little closer to him again, and he moved still a little further near the end of the bench. And then, when one of us wanted to move still closer, he said, 'I'm coming to the end of the bench. You're pushing me off!' And we said to him, 'Don't you realize that is what you're doing to us? You say you just want a little more land, and a little more land, and a little more land. Eventually, where are we to go to?'

It's a sad story, but there's a hopeful side. Some of our women ended up marrying those settlers, and their children were only half like us and I guess more like them, but they carried some of our traditions on. They liked to wear shoes on their feet, and we showed them how to make a wonderful light shoe we called a moccasin and some of them decided they liked moccasins best of all to put on their feet. And they liked some of our words and they started using them. So maybe, maybe, we could learn to live together. Maybe. We have to try.

Editor's note: in 1609, when Henry Hudson first sailed the *Half Moon* into the mouth of the Hudson river, there were about ten thousand natives living along the shoreline. They spoke the Agonquin language. The Lenape lived to the south, the Wappingers were on the central Hudson and the Mohegan lived to the north. The Mohegans named the river *Mahicanituk*, which means 'the river that flows both ways.' The Algonquins believed in Manitou, a 'great spirit' that resides in all things, so everything upon the earth was sacred and deserved proper respect and care.

THE GREAT PEACE

It was about four or five hundred years ago that a young man way up in Canada got in trouble with his own people. His name was Deganawidah. He came from the Huron tribe, and they sometimes fought with the people on the south side of the big lake. There were six nations, six peoples, who spoke pretty much the same language, but they sometimes got to fighting with each other. This young man said, 'I think people should learn to live in peace.' But his own people said, 'Get out of here, that's women's talk, *peace, peace, peace!*'

Deganawidah decided to paddle his canoe across the big lake, and then he started walking. At the first village he came to he talked about peace. He said, 'People within a village should not be killing each other, and different villages should not be killing each other.' But the war chief, whose name was Atoharyo, said, 'Get out of here, I am the war chief. That's women's talk. Go!'

Deganawidah walked to another village. There he met a man who was very sad because both his wife and his daughter had died, and he was all alone. His name was Hiawatha. When Hiawatha heard Deganawidah talk of peace, he said, 'Let me go with you. I too want to see peace between the villages.' The two men went from village to village and people were doubtful even though the two men talked well. Many people said they would like to see peace too, but only if all the villages would agree.

At one village, Deganawidah got an idea. He told the people to look at the sky the next day in the afternoon. Deganawidah did this because he had always looked closely at the sun and the moon, and he knew they were getting very close. He held his finger up close to the moon and he said, 'I think tomorrow afternoon the moon is going to be so close that it will black out the sun. Watch the sun tomorrow afternoon.' Sure enough, Deganawidah was right. The whole Earth started getting dark for a few minutes, and the people said, 'You must know things we don't know. We will do what you want us to do.' And the skies got light again.

Now, people from every village came with Deganawidah back to the first village. And now Atoharyo said, 'But if there is going to be peace, what is there for me to do?'

Deganawidah and his friends co-opted him. They knew how to make Atoharyo feel good. They said, 'You're in charge of the great peace. When there is a meeting once a year, you will call the meeting together. It will be underneath the great tree, and the white roots of peace will go to the north and the south and to the east and the west, and the eagle will roost in the very top of this great pine tree. You will call the meeting to order. When someone proposes something that needs to be done you will get them always to sleep on it before voting on it. Who will choose the people at this meeting? Why the women of course. The women are the heads of the clan. They know who is in the clan. They know who is the father of the children. They know who is best to be chosen. So the women will choose the men who will meet in the longhouse once a year under the great tree of peace with the white roots pointing in all directions.'

• • •

This was a long time ago—nobody is sure exactly how long. But many years later, an Irish fur trader married a young Indian girl, and he built a house for her near the little town of Fonda, about fifty miles west of Albany. He wrote a letter to Benjamin Franklin, who was postmaster general of the colonies, and he described the kind of government that kept the peace between six nations: the Seneca in the far west; the Cayuga, the Tuscarora, the Oneida, the Onondaga, and the Mohawks in the east.

A little more than twenty years later, it was 1787, and Benjamin Franklin was at a conference, trying to put down on paper the rules for a constitution for the new republic of the United States of America. People couldn't agree, and they were ready to give up, and Benjamin Franklin says, 'Let me read you this letter from the fur trader Mr. Johnson. He is dead now, but this is his letter. These are the rules of these people the French called Iroquois, but they call themselves the Haudenosaunee. We call them savages because their ways are different from ours, but they have kept the peace for hundreds of years. If they can keep the peace, why can't thirteen English colonies learn to keep the peace between each other?'

And so Franklin shamed all the delegates to sit down and try to find compromises so they could stick together, and they finally got a constitution. When they finished, Ben said, 'I don't agree with everything in this constitution, but I think it's the best we can get, and I think if we all will agree to obey the rules of the constitution, maybe through time we can make it better.' Ben was an old man of eighty-one years at the time. He didn't live much longer. When the constitution was finished, a woman said to him, 'Mr. Franklin, what kind of a government do we have now?' And old Ben said, 'A republic. If you can keep it.'

• • •

William Johnson was an Irish fur trader. His first wife died when he was about thirty years old. In what was then the little town of Albany, maybe one or two thousand people, the English had kind of a festival day. The officers were racing their horses, and a teenage Indian girl leaped on the back of the horse of one of the officers. The officer got his horse to rear up in the air and tried to get it to buck, but she wrapped her legs so strongly around the horse that he couldn't shake her off. Finally, he just gave up. Johnson, the fur trader, stepped up and he offered his hand to the Indian girl, and he paid court to her. When they married, he didn't want her living in Albany and being snubbed by all the white colonial women. He took her west, into the country where her father was a chief. That was way out west, fifty miles away, and you'd have to walk several days to make that distance. There he built her a big stone house that still stands. It's called

Johnson's Fort, near the Town of Fonda. It was from there that Johnson wrote a long letter to Benjamin Franklin describing the Iroquois system of government—the idea of women choosing the men, and the men having a meeting once a year and not agreeing to do anything unless they would sleep on it overnight, at least, before acting on it.

Benjamin Franklin got to know Johnson because he had been appointed postmaster general of the colonies. It was his job to see that the King's mail would get from New York up to Albany in time. With his teenage daughter, he rode horses from New York to Albany, deciding which little farmer's road should be improved into a post road. Maybe one road was straighter than the other, or not so steep. When they came to a stream, they would decide if they would put a ferry there; or, if it was a very narrow stream, they would try to put a bridge.

MADAME BRETT

It was in 1664 that English ships sailed into New York Harbor with their big guns. When they fired off one of their big guns, if a cannonball hit a house, there was no more house left! You would have to rebuild it. So, with relatively little violence, the Dutch surrendered to the British, and New Amsterdam became New York.

The new people in charge of New York spoke the English language, not the Dutch language, and upriver they decided to name some of the land after the Duchess of York, so it became Dutchess County. Over the years, I've loved to tell this story about the area right near my home in the southern corner of the county:

I was sixteen, a Dutch girl. I was married to an English Captain. Captain Brett, a sailor. He found that I inherited a precious piece of paper from my father. In return for money he'd given King Charles II, he now owned about twenty-five thousand acres of land—a huge triangle along the Hudson.

It was the summer of 1708 when my husband and I decided we would like to settle up here, and not only settle up here but sell land to other people. We bought a sailboat, and we got some saws and axes and shovels and drills and all sorts of tools to shape wood, and we sailed up to the mouth of the creek that we now call Fishkill Creek. There we found a French trapper.

His name was Paul Dubois. He trapped animals for food and sold the fur skins for money. He didn't go out hunting like the Indians did, with a bow and arrow, but he trapped the animals—little ones, rabbits, big ones, small bears. We showed him our piece of paper. It said we have the right to settle the Hudson on the east side from a few miles south of Fishkill Creek going northeast to a range of mountains, and on a straight line surveyed from north of Wappingers Creek southeast to the mountains. But we decided this man, Dubois, knew a lot about the land, and he could teach us a lot. So we said, 'Please, you stay here. You and your family can stay here, and we will put on the map where your house is, and say this is your land, and we will not sell any land right near it. Now, tell us what are the Indians like? What are their names?' Dubois knew the Indians well, and they knew him.

We selected a place a mile up the creek where we could put up a house, and the first thing we did was to build that house. We needed a place to live because I already had two little children and the third one was on its way. It came earlier than we expected. It was born on the boat when we were making a trip up the river, and so we named him Rivery.

My name was Catheryna, and my father and grandfather were Dutchmen. Their paper from the English King said they had a right to all the land between Fishkill Creek and Wappinger Creek. Wappinger was where the Wappinger Indians lived, but we told the Indians that we wouldn't sell land in the mountains and that they could live in the mountains the way they had always lived, and we would just sell the land along Fishkill Creek.

We'd only been up here five years when my husband was sailing with his servant, a black slave up into the harbor of Fishkill Creek, and he wasn't looking when the wind changed direction. The boom of the boat swung against him and hit him in the back of the head and knocked him into the river and he drowned. His manservant took his body and carried it one mile up to the house and said, 'Here is my master.'

What was I going to do? I know both my family and his family in New York thought I would give up this ambitious scheme, but I didn't. I was strong. I was young. I got some other woman to take care of the three children, and even though I was only twenty-six years old, I got on horseback—sidesaddle, of course, to be modest—and I went around with men who knew how to survey the land, and we decided, Let's sell a farm here and let's sell a farm there. When settlers came up from New York—whether they walked, rode a horse, or sailed a boat—we showed them where they could live with their families if they worked hard.

We put a dam on the Fishkill. We threw some big trees across the creek. We rolled some stones and found a place where a wheel would turn, and that wheel could turn a millstone or make a saw go up and down. A lot of people helped on this, and I had to pay them money, but whenever I sold a farm, I got some money. I put into every one of my pieces of paper when I sold a farm, 'You will build no other dam or mill on the Fishkill.' I didn't want competition. So, when they grew grain, they took it to my mill to run, and when they needed boards sawed up at length with a fast sawmill, they brought the logs to me, usually in a homemade wagon or in a homemade sled pulled by horses or oxen. Germans settled across the river and called their town Newburgh. A sailing ferry helped us trade together.

Within just a few years, there were hundreds of people, and then, later, thousands of people living by Fishkill Creek in the valley. So I was able to show them a woman could do things that people never thought a woman could do. This was my life's work, building the town of Fishkill Landing, where boats could safely land, and building a farming town called Fishkill right near Fishkill Creek and other towns further up like Stormville. I had three sons, and when I died, they carried on. I hope my house will not be torn down. They called me Madame Brett because my husband was Captain Roger Brett, even though, before I married him, I was just Catheryna Rondout, a Dutch girl.

• • •

I suppose I could call this story 'Madame Brett's Ghost' because I tell it as if her spirit is recounting her lifetime. Incidentally, some of the first settlers on Brett's lands were two young men that came up from Yonkers. Their father had paid some money for land on Fishkill Creek. Their name was Storm. The oldest was only fourteen, the younger one was only twelve, but they were strong; they hiked up Fishkill Creek, where they found some nice place where they thought they could have a farm, and they cleared the land all summer. When their father came up, he complimented them on the number of trees they cut down and the cabin they built. Garrett Storm was the name of the fourteen-year-old, and they called that town Stormville. Until recently, there was still a business in the City of Beacon called Garrett Storm.

Madame Brett's original house was built in 1709, and seven generations of her family lived there. It's still here in Beacon today, near Main Street and Route 52, and it's been kept up as a museum.

Here's a short story that follows from that:

We are the people who lived here long before any palefaces came. When they came here, they said we could live in the mountains and they would just live in the flat country. We did for many years, but there were more and more white people coming, and finally they had taken over the valley, and now the woman that sold us this land was dead and her son was taking over. But there was no more land in the valley to sell, and he started to sell land in the mountains where we were. Where were we to go if he sells all the land in the mountains?

We tried to take him to court. We found some white lawyers who would plead our case, but there wasn't a chance. We were just Indians. That's what they called us. Where would we go? There were Indians out west, but we didn't know them. If we went there, we might get killed. There were Indians to the north and the east, but there were white people there too. Where would we go?

We went down to a little settlement where Madame Brett had allowed some black-skinned people to live. The black-skinned people had once been slaves but they got free, and they came up to Madame Brett and said, 'We would like some land too; we have a little money we could give you.' And she sold them some land and they called it Green Haven. We went down to the black people and said, 'Could we live here too with you? We will learn how to become farmers, but we don't want to live with the white people as they are not always understanding to us, but you understand us. You know how the white people do not always treat us right, but if we stick together, maybe we could all live here.'

That's why there were many people who were part Indian and part African living in the town of Green Haven. In World War II, New York State bought the Town of Green Haven and made a big prison. I told this story when I was singing at the prison there, and one of the prisoners said, 'Yeah, Green Haven is still mostly black people.'

SHAKESPEARE AND KING JAMES

The Bible is not read by ordinary people all around the world as much as it is in English-speaking countries. Why? The King James version is such superb poetry. After reading Richard Lederer's book *Classic Literary Trivia*, I think I might know why. Lederer has a whole chapter on William Shakespeare. It turns out that Shakespeare didn't invent a few dozen words or a few hundred. They've traced over two thousand words which, so far as they know, were never used in the English language until Shakespeare used them. It's possible he got them from the countryside and put them in his plays. Just as an example, in the middle of a battle scene, someone shouts, 'I'll unhorse you!' Well, there's never been a word like *unhorse*. Some of these words appear in the King James version of the bible, so for hundreds of years, people have wondered if Shakespeare had anything to do with the King James translation. After all, he was a famous writer. They could have gotten his help. But there is absolutely no paper trail whatsoever, and they've examined every single piece of paper connected to the King James Bible to see if it was connected with Shakespeare.

A few decades ago, a young woman said to herself, 'Hmm, Shakespeare was forty-six years old in the year 1610, when the King James version was being completed and being prepared for publication.' She looked up the forty-sixth Psalm of David and counted forty-six words from the beginning. There's the word *shake*. She counts forty-six words from the end. There's the word *spear*! Now, that's too much of a coincidence. One of them could be a coincidence, but not two of them, and as Sherlock Holmes used to say, 'There is no such thing as a coincidence.' In my mind's eye, it could have happened like this:

It's after dark in London. A coach and horses clip-clops up to Shakespeare's door. A man in a long Ecclesiastical robe gets out and knocks on the door.

The servant pulls open a little window.

'Who is it?'

'Is Master Shakespeare within? Tell him that Canon Richardson of Oxford would very much like to speak with him.'

'I'll ask my master.'

Click goes the window. A few minutes later, he comes back.

'My master would be glad to see you.'

As he walks into the living room, Shakespeare rises from a chair near the fire and extends his hand, 'Well, to what do I owe the honor of this visit Canon Richardson?'

'Master Shakespeare, I came after dark because it would not be approved, and I am a member of a sacred profession. You are a member of a scandalous profession, but I need your help. I am on the committee charged with making a better English translation of this great, great old book. The great old book, and our attempts are so ugly I am ashamed of them. The original Hebrew is beautiful, it has rhythm and sonority, and even the Greek and the Latin are beautiful. But as for our attempts, there is no other word but ugly. Would you be willing to help us a bit?'

'Why, certainly, I'll be glad to. And Canon Richardson, I will pledge with my heart and I lay my hand upon this bible and pledge that I will not tell a word of this to anybody. I will pledge my manservant to silence, and I will never mention to anybody whoever came here. Now, let's look at those papers.'

• • •

Now, whether he came once or ten times or more, we don't know. All we know is that at least one time, there must have been contact somewhere, somehow.

Editor's note: the Authorized King James version of the Great Old Book was first published in 1611. James had approved fifty-four scholars work on it, and forty-seven of them worked in six separate groups at three different locations for seven years. With so many people involved, the chance that one or more of them might have consulted Shakespeare is not as remote as one might think. As for the 'coincidence,' the 46th Psalm of David is below. You can count it for yourself. Exclude the word *Selah* at the end, which is a Hebrew word for *Amen*. It appears repeatedly at the end of psalms or phrases within the psalms and is not technically part of the text, which reads:

God is our refuge and strength, a very present help in trouble. Therefore will not we fear, though the earth be removed, and though the mountains be carried into the midst of the sea; Though the waters thereof roar and be troubled, though the mountains **shake** with the swelling thereof. Selah. There is a river, the streams whereof shall make glad the city of God, the holy place of the tabernacles of the most high. God is in the midst of her; she shall not be moved: God shall help her, and that right early. The heathen raged, the kingdoms were moved: he uttered his voice, the earth melted. The LORD of hosts is with us; the God of Jacob is our refuge. Selah. Come, behold the works of the LORD, what desolations he hath made in the earth. He maketh wars to cease unto the end of the earth; he breaketh the bow, and cutteth the **spear** in sunder; he burneth the chariot in the fire. Be still, and know that I am God: I will be exalted among the heathen, I will be exalted in the earth. The LORD of hosts is with us; the God of Jacob is our refuge. Selah.

EINSTEIN AND MOSES ASCH

During the 1950s and 60s, I would very often go down to Moe Asch's little studio on 48th Street and sing one song or another, and sometimes a whole batch of songs, into his microphone. Moe ran a little record company he called Folkways from 1948 until his death in 1986. Moe never made very much money, but he recorded all sorts of music that the big commercial record companies wouldn't touch. Because of him, we can now hear recordings of people like Woody Guthrie and Leadbelly, and Southern blues players such as Big Bill Broonzy and Elizabeth Cotton, and mountain musicians like Doc Watson and Jean Ritchie and Roscoe Holcomb.

Moe recorded good music no matter where it came from, whether it was African American spirituals or railroad songs or Cajun ballads or Native American flute. His was really the first 'world music' company. But did you know that Albert Einstein helped get Folkways Records started?

In early 1939, Sholem Asch, the great novelist, asked his son Moe, 'You bought a recording machine; can I put it in the trunk of my car?'

Moe says, 'I think so. Why?'

'Because we've got to go to Princeton and record a short message for Dr. Einstein which can be played on WLIB and WEVD and other New York radio stations urging American Jews not to waste a minute, but to get their relatives out of Germany now!'

So they went down and recorded the message, and, over supper, Einstein says, 'Young Mr. Asch, are you a writer, like your father?'

'No,' says Moe, 'I make a living installing public address systems in hotels, but I made enough to buy this recording machine, and I'm fascinated with what it can do. I met a great Negro folksinger named Leadbelly, and nobody's recording him because they say he's not commercial. He's recorded for the Library of Congress, but you have to drive to Washington to hear the record. I think these records should be available for sale.'

And Einstein says, 'You're absolutely right. American people don't appreciate their own culture. It'll be a Polish Jew like you who'll do the job.' (Moe had come into the United States in 1912 through Ellis Island. He had been raised by his aunt, who was a friend of Lenin; she was in the Jewish Bund that was wiped out by Stalin.)

Moe Asch recorded Leadbelly in 1939. He only sold a hundred copies of the record in the first year. He went bankrupt two times before he started Folkways in 1948. Disc Records went bankrupt, and Asch Records went bankrupt. Then the invention of LPs made it possible to ship a record with nothing but a piece of cardboard, where before you had to pack a 78rpm record in three inches of sawdust because they were fragile shellac records. Now Moe was able to make a modest living selling good music on his Folkways label, and that's what he did for the next thirty-seven years.

Editor's note: Pete often spoke of the accomplishments of Moe Asch. Over the years, Folkways and its tiny staff managed to release some 2,168 albums, and Moe prided himself on the fact that every record in the catalogue remained in print and available for purchase, whether the demand was one record per year or a thousand. Moe also started the Broadsides label and released some of the early songs of people like Phil Ochs and Bob Dylan. After his death in 1986, Moe's family arranged to donate his entire catalogue to the Smithsonian on the condition that every recording would remain forever 'in print.' You can now obtain any Folkways recording and many other fine recordings from Smithsonian Folkways Recordings, 600 Maryland Avenue SW, Washington, DC, 20024, or folkways.si.edu. See also smithsonianglobalsound.org.

CHAPTER 02 SOME FAMILY STORIES

IS THERE A QUAKER IN THE HOUSE?

I hope sometime you try telling stories to children. At bedtime, you could sing them a song, or you could tell them a story about your own family. Nearly every family has some kind of story. How did Grandma meet Grandpa? Why did we move to this town? Was it because we needed a job and we heard that there were some jobs here? Or maybe we moved here because we heard there was land and we wanted to get land for a farm. However we got where we are, there are always stories you can tell.

Sometimes I ask kids if they ever think about how many ancestors we have if you go back far. We all had two parents. We all had four grandparents. We all had eight great-grandparents. Unless one or two people married cousins, that would be sixteen great-great-grandparents. Keep doubling: sixteen, thirty-two, sixty-four, one hundred and twenty-eight, two hundred and fifty-six, five hundred and twelve, one thousand and twenty-four in only ten generations! In ten more generations, over a million! So you can see how quickly you have a lot of ancestors. I wrote a song about it. It says, '*We've all been a-doubling down through the years.*' If you go back far enough, you're almost sure to find different kinds of people are in your ancestors.

You might have thought all your ancestors were Italian or all your ancestors were Irish or German or English or African, but somewhere along the line maybe somebody married somebody else, or somebody's parents came from two different places. If you go back really far, you'll probably find everybody in the world is a distant cousin. Most all of us are a little from Africa, a little from Asia, a little from Europe, and who knows where else. If you're part Indian, you might be from North America or South America and of course, the Indians originally came from Asia thousands and thousands of years ago.

So, here's a Seeger family story that I've told to my own grandchildren.

My older brother John was a pacifist. During World War II, he writes to my grandmother and says, 'Don't we have some Quaker ancestors from back in Pennsylvania? I've got to persuade my draft board that I am a real pacifist and not just somebody trying to avoid the draft.' My grandmother wrote him a short but very firm letter:

> *One should not have to have Quaker ancestors to be against war, but it*
> *so happens you do.*

Way back in the seventeenth century, a man in Wales was named John Op Bevan, and he became a follower of George Fox, the man who started the Quaker religion in England in the middle of the seventeenth century. Fox was appalled by Englishmen killing Englishmen simply because they had different religious beliefs. He started his new religious belief, the Society Of Friends, and because they got so excited, people called them Quakers. When they were speaking, they would shake full of emotion.

John Op Bevan became a Quaker, but his wife was more conservative. She kept going to the regular Church of England services. But there one day the minister inveighed against her husband, 'That man Op Bevan is going to fry in hell for all eternity!' She ran home in tears and threw herself in her husband's arms: 'Darling, tell me about this new religion of yours. I would rather go to hell with you than to heaven without you.' She became an enthusiastic Quaker.

A few years later, William Penn made a deal with King Charles II. It seems that William Penn's father had loaned King Charles a huge amount of money—something like a million dollars today—and the king now owed this money to young William Penn. William proposed a deal: 'Give me permission to sail a boat to your new colony across the sea, and I will found a good English city.' The king probably thought, *I will get rid of him, these Quakers give me trouble.* He signed a piece of paper, and in return for getting out of the debt, King Charles let William Penn put a boatload of people together to sail to the New World.

On that boat were John Op Bevan and his wife. They were young and they sailed up the Delaware River, which the Dutch called the South River. (The Hudson was the North River.) The year was 1784 when they landed. William Penn made a deal with the Indians for some land. He gave them things they wanted, like knives and hatchets and iron pots. However, William Penn died, and his son was not so generous a man and he cheated the Indians. Young Ben Franklin hated him and made fun of him in his newspaper.

After some time had passed, John Op Bevan and his family became sad because the Quaker city did not turn out to be quite what they hoped it would be. They returned to Wales as older people to die where they had been born. But they left their children here, and one of their great-granddaughters married a Captain Stacey from New England, and their son married a Dutch girl, and that's how come our mother was also part Dutch.

I think that made my brother one thirty-second Quaker. All during World War II, he worked in a hospital changing bedpans and doing the dirtiest kinds of work for three and a half or four years.

Incidentally, my mother had a French grandfather and an Irish grandmother, and she was also one eighth Dutch, so she was only three eighths English, descended from a little town of Chester, Pennsylvania.

WE'LL ALL BE A-DOUBLING *Pete Seeger*

Chorus:
We'll all be a-doubling, a-doubling, a-doubling,
We'll all be a-doubling down through the years,
We'll all be a-doubling, a-doubling, a-doubling,
We'll all be a-doubling down through the years.

Two times two is four.
Two times four is eight.
Two times eight is sixteen,
And the hour is getting late!

Twice sixteen is thirty-two.
Next comes sixty-four.
Next comes a hundred twenty-eight,
Do we need to hear more?

Next comes two hundred fifty-six.
Next five hundred and twelve.
Next, one thousand twenty-four,
So figure it out yourself.

Keep doubling ten generations.
You can have children over a million.
Keep going another twenty.
Your children would be over a trillion.

At this point in the song, I usually say, 'Hold on—there's never been a trillion people in the world. At least not yet. So some of us must have married cousins, and you and I are all distant cousins of each other.'

Either people are going to have to get smaller
Or the world's going to have to get bigger;
Or there's a couple other possibilities,
I'll leave it to you to figure.

I know I shouldn't a been born!
I was my mama's third child;
But now I'm hollering around the world,
And I drive the Birchers wild!

MEETING TOSHI

I dropped out of college in 1938, when I was nineteen years old. I got too interested in politics and lost my scholarship. I was ahead of my class, but I was immature in more ways than one. I spent the summer on a bicycle, painting watercolors, and thought I'd be an artist. I went to art school in New York. I also thought I wanted to be a journalist because I'd run school newspapers for six full years: at age twelve and all through prep school, and in Harvard for a year, working with Arthur Kinoy.

I had an aunt in New York who taught school. She found out I was dead broke and was not making any kind of living as an artist, nor was I making any kind of living as a journalist, and my aunt said, 'Peter, come sing some of your songs for my class. I can get five dollars for you.'

Five dollars! Most people had to work all day or maybe two days to make five dollars in those days. And I would get five dollars just for having fun for an hour? It really seemed sinful, but I went and took the money. Then I found another school that paid me three dollars. That was still good pay for an hour's work. And one of the teachers in this other school led a teenage square dance club, and she asked if I'd come sing some songs at her club. It was called the American Square Dance Group. Margo Mayo was the director of it. I came to sing and came back the next week to dance. There were about twenty or thirty of us, and one of the dancers was Toshi Ohta. But we didn't start going together. Like I say, I was very immature in many ways.

Many people somehow got the impression that Toshi and I met at the World's Fair. We had already met at the square dance club by that time, but our paths did cross at the fair, and that was because of my uncle.

I had an uncle who was a press agent for theaters. He'd graduated from Harvard in 1904, and he spoke French like a native because his grandfather ran a prep school in New York that taught French to its students.

One of my great-grandfathers was born in France. His name was Elie Charlier. He must have been a smart kid because he got a scholarship to an expensive school in Switzerland. There, he made a discovery that rich people paid a lot of money for their kids to go to a good school. And he arrived in New York with enough money to print a piece of paper saying, 'If you want your sons to enter the diplomatic service, they must know

French! Send them to Professor Charlier.' And he gave an address in a posh district where he'd rented a room. Pretty soon, he was hiring other teachers, and before long, the Charlier Institute was born, and for forty-five years it was New York's leading preparatory school. The sons of John Jacob Astor went there and the sons of Hamilton Fish and the Roosevelt family including Teddy Roosevelt all went to my great-grandfather's school. My grandmother, his daughter, spoke French like a native because they spoke French in their home, and so her son, my uncle, spoke French very well.

When Sarah Bernhardt came touring America, my uncle took his college French club down, and they all sat in the front row and they laughed at all the right jokes at the right time. They went back to see Sarah Bernhardt in her dressing room. And she said to my uncle, 'When do you graduate?'

'Oh, in just a month.'

And she says, 'Well, if you need a job, I have one for you.'

My uncle became a press agent for Sarah Bernhardt. Within ten years, he knew the cities of America, traveling by train from city to city arranging for press interviews and so on. During World War I, he was press agent for the French army band that was touring America. During the twenties and thirties, he was a press agent for Broadway plays. He ended up being press agent for the Guggenheim Museum when Frank Lloyd Wright built his fancy new building. He was in his seventies by that time.

But at the time of the World's Fair, he was press agent for the Merry England Exhibit, because Margaret Webster put on Shakespeare plays there. She had shortened versions of Shakespeare plays that were put on in a historically accurate replica of the Globe Theatre. It was open to the sky and had two balconies and it seated maybe three hundred people. And my uncle, finding I was out of a job, got me a job there, picking up cigarette butts. And Toshi was needing a job, and she got a job serving food in the Japanese exhibit. This was 1939, just two years before Pearl Harbor. But we still didn't start going together.

Two full years later, in early 1942, The Almanac Singers had been singing for a year. We had a big collection of songs and they needed to be alphabetized and put in decent order, and I needed some volunteers. I asked at the square dance club if anyone would volunteer. Well, Toshi Ohta volunteered. After a couple of weeks, finally, we were going together steady.

I went into the army in July 1942. She said she'd wait for me. We wrote letters back and forth. Then the military intelligence decided I was a 'lefty' and should not be sent overseas—just keep me pickin' up cigarette butts somewhere—and I said, 'If I'm not going overseas, we might as well get married and we can live off the post.' I got a week's furlough after being in the army for a year. We arranged and got married during that week's furlough, and that was that.

THE INCREDIBLE ODYSSEY OF TAKASHI OHTA

I suppose it's only fair that I also tell you a story from my wife Toshi's side of the family. This is the story of her father Takashi, whose life would make a great movie.

Over a hundred and fifty years ago in Japan, the young emperor Meiji won a civil war against the Shogun using the slogan, 'Keep the foreign devils out!' Then, having won it, he westernized Japan as quick as he could. He sent young students and aristocrats to study in Europe and America and other places. One of three young aristocrats sent in the 1860s was my wife Toshi's grandfather.

One of his three fellow students came back and said, 'Japan should follow the example of Prussia. Get a strong army and navy, and then we'll get colonies and we'll have power.' He started the Japanese fascist movement that took power in the 1920s, and they eventually took over Manchuria and so on.

Another of the three students came back and said, 'Japan should follow the example of England. You wheel and you deal, and take advantage of your enemies' dissensions, and little by little you can take over without having to fight too much.' He became prime minister about a hundred years ago.

But Toshi's grandfather came back having witnessed the Paris Commune. He helped translate Marx into Japanese and helped the striking copper miners, and he stood up for those who the government was not treating well.

In 1911, he was raising money for Sun Yat Sen to help start a Chinese revolution, and a shipload of munitions was discovered by the British. The British were furious because they were going to take over China like they'd taken over India. They demanded the culprit be punished, and Toshi's grandfather was arrested and sentenced to be exiled forever.

Toshi's grandfather had a small business and a family to support, and he did not want to leave Japan. There was an old Japanese tradition that said that a son could take his father's banishment. Toshi's grandfather had thirteen children; some were grown up and had kids of their own, some were just babies, but there was a seventeen-year-old named Takashi who was young and strong and good at Judo. Takashi bowed low and said, 'Father, I will take your punishment. I will go and be exiled, and you can stay here.' So, Toshi's grandfather stayed in Japan, although little by little everything was taken away from the family. They had been prosperous, but they ended up penniless.

Takashi went to China, and first he fought under Sun Yat Sen, but his branch of the army was defeated, and so they went to the hills and became bandits. Once a month they'd come down and take over some rich man's house, and they'd give away all the good jewelry and other valuable things and they kept the food and the clothing, which they needed, and then went back to the hills. The people loved them because they got the other things.

Then, one day, some Japanese Buddhist Monks were coming down the road on their way to Tibet, because they wanted the Grand Lama to help settle some obscure theological argument about where Europe ended and Asia began. They needed a bodyguard, so Takashi told them he was a black belt in Judo and that he could protect them. Takashi shaved his head, put on sandals and a robe, and became their bodyguard. For two thousand miles, they walked across the Gobi Desert, over mountains and through valleys. It took them a year, but he safely delivered them from the north into Lhasa, the capital of Tibet.

Then Takashi took a chance. It was dangerous because he had no passport. He walked down into India and got a job peeling potatoes on a British ship that had sailed up the Ganges. In those days, sailing ships went far up rivers, and during the monsoon season, the Ganges was a deep-water river for five hundred miles.

For the next eight years, on and off, Takashi peeled potatoes on British ships. He spent time in the Mediterranean and many other places. For a brief period, he stayed in South Africa, but he didn't like it there.

For another brief period he lived in Brazil, but he almost got killed there. Takashi had found a job with a railroad that was cutting a line through the jungle. The local Indians were not pleased about the railroad coming through, and they were shooting poison arrows at them. The railroad hired Takashi to be a go-between with the Indians because they thought he looked a little like an Indian. The Indians liked Takashi, but he made a mistake. He made a little grass doll for a thirteen-year-old Indian girl, not knowing she was engaged to be married. Her fiancé was furious and put a poison snake in Takashi's lunchbox. When he opened his lunchbox, he was bitten. His fellow workers fed him whiskey for days, which was the only treatment they had, so for a week he was out of this world, having nothing but whiskey and more whiskey, but somehow he survived.

Back then, the railroad workers were like slaves. They were way out in the jungle, being paid hardly any money at all. Takashi knew geography. He said, 'Just over this range of mountains, there's a river that flows down into Uruguay. If we follow this stream, I think it leads through a gap in the mountains where we can get to the river.' For a week, Takashi led them through the jungle, and they got to Uruguay. There he got on another British Ship peeling potatoes again.

Takashi was quite a good translator. One time they were in the Mediterranean and a Japanese ship was there, and the two captains had to talk but they didn't have an interpreter, and somebody said, 'There is a Jap down in the kitchen.' So they put a suit of clothes on Takashi, and he interpreted with the two admirals. Then he gave back the suit and went back to peeling potatoes.

It was three years later, in 1919, when Takashi stepped off the boat and entered the United States. He had a British passport, and he had to go to Washington to get it revalidated. He was walking down the street and saw a sign that said, 'Dishwasher wanted.' Takashi was dead broke, so he knocked on the door and says, 'I can wash dishes.'

The kind southern woman who answered the door says, 'I'm running this tea house to keep my father alive. He is sick, and I can't pay you very much, but I've got a room you can sleep in.' Six months later, her father died, and she eloped to New York with Takashi. Her mother and the rest of the family were horrified that she had run off with a Japanese man. But she'd already left the family once before. During World War I, she had shared an apartment in Greenwich Village with a well-known actress named Eva

Le Gallienne. I used to tell people that Toshi's mother was a World War I hippie—they called them Bohemians then. But she was one more Virginian that didn't want to be part of the slave South, the male-run South.

Takashi married and had a family. Toshi was born in 1922. Takashi made a living for a time as a scenery designer, among other places for the Provincetown Theater, back when Paul Robeson was doing the first play by Eugene O'Neill, *All My Children*. Takashi and Robeson became good friends. Takashi's life had temporarily calmed down.

But then World War II came around. Takashi wrote a letter to Washington right after Pearl Harbor. He says, 'The only hope for Japan is to get rid of the Militarists.' Militarists had controlled the country since about the 1920s. They invaded Manchuria, and during World War I they were on the side of England. Takashi offered the government his services as a translator.

At first, the government ignored his offer. But they were dropping leaflets on Japanese troops, and they were so amateurish they finally took him up on it. Takashi put together a team of young people who were very anti-fascist. He and his crew flew over to the Burma theater, where they were in charge of designing pamphlets that could be dropped on a Japanese camp not far away. The pamphlets said things like, 'Your officers tell you that you are winning the war, but do you know that you've lost Wake Island, and you're losing the Philippines...'

At one time, they decided they should go there and see whether they were being read or not. They were going to be parachuted behind the lines. In the plane, the sergeant said, 'Where are your jumping boots?'

'I was never given any.'

'Well, what did you wear on your practice jump?'

'We never had a practice jump.'

'Heh, more snafus!'

Takashi was one of the men who had no trouble in landing. He knew Jujitsu well, and he knew how to roll, so when he hit the ground he just rolled right away. Now he walked into this Japanese camp, and he was in the showers with no clothes on and a Japanese sergeant looks at his feet and says, 'You're a spy!' This was because his big toe was right next to his other toes, as most Americans' is. But Japanese army shoes had a separate thing for the big toe and a separate thing for the other four toes. So their feet in the showers would be split, with the big toe sticking out sideways.

Takashi just said, 'I am not here to hurt anybody,' and he lit out running naked through the woods. After a mile or two, he came to a little road in no man's land. He started walking but he hears a jeep coming. He turns around and there is a jeep in the distance. He holds up his hands but they start shooting at him, so he rolls into the ditch and lays there without moving. When the jeep stops right near to him, he remembers hearing, 'Should I put another round in him?' 'No let's get the hell out,' and the jeeps roars away.

The next time he sees a jeep come in that direction, he lies on the ground on his back and shouts out when they get near enough to hear him, 'Take me to Colonel Sanderson.'

They kept their guns on him, but they did take him to Colonel Sanderson, in charge of the American camp. That was one more narrow escape.

Before he got working for Washington, Takashi was walking down Bleeker Street once and a man looked and said, 'Are you a Jap?' Takashi said no, but the man started swinging at him. With his knowledge of Judo, in about one and a half seconds the man was on the sidewalk with his arm up, tightened back, and he couldn't move, and a crowd gathered, and Takashi said, 'Will you please call a policeman? This man started swinging at me. I don't want to hurt him, but I don't want him to hit anybody.' So a policeman came and said, 'Where do you live?' and he said, 'Two blocks away,' and I guess they came with him there to make sure that was correct.

If they had been living on the West Coast, they would have been put in the internment camps, but on the East Coast the FBI came and took away the binoculars and the cameras and told them, 'Do not leave this part of Manhattan.' He couldn't go to New Jersey and he couldn't go to Brooklyn. At least Toshi and Takashi were allowed to live there.

After World War II, Takashi came back to New York, but it was difficult for him. He got one disappointing job after another—the kind of jobs that are 'supposed to be given to those ignorant Asians.' At one time, he was even hired as a butler for a well-to-do Manhattan couple. One night, they were going to have a special guest, and they told Takashi to be clean and to wear his best clothing and so forth. When he opened the door, it was an old theater friend of his. They were bosom buddies when they'd worked at the Provincetown Theater with Paul Robeson. The guest threw open his arms and says, 'Takashi!' and gave him a big embrace, and he spent the whole evening talking to Takashi and almost ignoring his hosts. Of course, Takashi was fired as soon as the guest left—they were so humiliated.

Takashi had a stroke about two years after Toshi's mother died. In '59, we got a telephone call from him. He said, 'I am lying on the floor'—he must have had just enough energy to knock the telephone down on the floor—'come save me.' Toshi called an ambulance. He got into a hospital and the verdict was he had a heart attack and a stroke. I was already building a room on the barn where Toshi and I have a bedroom now. In the warmer months of the year, that is where Takashi lived for ten years, but in the colder months he went out to stay with Toshi's brother's family in San Francisco.

The University Settlement in New York was the organization that ran a settlement house with a lot of people from Columbia University. About a hundred years ago they got land and a house given them in Beacon. General Howland had died, and his widow was giving away what she didn't need, and she kept the mansion to live in with her servants, but she gave away the farm on the other side of the street. They used the land as a summer camp for kids. I went down to sing for the kids and found they were looking for a caretaker. A lefty named Charlie Cook came up from New York and recognized me, and I said, 'My father-in-law would like a job up here. Do you have any kind of job?'

Although he was getting on in years, Takashi was in very good condition. He could swim underwater the length of the pool. He ran the lawnmower, and if he saw a kid needed some help, he was like grandpa.

Takashi ended his life spending ten years as a caretaker at the University Settlement camp right here in Beacon, just down the hill from Toshi and myself. He said it was the happiest ten years of his life.

• • •

The astonishing thing about the present system in America is that they have not been able to exile people like you, or me, or millions more like us. During the blacklist, a few people went away. Sam Wanamaker, the actor, went over to London to make a living, as a number of others did. I have friends who went to East Germany and to the Ukraine. But by and large, people have come to this country, with all its problems, and stayed here, because at least you can speak. Maybe people don't always pay much attention to what you say, but you can say things. That wasn't always the case for blacks in the South, but Martin Luther King Jr. helped change things. That's why I'm actually so optimistic now because I've seen this country change. And they haven't been able to banish us the way they've done in other places.

CHARLES SEEGER AND THE TRAILER

My father started off life as a musician. As a teenager, he could look through the music for a symphony while it was playing, and he could tell if somebody missed a note. Then he went to Harvard and got an A+ in music, but only Bs and Cs in the other subjects. He was rather bored by the rest of his studies. But he went to Germany to do graduate work. There, he ran into radical composers. And he also met the president of the University of California, who happened to be in Germany. And this very self-confident twenty-year-old says, 'If I were teaching music, I would do this and I would do that.' Well, he hadn't been back here very long before the University of California asked him if he would come work there. He would be in charge of the music department. They didn't have much of a music department. They had one man who took students to listen to a symphony and said, 'See what Mozart did,' and then take them to another symphony and say, 'See what Hayden did.' But my father, with great youthful confidence, set about setting up a music department.

But he met other professors who said, 'Seeger, you may know a lot about music, but you're an ignoramus when it comes to history and economics.' And, pretty soon, he was a socialist. When World War I came, he was making speeches against imperialist war. He went to speak for the Wobblies, and they wanted him to join. He said, 'Well I'm not a worker, I'm a professor.' But he spoke to them. And pretty soon he was fired. He was given a sabbatical, and they said, 'Don't come back.'

That's when he thought of this grand idea. He and my mother would play classical music through the countryside. And he built this trailer—tongue-and-groove maple, brass screws, fourteen feet long, five and a half feet wide. I was just a baby. I thought it was a huge trailer. My cradle hung from the hoops that held the canvas up. My two older brothers had tiny bunks at one end. My father made a place where the whole side of the trailer folded out two feet, so he had a seven-foot-long stage with canvas over it, and when they traveled, it folded back. It was really quite an ingenious trailer.

My grandmother wanted her daughter to be a famous violinist, and so, even after she had three children, when my father built this trailer and went down south, she and my uncle rented a fancy theater, the Belasco Theater in Washington, and got some fancy sponsors, including Mrs. Coolidge, the vice president's wife. This was 1921, and Calvin Coolidge was our vice president. And they put the trailer on the stage, looking very picturesque, and my father played the little pump organ and my mother played the violin. They camped out in Rock Creek Park, which was a wilderness of weeds then. They cooked their meals over a fire while a few tourists came to gawk at them. They made maybe a few thousand dollars from the concert, and that's what they lived on trying to get down to Florida.

My father's basic idea was, 'Why should we play our great music for rich people in the cities? Why don't we take our good music out to good people in the country?' But the trip was not easy. In North Carolina, they gave up. Roads were not paved in 1921, except in cities, and after one hair-raising experience with a flood, my mother put her foot down and said, 'This is not going to work out.'

It was so late in the year, around November. They woke up the next morning with six serious white farmers with guns around the trailer saying, 'We don't want no gypsies 'round here.'

And my father, in his New England accent, says, 'We're not gypsies, we're musicians.'

'You're what?'

And my mother brings out the violin, and he brings out the little pump organ.

'Well, I'll be gol-darned!'

And my father said, 'Actually, we need a place we can camp out for the winter. The roads are so bad we can't get back to New York. Do you know any place we can camp out?'

And one farmer named McKenzie says, 'Oh I got a wood lot you can park it in. You can camp out there if you want.'

And my father chopped down some trees and made a framework

sixteen-foot square and got a squad tent at an army surplus store, and they got a stove inside it. So, for three or four months, they camped out. It was probably March or April when they started north.

And one night before they left, they took their classical music up to the McKenzie's farmhouse, to show them what kind of music they played. And the McKenzies were very polite, and they said, 'Oh that's very nice, we play a little music too.' And they took down banjos and fiddles and played up a storm. And my father says, 'For the first time in my life, I found out that the people had a lot of good music themselves. They didn't need my good music as much as I thought.'

...

My father studied most of his life calling himself a musicologist, although an 'ethnomusicologist,' because the European musicologists wanted real musicology to be 'classical' musicology. But he once said, 'Truth is a rabbit in a bramble patch. You can't lay your hands on it. All you can do is point as you circle around the bramble patch. It's somewhere in there, but you can't put your hands on its pulsing little body.'

FRANK'S MUSIC SCHOOL

My grandfather was a mild-mannered doctor, and my grandmother kept running up bills he couldn't pay.

'You're a doctor. Go earn some money and pay these bills,' says my grandmother.

They fled the bills and went out to Denver, where my mother, Constance, was born. And my mother proved to be very musical.

Out in Denver in 1889, my grandmother went to a music store to get some music for this talented daughter, and she got very well acquainted with the young man behind the counter. His name was Frank Damrosh. And one day, my grandmother says to him, 'What are you doing waiting behind a counter at a music store in Denver? You should be in New York, running a music school. I know a lot of people who can help give you some backing.' She did, because her father ran a very successful prep school, and she knew all sorts of well-to-do people. They had lived on Gramercy Park. They knew the Moore family of Clement Moore, who wrote 'The Night Before

Christmas,' and they knew some other wealthy families who were into music.

So, in 1905, Frank Damrosh started the Institute of Musical Art in New York City. And years later, when my mother and father decided to end their trailer trip to the south, my mother says, 'Charlie, this is not going to work. We're going back. Damrosh says I can get a job teaching, and I'm sure he'll give a job to you too.'

My mother taught at Frank's school for fifteen or twenty years, and my father taught there for about ten years until he split with my mother.

Later on, the school wanted to get more money, and they took the Julliard family money and changed the name to Julliard. By this time, Damrosh was very old. But in 1905, he was a younger man, and he ran the Institute of Musical Art on Claremont Avenue and 122nd Street, right across from where Riverside Church is now. They moved it down to Lincoln Center ten or twenty years ago.

THE AVON OLD FARMS SCHOOL

Editor's note: before attending Harvard (and then dropping out of Harvard), Pete had a prep-school-style education at a small Connecticut boys school called Avon Old Farms School. The school still exists; sometime in the 1990s, Pete visited there, and it sparked some old memories.

I'll tell you about this unusual school I went to, where you had to wear wing collars and bowties to supper every night. And speaking of unusual people, she was christened Effie Pope. But she changed her name from Effie to Theodate because she had a Quaker grandmother up in New England named Theodate. Her father had invented a way of making malleable steel for railroad car couplings and became a multimillionaire. With his patent, the Pope Steel Company made bicycles and other things out in Cleveland.

His wife was from New England, and I'm sure she said to her husband, 'You must realize that Effie's a very unusual girl. She's determined to be an architect.'

In those days, women were not architects. But her father helped her get training. He got McKim, Mead & White to take her in as an apprentice and teach her. By the time she was in her thirties, she was a well-trained architect. She designed a mansion for her parents around 1903. It's a Mount

Vernon-type building with big white pillars. As far as I was concerned, she was one old lady who had more money than any one person should have, spending millions on a mansion for her millionaire parents to retire to, but she did a good job.

Next, her father financed the building of a school, and Theodate designed all the buildings for the school. When her parents died, in 1916, she now had a fortune, and she said, 'Now I'm going to design my own school.'

Just as I went back to the Kentucky mountains for my favorite banjo picking, Theodate ignored Greece and Rome, and she ignored Gothic. She went to the Cotswolds area of England, where they loved to build wavy slate roofs, and she built her school in the Cotswolds style of architecture. There's nothing else in this country like it. It's imitation, but very good imitation. Thick stone walls, oak interiors, quite dark.

She had the school about two-thirds built, with a huge refectory and a dining hall with big wooden arches, when her financial advisors, in 1927, said, 'Mrs. Riddle, do you realize you'll be flat broke in six months if you keep on spending money like this?'

'Oh,' she says, 'I had no idea this would ever happen.'

The next day, everyone was fired. Water filled the quarry, and the equipment rusted away at the bottom. And, that coming fall, she opened with ninety students from wherever she could get them.

She had a good director who'd been a director of another school, and she paid him a good lot of money, and he got a good staff. But three or four years later, he quit. She would come in the school and say, 'Do this' and 'Do that,' and he said, 'I can't run this school with this crazy old woman coming in.'

The next headmaster, which is when I joined the school in 1932, made her sign a contract: 'The founder will always be accompanied by the headmaster every time she's on the campus.' She felt like a prisoner. She couldn't visit her own school unless he was at her side.

The school was called Avon Old Farms, and now it's called Avon Old Farms School. She'd bought a batch of old farms that were along the Farmington River. They had fields down near the river and woods back in the mountains and ended up having three thousand acres of woods and fields. I loved it because I could go hiking in the woods and track animals and put my teepee up and so on.

My parents had known a family that sent their son there. The Finke family. They were rather wealthy old socialists, and they funded Manumit School and Brooklyn Labor College. Their son, Ben Finke, ended up rooming with my brother in college. But before that, he was going to Avon and gave fairly good reports. He said, 'It's a little unusual school, but it's got good teachers.'

And that was it—they had very good teachers. The English teacher was a friend of Edna Saint Vincent Millay, and we put on very good plays: *Hamlet, St. Joan, Candida, The Adding Machine, Aria Da Capo.* I played Columbine in *Aria Da Capo* because I was a little shrimp and they let my hair grow long, and they curled it up so it stood out in a bush, and I'd wear falsies and played girls' parts in the plays.

In my second year, I started this little newspaper because I was short of cash. I tried shining shoes for a nickel a pair and only made about thirty dollars my first year. In my second year, the school gave me permission to use the mimeograph machine, and every Tuesday out comes the *Avon Weekly Newsletter.* I collected the news and I typed the stencil and turned the crank and sold the copies for a nickel apiece and kept the money. I think my total circulation was about eighty or a hundred copies. I'd tell the students, 'If you send this home, all you need to say is, *I'm fine, how are you?* and all the news of the week is right there.'

I think it was the headmaster who said, 'Peter, I think Mrs. Riddle would like to see a copy—why don't you mail it to her.' I sent her a gratis copy, not realizing anything. Son of a gun, she liked it! And that's why I stayed there another three years, free of charge. I didn't realize 'til after I was out of the school. That's why I got a scholarship. It wasn't because of my high marks. I knew my parents were broke, so it was that foolish little newsletter.

When I went back to visit, I realized Mrs. Riddle was more unusual than I thought. She was very wealthy, and she was a friend of Franklin Roosevelt. One of his nephews went there. She was very much very upper class— her charter said, 'Avon is a school for the sons of the gentry.' Nevertheless, she had some very good teachers who attended the Progressive Education Association every year—John Dewey's outfit.

They're not co-ed now, but they do take in a wide variety of students, not just Jews and Catholics but Africans and Asians and Latinos and so on. I went back for the first time for five whole days and went to classes, and I had to laugh that Mrs. Riddle's crazy architecture was no crazier than my Kentucky mountain banjo picking. Except it was too expensive.

She had a shop called a carpentry shop. It was one of the first buildings built, because the carpenters would work there while they were working on the other buildings. It got three-quarters built and she decided it was not being built right, and she had it torn down—a hundred thousand dollars is what I was told. That's the equivalent of a million dollars now. True, the building is now being used as a chapel—you can squeeze two or three hundred students in it—but it's built with sticks in the roof, and on top of that slate and hand-hewn beams. This was in the Depression, when people were starving to death.

Well, this is the money that's in the world. Now, how do the rich people change their minds?

THE WOODS

I was a nature nut as a kid. My older brothers were reading, and I wanted to be like them. And I was an early reader at age six. At age seven, I was given a book by a man named Earnest Thompson Seton called *Rolf In The Woods*. Seton was a nature writer. He wrote *The Wild Animals I Have Known* and *The Life Of A Grizzly* and *Lobo The Wolf* and so on. And I decided that's how I was going to spend my life. I was either going to be a forest ranger or something where I could be in the woods. Even today, if I go walking in the woods, that's like going to church for me.

However, at age sixteen, my mother was teaching violin to some teenagers in a Jewish family, and when, over supper, it came up about what I was going to do with my life, I said, 'I'm going to be a hermit. It's the only way to stay honest in a world of hypocrisy. The moment you participate in the world, you start becoming a hypocrite yourself, and I don't want to become a hypocrite, so if I can't get a job in the woods, I'll just be a hermit somehow.'

And they jumped on me like a ton of bricks. They said, 'That's your idea of morality? You're going to be nice and pure yourself, and let the rest of the world go to hell?' And they posed their ancient Jewish social conscience against my more Henry David Thoreau way of thinking. I had read Thoreau when I was twelve years old. I decided they were right, and I decided to get involved. And I have been involved ever since.

CHAPTER 03 SOME BANJO

I played a tenor banjo first. Tenor banjo was played back before amplification was invented. Jazz bands needed rhythm, and they wanted more than just drums. Well, piano was good, but a banjo was as loud as a piano. If you ever hear Duke Ellington's famous record of 'Mood Indigo,' the band is playing these wonderful chords, and right beside the saxophones and trumpets you hear this *pluck, plunk, plunk, plunk, plunk.*

I wanted to be with my peers when I was in prep school, so I switched over from a ukulele to a tenor banjo. I think I still have the letter—my mother saved it—trying to persuade her, 'Mother, can't I have twenty-five dollars? That's what my teacher is willing to sell it for.' My teacher had briefly played the banjo himself, but now he was glad to sell it to me. And it's all just chords, like a ukulele plays chords, but now I played banjo chords.

Then, in 1935, my father took me to a square dance festival in Ashville, and I suddenly realized what a wonderful instrument the five-string banjo was. My father felt that I should hear the five-string, which he had heard on records, and decided that I should come down south with him. He took the whole family. My sister Peggy was only one year old, Michael was three, and my stepmother, Ruth, was there. We got a friend to go with us, and between her and Ruth the two women took turns taking care of the babies.

But it was an education for me! How could I get to be in college and not have realized what widespread poverty was in America? We drove a shortcut to Ashville. Instead of taking a nice modern highway, we went by a one-and-a-half-lane road. It might not have even been paved. But we went down a valley, and I looked out the window at these families living in little shacks with naked children and laundry out on the line, and it was obvious these people were living hand to mouth. But it didn't seem unusual. They didn't have money but they lived as best they could. And I suppose if the husband could scrabble up a few dollars here or there, he could buy something at the store, but these families couldn't have been living on much more than a few dollars a week.

Then we get to Ashville, which was a small town in those days. A local lawyer named Bascom Lunsford had for several years run an annual mountain song-and-dance festival. He got the local baseball field, which could hold maybe two or three thousand seats, but for this, I don't think there were more than one thousand seats filled. And he had a wooden stage set up about thirty feet wide, and he did a very smart show-business trick. He'd have one band playing on stage right, and while they were playing, he'd walk over to the left-hand side of the stage, twenty-five feet away, and he'd get the next band up onstage, and he says, 'Now are you in tune? Do you know what song you're going to play? Now here's where you stand, and here's where the fiddle stands.'

He'd have three or four people grouped around one microphone.

'Now, when the light hits you, you start playing.'

'Are you really sure you're in tune, you know what you're going to play? Okay.'

He knows that the other group on stage right is about to finish. And he walks into the circle of light and says, 'Give 'em a hand, folks, aren't The Bog Trotters great? Oh, they're wonderful. Now, over here, we have The Coon Creek Gang.'

And he'd walk twenty-five feet and the spotlight would follow him, and he points his finger at them. So he had a fast-moving show, without a whole lot of people talking and tuning up. It's what should be learned by more people.

Now that's where I first heard the five-string banjo. Bascom Lunsford gave me my first lesson: 'Now you pick up on the third string, and now you pick up on the first string, and then you bring your thumb down on the fifth string, *tick-a bump-ditty bump-ditty bump-ditty.*'

One of the people I was also impressed with was a fifty-year-old woman who sat in a rocking chair, and she had painted butterflies and flowers all over the head of her banjo. I found out since then that she had been a country music recording artist fifteen years earlier, in the 20s. Her name was Samantha Bumgarner, and I later put a picture of her in my banjo book. She came from Gatlinburg, Tennessee, which was about thirty miles to the west of Ashville, and she was quite a well-known performer. As a matter of fact, later on, when I was in the US Army, I met a man from Gatlinburg and I asked him if he had ever heard of a woman banjo picker named Samantha Bumgarner, and he says, 'Oh, yes! She's famous!' She was one of the first country women recorded back then. The northern record companies found their jazz records weren't selling down south, but they had what they called a hillbilly catalogue, and they put out fiddlers and banjo. They also put out what they called a 'race' catalogue, which was in two parts, one for blues and one for gospel, and that was sold to black people. But the hillbilly catalogue was what they sold to white people.

The record companies recorded down there. They sent a man named Ralph Peer who would put a recording machine in a van, and he'd go down to a place like Knoxville or Nashville, and he would set it up in a hotel room. He'd let the hotel know what he was doing, because he would advertise in the local papers: 'He's from Vocalion Records'—that was one of the big companies—'and he's recording. Anybody whose recording is accepted will get twenty-five dollars.' Well, the next day there'd be fifty people with instruments lined up in the hotel hallway. And one after another he'd record them, and he'd either accept it or say, 'Sorry, no,' and they were out. But he ended up recording hundreds of country people, and he could have recorded Samantha down there.

So, I heard Bascom Lunsford and Samantha Bumgarner first, but I heard others too. Then I listened to some records. Almost no one played the five-string banjo up north in those days. Alan Lomax did find one man who had started in the South, but he'd gotten a job up New York, and he recorded him. And there was an elegant student named Rebecca Tarwater, who Alan had recorded playing 'Old Joe Clark' very elegantly, and she lived in New York, although she was probably from the South. But I learned from Bascom and Samantha and from the others down south. Then I also learned how to slow a record down. I've forgotten quite how I did it, but I can remember finding a record and writing down the notes, one at a time, *bum, bum, bum, bum, bum…*

But I didn't learn much more. I was still a very amateurish banjo picker in 1940 five years later. I hadn't really learned that much. But then I spent six months hitchhiking around the country—especially three months in the Appalachians, West Virginia, Kentucky, Tennessee, and Northern Alabama—and every time I met somebody who could play a banjo, I'd say, 'Hey, you play something.' And I'd watch them closely, and by the end of that year, I was a two-hundred-percent-better banjo picker.

I had been living with my older brother and his roommate in New York City on East 11th Street, between Third and Fourth Avenue, and that's where I bought my first five-string banjo. Down at the end of the street at Third Avenue, around 12th or 13th Street, they had a five-string banjo there for only five dollars. It was an S.S. Stewart, made probably around the turn of the century. Stewart was the man who wrote his own banjo instruction book and said, 'Only a bore would use steel strings.' He had gut strings on his banjo. But I put steel strings on mine—I hadn't read his book yet. And I met Paul Cadwell, who was a classic banjo player. He played strictly by written notes. But he liked what I was trying to do, and although he was a conservative, he would get together with me occasionally, and we would compare our different things that we were doing. He was very good at fingerpicking.

This was in about 1939. And then I went off with that S.S. Stewart banjo, and Woody Guthrie had taught me how to sing in saloons, and how to ride freight trains. But the first time I jumped off a freight train in the town of Lincoln, Nebraska, I didn't know how to jump off correctly. And *WHAM!* I fell on the ground. Luckily I didn't hurt myself, but I did hurt the banjo. My lovely S.S. Stewart had a broken neck. I mailed it back to a girlfriend I'd met and never saw her again, and never saw the banjo again, although forty years later she called me up, and she did faintly remember that I had sent her a banjo, but she didn't know what happened to it.

I went back to the same pawn shop and bought a Vega Whyte Laydie for only ten dollars. I took the Vega when I traveled with The Almanac Singers, and I went through World War II with it. But in 1949, I happened to be in New York City, and I was thirsty and went in for either a bottle of beer or a cup of coffee, and I didn't lock my car. It was double parked right outside, twenty feet away from me, but I came out and the banjo was not in it.

Before the Vega was taken, I had made a long-neck banjo out of it. I needed a longer neck because I wanted to play 'Viva La Quince Brigada' in C minor fingering, and I couldn't sing it as high as C. John D'Angelico had a repair shop down on the Lower East Side, and his assistant, George, sawed off the neck of my Vega White Laydie and put pegs in and glued it back with two extra frets. Now I could sing it in B flat. This was during World War II, because that's when we recorded those songs of the Abraham Lincoln Battalion.

I spent my first year in the army in the South, in Biloxi, Mississippi, learning the hydraulic system on a B-24 bomber, but then I got transferred up to a Special Service outfit. They'd found out my leftie background, and so the rest of my outfit had gone on to glory and death, but I was just picking up cigarette butts in Keesler Field. Then I got furlough, and I did something I'd always disapproved of. I used 'pull.' My father knew a major in the Special Service and got me an appointment. I walked up to the Pentagon, walked up to the second floor, found the major's office, and I said, 'I'm a good song leader. I think I could be more use to the war effort than sitting down there picking up cigarette butts.' And he says, 'Well, I don't know. I can't promise anything, but I'll do what I can.' And, sure enough, one week later, I was transferred to a Special Service company in Fort Mead, Maryland, twenty miles from Washington and twenty miles from Baltimore—and just a few hundred miles from New York.

While I was there, Bess Hawes and her husband, Butch, and Tom Glazer asked if we could record some of the songs of the Abraham Lincoln Battalion for Moses Asch. The Abraham Lincoln Battalion was made up of volunteers who had gone to Spain to fight fascism in the 1930s, and many of us on the political left had been singing some of their songs. So I arranged for a weekend pass. I left on Friday night, took a train to New York, and on Saturday morning I was up at the Folkways recording studio with these three other friends. We rehearsed six songs. In those days, three

78rpm records was one album. We rehearsed on Saturday and recorded the six on Sunday, and Sunday evening I took the train back to my job in Fort Mead, Maryland, doing close-order drill and other things. So, I was able to make that recording with the long-neck Vega Whyte Laydie before it went missing in 1949.

In 1948, Lee Hays said to me, 'Do you think we can start another singing group, and this time do a little rehearsing?' Because that was the Almanacs joke. Woody said, 'This is the first singing outfit I've ever been in that rehearses onstage,' because we'd be up onstage and I'd say, 'Hey Lee, take this note in the bass,' and I'd say, 'Woody, take the high harmony.'

I had started with The Weavers using my Vega. Then I tried several banjos, and they cost, now, hundreds of dollars, but I wasn't satisfied with them. They didn't have the kind of *plunk* that the Whyte Laydie has. In 1949, The Weavers didn't get many jobs, so I had some time on my hands, and I had to get a new banjo. Vega was going out of business. But I contacted a nice guy at Vega and said, 'Can you sell me at least a pot?'—that's the round part of a banjo with the drum—'and I'll see if I can make a neck for it.' I bought this very expensive wood. If you ever took a train up from Grand Central, right on the north side of the Harlem River was a sign saying, 'Monteath Brothers, Tropical Hardwoods.' It's been out of business for many years, but that's where I bought this piece of lignum vitae, which is a very hard wood. And I got John D'Angelico to rough it out. I asked him just to saw it in the shape of what it looks like from on top and what it looks like from the side, and I said I'd round it off myself. And, with files, I went back and forth and rounded the whole thing off, and then a finer file, and finally I was using sandpaper to make it smooth. And this time I had a three-fret longer neck. I was singing in colleges then, and up in MIT there was a banjo picker that put four extra frets on, but it'd take a tall person to reach out there. I finished the lignum vitae banjo in a few months in late 1949 or 1950 and played it while I was touring the country with The Weavers.

A few years later, I began writing words on my banjo head.

For years, Woody had a sign on his guitar, 'THIS MACHINE KILLS FASCISTS,' and we'd say, 'Woody, Hitler's dead—why don't you take the sign off?' And he'd say, 'Oh, this fascism comes along whenever the rich people get the generals to do what they want.' It's a good definition of fascism.

But then Woody went into the hospital, and that's when I decided to put something on my banjo, but I thought it should be a little different.

THIS MACHINE SURROUNDS HATE AND FORCES IT TO SURRENDER.

It was 1952 when I first put that on my new banjo, and I've kept it on my banjo head ever since. Sometimes I put it on well, but other times I'm very sloppy.

• • •

For almost sixty-four years, Pete played the long-neck banjo with the arbor vitae neck that he first began playing with The Weavers around 1950. In 1988, Pete's friend Ralph Storm built him a new banjo with a neck made of dogwood from the woods near Pete's home. For a short period of time, Pete also played a long-neck banjo that I lent to him after his main banjo had broken several times. That banjo had been gifted to me by our good friend John Fisher. As far as we know, these are the only three instruments upon which Pete wrote 'THIS MACHINE SURROUNDS HATE AND FORCES IT TO SURRENDER.'

After Pete's arbor vitae banjo was repaired, he arranged for the banjo he'd borrowed from me to be exhibited at the Grammy Museum in Los Angeles as part of their opening exhibit entitled *Songs Of Conscience, Sounds Of Freedom*, where it was in good company with instruments played by Woody Guthrie, Bob Dylan, Odetta, and others. It has since been transferred to the Woody Guthrie Center in Tulsa, Oklahoma.

But that's the way it was with Pete. Banjos came and went. Pete didn't view them as cherished items to protect but more like a carpenter might view their hammer. You might have your favorite old hammer that fits your hand just right, but if something happens to it, or it goes missing, you pick up another and keep working. And if one day you find yourself alongside a fellow carpenter who needs a hammer, you reach into your toolbox and give him one.

Sometime around 1997, Pete heard that I wanted a better long-neck and offered to lend me his dogwood banjo. It was an honor to have it for a time, but people thought I was imitating Pete because of the words written on it. That's why it was almost a relief when Pete called one day and said he needed to 'borrow it back' because he had lost his main banjo.

This was in August of the year 2000. Pete had sung at a fundraising concert up near Rosendale, New York, and was tired after the concert, so he put the banjo on top of his car and lay down in the back seat for a rest. He woke up refreshed and drove off, and the banjo slipped from the roof and landed in a ditch somewhere. For weeks that summer, articles appeared in newspapers around the country, lamenting Pete's lost banjo. It was eventually found and returned.

But the arbor vitae banjo wasn't the only banjo to find its way back to Pete— or at least so we think…

While recording for this chapter, I was particularly intrigued by Pete's story of breaking his S.S. Stewart banjo while jumping off a freight train with Woody Guthrie. This was because, some fifteen years earlier, I had purchased an old S.S. Stewart in a small repair shop in Newburgh, New York, that very much matched Pete's description of the one he broke. I remember asking the owner, Gary Emmons, why he was selling a nice old Stewart for only two hundred dollars. He turned the banjo over and pointed to a glue joint at the heel of the neck and said, 'It's because the neck has been snapped and reglued, and I don't know how or when that happened, so I can't stand behind it.' Gary was always scrupulously honest, and he never charged enough for his great repair work.

I told Pete about the banjo, and he wanted to see it. He examined it closely, tracing the line of the break with his finger, and remarked, 'This is exactly how mine snapped. I think this might be my banjo!'

After some seventy-one years, I like to believe that Pete's first five-string banjo had found its way home.

CHAPTER 04

SOME WOODY GUTHRIE

I remember very well when Woody Guthrie and I met. It was in 1940, at a midnight benefit concert for California Migratory Workers. They called them Oakies. Will Geer, the well-known actor, had arranged for the concert in a small theater off Broadway, only a block from Times Square in New York City—the center of the entertainment district. This was March 1940, just a year after the famous novel *The Grapes Of Wrath* by John Steinbeck had come out. There was a Broadway play called *Tobacco Road* about sharecroppers in Georgia, and Will Geer was the lead, and he got permission from the producers.

The stage had just one set, a lot of red clay curving up to some sharecroppers' shacks, and then one of the shacks had a little porch on it, which was almost like a little stage inside a stage. Woody had been living in Los Angeles, and Will had met him a year before, in Hollywood. Will had written Woody, 'If you can get here by March some people will hear you and you will get some jobs.' So he hitchhiked into New York from Pennsylvania in the month of February.

What Woody didn't know was that Alan Lomax, the folklorist, would drive up from Washington DC with me. I was working for Alan at the time at a small salary, going through records at the Library of Congress, and he drove me up in his car. He insisted that I sing at least one song in the program. I sang an outlaw ballad named 'John Hardy' very amateurishly, and I got a smattering of polite applause and retired in confusion. But there were some famous people on the show. Leadbelly sat on that little porch and sang some songs, Josh White was there, and The Golden Gate Quartet, Burl Ives, and a square dance by Margo Mayo's American Square Dance group, and my future wife was one of the dancers.

Then there was this short, curly headed guy named Woody telling his stories and jokes and singing a few songs. Nobody had ever seen him onstage before and Woody had the whole crowd laughing. He would sing a song and then tell a joke:

Oklahoma is a very rich state, you know. You want some oil, go down the hole and get you some oil. You want coal, we got coal in Oklahoma—go down the hole and get you some coal. You want lead, go down the hole and get you some lead. If you want food, clothing, groceries, go down the hole—and stay there.

Next, he would sing another song, and then, 'There was a dry spell in Oklahoma. I saw three telephone poles chasing one little dog.'

For about twenty minutes, Woody held that audience absolutely spellbound. Here was the real thing. Alan Lomax got backstage and says, 'Woody I have a recording studio down in Washington. You have to come down and record all these songs and more, all the songs you know, all the songs you made up.'

Recording studios were rare things in those days, and Alan demanded they give as much time as necessary. I think they recorded for three days, rambling on. Alan recorded his whole life story and all the songs he could think of, and he said, very forcefully, 'Woody, you are a great songwriter. Don't let anything distract you from what is your life's work of writing songs.' And he said it so forcefully that Woody took it to heart, and he did it. He just wrote new songs every day, practically.

I met Woody in Alan's house, and he found that I could follow him in any song he played. I had a good ear and I stayed in tune—played the right chord, didn't play anything too fancy. Woody was always cracking jokes, and when he met me, he couldn't quite figure me out. He once said, 'That Seeger guy is the youngest man I know—he don't drink, he don't smoke, he don't chase girls.' I was twenty years old, but a very immature twenty. But he must have liked me, because I had a good ear and I could accompany him in any song he sang the first time I heard it, if not the second time, so pretty soon I was tagging along with him.

• • •

I remember one night, Woody said, 'Are there any mountains near us?'

I said, 'Yeah a couple of hours drive, they're called the Blue Ridge Mountains of Virginia.'

He said, 'Let's go visit them.'

Near midnight, we start off. There was an old woman carrying a big sack of clothing, and we slowed down and said, 'Ma'am would you like us to give you a lift, that bag must be heavy?'

And she said, 'It sure is.' She got in the back seat and said, 'Where are you boys going, this time of night?'

'Oh, we're going out to visit the mountains.'

She said, 'Boys, will you let me off, please.'

'You're not going to get another lift tonight.'

She said, 'Boys, let me off!'

She didn't want to be in a car with any men who were going to visit the mountains at one o'clock in the morning.

MY BIG EDUCATION

Woody was like my big, big education, learning about America. I'd gone to private schools all my life. I was twenty-one in 1940 and he was twenty-seven. He said, 'Pete, you ever been West?' Well, I had to confess. 'Never.' I'd been to Washington, and I once took a trip south to a folk festival in Ashville, North Carolina. We drove down some little mountain roads where there was absolutely no money. I thought I knew slums from seeing the slums in New York, but these mountain slums were two times worse. But that's all I knew. So Woody said, 'Well, Pete, I got to drive out to see my wife and family out there in Texas. Tag along.'

I went out west with him to the panhandle of Texas, and along the line, he taught me how to sing in the saloons.

He said, 'Pete, sling your banjo on your back, go in and buy a nickel beer, and sip it as slow as you can. Sooner or later someone will say, *Kid, can you play that thing?* Don't be too eager. Say, *Maybe a little*, but keep on sipping your beer. Sooner or later, somebody will say, *Kid, I got a quarter for you if you pick us a tune.* Now you swing it around and play your best song.'

With that kind of instruction, I couldn't go wrong. I never went hungry, making my way out to Montana and going back again down to Florida later that year.

Woody also taught me how to hitch a ride on freight trains, when the hitchhiking was going slowly.

'You don't get on the train right in the station, they'll kick you off, but wait a couple of a hundred yards outside of the station, and while it is picking up speed, it is only going two or three miles an hour, you see an empty boxcar, toss your banjo in it, and then you hop in after it. When it slows down for another station and it slows down to two or three miles an hour, then you hop off it.'

Of course, the first time I tried it, I was not that expert, and I fell. But about a month later, I managed to go out as far as Butte, Montana, and sing for the copper miners there. Then I hitchhiked back and went to the north part of Florida, where a whole lot of people were building an army camp. In the evening you could hear fiddles and other instruments having a little party, and two musicians would meet each other, and they don't even ask each other's names but they start to play music together.

I spent most of my time going up and down the Appalachians from northern Alabama to the highlands of Tennessee, up to Southeastern County, Harlan County of Kentucky, even touched West Virginia for a while. I met some wonderful people. That's where the song 'Which Side Are You On' was made up, by a woman named Florence Reece. Her husband, Sam, was a rank-and-file organizer, and they had a strike of the coal miners, and the company sheriff sent his men down to literally kill him. But he was warned in time. He got out the back door. They came in, stuck their rifles into the closets and under the beds and, Mrs. Reece told me, even into piles of dirty laundry. Her two little girls started crying. The men said, 'What are you crying for? We're not after you, we're after your old man.' They never did find him. He escaped and didn't come back—he left Harlan County. But Mrs. Reece was so outraged she tore her calendar off the wall, and on the backside of the calendar she wrote these verses:

Come all of you good workers, good news to you I'll tell
Of how the good old union has come in here to dwell
Which side are you on, which side are you on?

They say in Harlan County, there are no neutrals there
You'll either be a union man or a thug for J.H. Blair
Which side are you on, which side are you on?

When I was hitchhiking through there a few years later, Sheriff Blair himself was assassinated. They found him somewhere. He'd made a few too many enemies. However, I was warned about him. They said, 'If you are riding on the top of a freight car, find some way to get off before you're in the town of Hazard'—the main town in Harlan County. 'There's a sheriff there, likes to shoot hobos off the top of the freight trains.' So I got off.

I managed to cover most of the states. The only ones I missed were the far west, Idaho and Utah, and from there west. But I went down to Florida, went through Alabama and Georgia, and up to Maine. And I remember thinking, in 1940, I would've graduated from Harvard, but I learned a whole lot of things about my country that I never would have learned if I had stayed at Harvard.

WOODY'S EDUCATION

Even as a kid, Woody was curious. In the little town of Okemah, the librarian was amazed. Here is this kid of ten or eleven years old, just reading one book after another, after another, after another. Books that would normally be read by adults, and he was still a kid. At age twelve, he visited his mother in the mental hospital, and he came back and threw himself on the floor crying and said, 'She didn't recognize me.' For the next three years, he lived with his uncle, who was a musician, and I think that's where he learned how to play the guitar and mandolin and fiddle and a couple of other things. But at age seventeen, his father remarried a woman in Pampa, Texas, a little oil boom town in the panhandle, up north of Amarillo a ways. There he went to high school, and there again the local librarian was amazed at this kid who read voraciously, and she said, 'Have you seen this book, have you seen that book?'

'No, I read that three years ago.'

I was with him in New York when we visited my sister-in-law, and she had a book of the French writer François Rabelais—in translation, of course—and Woody dipped into it and said, 'Can I borrow this?' He borrowed it for a day or two and read through it. In the following weeks I could see his writing borrowing some of the ideas of Rabelais, namely piling on adjectives by the dozen. So, Woody was a real intellectual. If he had been born into an intellectual family, he probably would have gone into academia in some way. But he loved music, and he was convinced that with music he could reach people better than he could with just prose. He did write a couple of books, but late in life, he said, 'No, the songs were the best thing I ever done. The prose you read once or twice, the songs you sing over and over again.'

Not that all his songs were successful. He wrote not just hundreds but probably thousands and lost half of them. He was once on an airplane ride with me and Lee Hayes. We were singing for the Westinghouse strikers in Pittsburgh, and we got in the airplane and Lee went to sleep, although it was only an hour and a half ride, and I was busy reading a magazine. Woody was scribbling on a piece of paper. He would look out the window and see a little town and write a verse wondering what the people were thinking as this metal bird went over their heads. And then he would look at the pretty hostess and wonder what she would do that night, whether she was friendly with the pilot or what. And then he would write a verse about the electrical workers who were on strike, who we were going to sing for, wondering what they would think about our songs. Then he gets up and he leaves the piece of paper in the seat. I picked it up and I gave it to him after we got out of the airport, and I said, 'Woody, do you realize how Lee and I envy you, the way you just write verses, verse after verse after verse wherever you are.' But he'd done that for a long time.

Woody first got in close touch with the Communist Party in 1939, when he worked on a tiny little radio station somewhere on the outskirts of Los

Angeles. The owner of the station really believed in the First Amendment, and he thought that everyone had a right to be heard from, so he let a Communist have fifteen minutes on the air every day, and Woody was also allowed fifteen minutes on the air every day. Woody was a reader of newspapers, and so he'd occasionally have songs about what went on in the news. He got paid all of one dollar, but he mimeographed a little songbook, and he said, 'I got my songs in this book. If you send me twenty-five cents, I'll send you a copy.' So he made a little extra money by selling his twenty-five-cent songbook. It was called *On A Slow Train Through California*, which was a takeoff on the book of jokes sold in the Midwest, *On A Slow Train Through Arkansas*.

One day, Woody said to the Communist commentator, whose name was Ed Robbins, 'Ed, do you ever listen to my program? I listen to yours.' And Ed was a little apologetic, and he said, 'Woody I have to confess. I don't usually listen to country music, and you're on before me, and I usually just arrive in time for my program.' And Woody says, 'Well, you come early tomorrow and listen to my song. I think you'll be interested.'

Next day, Ed heard:

Mr. Tom Mooney is free
Mr. Tom Mooney is free
Done got a pardon from that old jailhouse warden
Governor Culbert L. Olsen's decree

After the program, Ed said, 'Woody that is a great song! Do you know there's going to be a big mass meeting tonight? Tom Mooney's going to speak there. They would love to hear your song. Would you come?' Then he had second thoughts, and he says, 'Huh, erm, Woody, it's a little left wing.' And Woody said, 'Left wing, chicken wing, don't bother me none. I've been in the red all my life.' So he went with Ed to the rally. There were a thousand people listening to speech after speech, after speech, after speech, and Woody fell asleep. Ed had to walk across the stage and shake him— 'Woody you're on!' Woody shook his head, picked up his guitar, walked to the microphone, and he sang his song. He got a standing ovation—he had to sing his song twice.

Will Geer, the actor, was in the audience, and he goes up to Woody after the program, and he said, 'Woody, I'm going up tomorrow to put on a program for the striking workers in the lettuce fields, up near Bakersfield. Would you come with me? They're mostly Okies like you, they'd love your songs.' So, pretty soon, Will and Woody were a team, and they sang at fundraising parties in Hollywood, as well as up in the lettuce fields and so on. That's when Woody made up more songs, like 'Do Re Mi.'

Woody called himself a Communist, but he was never one of these people to go to meetings. He just read the *Daily Worker*, and once he had a column in that paper, and he wrote little things like Will Rogers wrote. Will Rogers sent telegrams that were printed by newspapers all over the country, in the *New York Times* and so on. Woody had a column in the Communist newspaper called 'Woody Sez' and, for example, when he went down to Washington where Alan Lomax recorded him, he writes:

> Went down to look at the Potomac. Quite a broad river. They said George Washington threw a silver dollar across it. But of course then, a dollar went further in those days.

That's the kind of column he had every day in the *Daily Worker*, but Woody was not a member of the party. I think he applied and was turned down. He and I weren't regular people who took on assignments. We sang our songs, and I guess the party was glad we sang them.

HOW WOODY WROTE SONGS

Woody really liked a number of good old songs, whether it was 'John Henry' or songs The Carter Family sang. He loved them. He played their record about an outlaw named John Hardy over and over again and finally put the new words to it about Tom Joad. He also liked the way they sang an old favorite, '*Takes a worried man to sing a worried song, I'm worried now but I won't be worried long …*' He also loved the songs of Jimmy Rogers, the yodeling break man, '*T for Texas T for Tennessee …*'

Woody also loved some of the blues. I especially remember Big Bill Broonzy and Blind Lemon Jefferson. These were blues singers back in the 1920s. Woody would take one of their blues and sing it over and over and change it a little here and change it a little there, and change it a little more until it was almost a new song. Blind Lemon sang, '*I'm broke and I ain't got a dime,*' and pretty soon Woody would sing, '*I was broke and I did not have a dime.*' By the time he'd finished with that, he had 'New York Town.' My guess is there must have been tens of thousands of beginning guitar players who couldn't sing anything fancy, but they could sing that song.

• • •

When Woody and I were on the way to Texas to see his wife, we stopped off for a week in Oklahoma City, and the left was trying to organize a union of oil drillers. It was a small meeting, about sixty people, but the wives and the children were there. They didn't have money for babysitters. And six men came in with overcoats on and stood along the back wall and didn't take their overcoats off, and the organizer said, 'I don't know who they are, it's an open meeting, but they might be intending to break us up. See if you can get the crowd singing.'

And we did get the crowd singing—the women and children, too. And sure enough, after the meeting was over, they said, 'Yeah, we did intend to break this up, but this is a little different than we were told.' They had clubs underneath their overcoats. Then they said, 'You should have an American flag.' And the organizer said, 'You're right. Next time, at all our meetings, we should have the American flag.'

But they never did break us up, and maybe it was the presence of women and children there that stopped them. Well, the organizer's wife said, 'Woody, all of these songs are about *brothers* this and *men* that. Can't you make up a song for the union women?' Next morning in the union office, there was Woody, tap, tap, tapping on a typewriter, and then he'd get up and try out a verse with his guitar and then sit down tap, tap some more. And he'd say, 'Pete, what do you think of this?' And I'd say, 'Sounds pretty good to me.' He claimed I helped him write it, but I was just there when he wrote it. It had one of the world's greatest choruses. He'd picked a famous old tune, a German folk song called 'The Happy Plowman' that somebody had made into a bawdy song about cowboys and Indians, '*Oh the moon shines bright on pretty red Wing.*' And now Woody had, '*Oh, you can't scare me, I'm sticking to the union…*'

UNION MAID *Woody Guthrie*

There once was a union maid, she never was afraid
Of goons and ginks and company finks and the deputy sheriffs who made the raid.
She went to the union hall when a meeting it was called,
And when the Legion boys come 'round
She always stood her ground.

Oh, you can't scare me, I'm sticking to the union,
I'm sticking to the union, I'm sticking to the union.
Oh, you can't scare me, I'm sticking to the union,
I'm sticking to the union 'til the day I die…

That song that he put together in a few minutes is now one of the best-known union songs in the English language, just because of that great chorus. We sang it at the Labor Day Parade in San Francisco a month later, and a crowd of people were singing it with us. You never know.

• • •

Woody and I hitchhiked on credit. He paid a down payment on a car in New York. Then we drove out to see his family in the panhandle of Texas, but the company caught up with the car. After that, Woody went back to New York and recorded some songs for Victor. That's when he recorded the *Dust Bowl Ballads*.

My own hitchhiking took me through New York briefly, and I met with Woody. I think this was August or September. He says, 'Pete, do you have a typewriter still?'

I said, 'Yeah, I'm staying with a friend over on the East Side.'

He said, 'Could I use it for a few hours? I got to write a song about *The Grapes Of Wrath*.'

I said, 'Have you read the book?'

He said, 'No, but I saw the movie.'

The movie scriptwriters did half his job for him, boiling down a long, three-hundred-page book to an hour-and-a-half movie. And then Woody boiled down the hour-and-a-half movie to a six-minute song, 'Tom Joad.'

It was on a 78rpm record, so half the verses went on one side of the record and half the verses went on the other side.

THE ALMANAC SINGERS

In early 1941, Lee Hays and his roommate, Millard Lampell, wrote most of the song 'The Ballad Of Harry Bridges' with just a little help from me. I probably chose the tune, an old Irish tune. I call it 'the great American folk tune' because it has been used for so many sets of words. Woody Guthrie had been out west, singing songs about the Grand Coulee Dam, and he hitchhiked east because I wrote him a letter and said, 'Woody, I am singing with two other guys. We call ourselves The Almanac Singers. We're singing for the unions, and we sang in Madison Square Garden for the striking transit workers, and I had the crowd singing your song, *Oh you can't scare me, I'm sticking to the union…*'

Woody had deserted his wife and kids one too many times, so his wife went back to Texas to get a divorce, and he knocked on our door on June 23rd, one day after Hitler invaded the Soviet Union, and I said, 'Woody, it's good to see you!'

The first words out of his mouth were, 'I guess we won't be singing any more peace songs, will we?' I said, 'You mean we have to work with Churchill?' And Woody says, 'Yep, Churchill says, All aid to the gallant Soviet allies.' I said, 'Is this the same Churchill who in 1920 said, We must strangle the Bolshevik infant in its cradle?' Woody says, 'Yup. Churchill has flip-flopped. We got to flip-flop.'

And so we did. We quit singing peace songs and stuck to union songs as we drove across the country.

We had recorded 'The Ballad Of Harry Bridges' at the request of the Harry Bridges Defense Committee about six weeks earlier, and soon after Woody joined us in June, we all got into an old car and drove out west. We stopped briefly to sing for the seamen who were having a convention in Ohio and for the Chicago Repertory Theater, and we stayed in the home of one of the young actors, Studs Turkel, and his wife. Then we stopped to sing in Denver briefly. We passed through Salt Lake City, and we may have gone through Reno.

We arrived in San Francisco just in time to sing at a meeting of Local

10. And when we walked down the aisle, some of the longshoremen looked around and said, 'Hey what's a bunch of hillbillies singers doing here? We got work to do.' But Harry says, 'Men, I think you'll want to hear what these men are singing.'

We sang 'The Ballad Of Harry Bridges' and got a standing ovation. We had to sing it twice through. And on the way down the aisle they were slapping Woody on the back so hard they nearly knocked him over. He was a small guy, about five foot four, as I remember. We sang it all up and down the West Coast during the next month—in Los Angeles, and of course San Francisco, and Portland, Oregon, and Seattle.

THE BALLAD OF HARRY BRIDGES *Lee Hays, Millard Lampell, Pete Seeger*

Let me tell you of a sailor, Harry Bridges is his name,
An honest union leader whom the bosses tried to frame,
He left home in Australia, to sail the seas around,
He sailed across the ocean to land in Frisco town.

There was only a company union, the bosses had their way.
A worker had to stand in line for a lousy dollar a day.
When up spoke Harry Bridges, 'Us workers got to get wise.
Our wives and kids will starve to death if we don't get organized.'

Chorus (sung after most of the verses):
Oh, the FBI is worried, the bosses they are scared
They can't deport six million men they know.
And we're not going to let them send Harry over the seas.
We'll fight for Harry Bridges and build the CIO…

A few months later, Woody wrote a song called 'The Sinking Of The Reuben James,' which is still such a great song. By October 1941, The Almanac Singers wasn't just Lee and Mill and me, it was Bess Lomax, and Butch Haws, and Sis Cunningham who later ran *Broadside* magazine and others. We read in the newspapers about the ship *Reuben James* being sunk off the coast of Greenland.

ABOVE Charles and Constance Seeger
with their children, Pete, John, and
Charles, on a trailer trip to the South.
Elie Edson, courtesy of the Seeger Family.

ABOVE The Almanac Singers visit the famed labor-union supporter Mother Bloor at her farmhouse in Pennsylvania c. 1941. A young Pete Seeger strums the banjo; to his right are Pete Hawes, Mother Bloor, and future Weaver Lee Hays. *Walter Lowenfels, courtesy of Judy Jacobs.*

OPPOSITE PAGE TOP Pete and Toshi Seeger on their wedding day, 1943. *Courtesy of Tinya Seeger.* **BOTTOM** The Almanac Singers in Greenwich Village, 1942. Left to right: Woody Guthrie, Millard Lampell, Bess Hawes, Pete Seeger, Arthur Stern, Sis Cunningham. *Courtesy of the Woody Guthrie Archives.*

ABOVE Pete Seeger and Leadbelly jamming at a party in 1948. The dark-haired man near the top right is David Bernz's father, Harold; the woman behind him is most likely Harold's future wife, Ruth. *Harold Bernz Archives.* **RIGHT** Leadbelly performing at the same event. *Harold Bernz Archives.*

OPPOSITE PAGE Woody Guthrie, Leadbelly, and Betty Sanders, 1948. *Harold Bernz Archives.*

ABOVE George Margolin leading an
early singalong in Washington Square
Park, Greenwich Village, New York,
c. 1948. *Ruth Bernz Archives.*

ABOVE The first issue of *Sing Out!* magazine, started by Pete and others as a successor to the earlier *People's Songs Bulletin*.

FOLLOWING PAGE A publicity poster on display outside a Weavers concert, c. 1952. *Harold Bernz Archives.*

DIRECT FROM NEW YORK

THE
WEAVERS
SENSATIONAL SINGING STARS
THEY INTRODUCED
'GOODNIGHT IRENE' and 'ONE OF THE ROVIN' KIND'
BEHIND LOCKED DOORS

Woody felt very certain that everybody in this world was important and their name should be mentioned, so he wrote a ballad with about twenty verses, and he put into those verses the names of all forty men who had drowned. When he sang it to the rest of us Almanacs, we said, 'Woody, nobody but you is going to sing that song. At least give us a chorus we can join in on.' He grumbled and grumbled and it took him a week, and he came back with that great chorus:

What were their names,
Tell me what were their names,
Did you have a friend on the good Reuben James?

He did a good job of shrinking down his twenty verses to five verses. He'd used the tune of 'Wildwood Flower,' an old Carter Family tune. He flattened out that tune, though, and when it ended he made up a chorus using the musical elements of the verse. That was such a good chorus that it's still sung now, sixty-five years later.

So, Woody was a musician as well as a word man, although he usually started with words and later on got a tune. He once said, 'I write some words and look around for some old tune that the people seem to like and that will fit my words.'

THE FIGHT AGAINST FASCISM STARTS RIGHT HERE

The Almanac Singers recorded peace songs and union songs in 1941, and then Hitler invaded the Soviet Union and we forgot about singing peace songs. Then, along comes Pearl Harbor and we quit singing strike songs, and it was 'win the war' for the next three and a half years. The Communist Party had influence in the labor movement then, and we put the emphasis on doing a good job to beat Hitler. I joined the army in July of 1942, got married in July 1943, and Toshi joined me living off the post. I went overseas in 1944 and 1945, and Woody went in the merchant marines.

Woody went through World War II with a piece of cardboard pasted to the top of his guitar, 'THIS MACHINE KILLS FASCISTS'. He really wanted his guitar to win the war against Hitler, no matter where he was. And he thought of the word *fascist* in the broadest sense. When Woody went to Baltimore around 1942, he was singing for a big rally to buy war bonds and beat Hitler. He and Sonny Terry, the harmonica player, and Brownie McGee, the blues singer, were singing: '*We're gonna tear Hitler down, we're gonna tear Hitler down ...*'

After they'd sung, the chairman said, 'Mr. Guthrie, we have a seat for you at the table here, and we have a table for your friends out in the kitchen.' And Woody says, 'What do you mean! We sang together, why can't we eat together?' And the chairman said, 'Well, Mr. Guthrie, this is Baltimore, you know.' And Woody shouted out, 'This fight against fascism got to start right here!' And he picks the whole big table up with all the silver and glasses on it and tips it over. *Crash!* On the floor goes everything. A second later, he walked to the table next to him and picks that up in the air. *Crash!* All the silver and glasses getting broken. They grabbed him by both arms. Brownie says, 'Sonny's blind, and I am lame—you're going to get us all in trouble.' And Woody kept shouting, 'This fight against fascism got to start right here!'

Woody sang a lot of old country songs, and years before he had sung what they call a 'minstrel song' full of what they used to call 'darkie' dialect. This was in California in 1937. The next day, he got a letter from a well-educated African American:

Mr. Guthrie, I believe you mean well, or I would not bother writing you, but do you realize that song I just heard you sing is really insulting to a lot of people like me?

It was a long letter, and he went into detail about how black people had been captured as slaves and made to work all their lives away, and how they were sold away from their families. He said, 'Think of what it was like to be sold and never see your mother again.'

Well, the next day, Woody reads this man's whole letter on the air. He said, 'Folks you just heard the man's letter. Now I know that song he was talking about. Remember I sang it a couple of days ago. I am holding that song up right close to the microphone. I want you to listen.' He tore the paper in half.

• • •

After the war, the Cold War broke out, and it was a bad time for the United States of America. But the funny thing was, it didn't make that much difference to me. I sang with little lefty groups here and summer camps and schools there. I didn't expect to get commercial work. At one time around 1947, Woody and Marge visited me in MacDougal Street and said we might try starting up the Almanacs again. But I said, 'Woody is raising a family and I am raising a family—it's not practical.' The Almanacs were like a family, all living in one place. So I turned him down.

And then, in 1950, totally unexpected, I had a new group—not The Almanac Singers but The Weavers, with Lee Hays and Fred Hellerman and Ronnie Gilbert. By one of these musical accidents, The Weavers got a Decca recording contract, and all of a sudden we had hit records. 'Goodnight Irene' was on top of the hit parade, week after week, month after month in the summer of 1950. Decca heard us singing Woody's song 'So Long, It's Been Good To Know Yuh.' The original is such a great song, taking a tragic story and finding humor in it, and I'm regretting deeply that we gave in to Decca Records. Decca said, 'No one is interested in singing about dust storms. This is 1950. Make up a song anybody can sing anywhere.'

Woody agreed—if he could write it. So he came in and sat on the floor at Gordon Jenkins' apartment at the Sheridan Hotel and grabbed a pen and made a batch of new verses, and it became just a funny song. They're not as good as the originals, and he probably knew it. We didn't sing them that much. We sang it for the recording company once or twice, but only a few people sing the recorded version, *What a long time since I've been home ...* They usually sing the way Woody originated it, *That dusty old dust is a-gettin' my home, and I got to be driftin' along.* The original as Woody wrote it in 1935 is a tragic song as well as a funny song.

The Weavers had a string of pop records, but then came the blacklisters. They probably said, 'How did we let those commie so-and-sos slip through our fingers?' They were as surprised as we were. They started cutting us down in late 1950, and cut us down more in '51, and by 1952 we were singing in Daffy's Bar & Grill on the outskirts of Cleveland, and we decided to take a sabbatical. As Lee Hayes said, 'It turned into a Mondical and a Tuesical.' However, it didn't really make much difference to me. I liked to sing for the left wing, just like Woody did.

THIS LAND IS YOUR LAND

When Woody first came out to New York in 1940, he didn't have enough money for a ticket the whole way. He hitchhiked through Pennsylvania in the month of February, and the verses he was writing said:

As I was walking that ribbon of highway
I saw above me that endless skyway...

Not long after I met Woody, I found a piece of paper among Woody's many pieces of paper and at the top of the page it said, 'God Blessed America.' I found that when he was hitching through Pennsylvania, he'd have to go in for a cup of coffee occasionally, a nickel cup of coffee it was in those days, and 'God Bless America' was a big hit at the time, and it was on the jukebox. So that was the last line of every verse:

This land is your land... God blessed America for me
As I went walking that ribbon of highway... God blessed America for me
I roamed and I rambled... God blessed America for me
And the sun was shining... God Blessed America for me

That's how he wrote the song in 1940. We never heard him sing it once, not me or anyone else. It just went into his files of unfinished songs. But somewhere in the next eight years, he added a few verses, and he got a new last line, *'This land was made for you and me.'*

In 1948, there was a tiny little recording company called Folkways that recorded the song. This was just about the time LPs were invented, but they were still selling 78rpm records, and the man in charge of the company, Moses Ash, said, 'Woody, you can only get two and a half minutes of a song on one side of a record. We have to cut a few verses.' And maybe that's why some of those verses didn't get in the recording. However, it was a good song anyway, with a good old tune that was probably the gospel song:

Oh my lovin' brother
When the world's on fire

Want to lay your head
Upon God's bosom...

On the other hand, that may have come from an older song still, that's the folk process, and now Woody had:

This land is your land, this land is my land
From California to the New York Island;
From the redwood forest to the Gulf Stream waters
This land was made for you and me...

The teachers in New York City liked the song, and they started teaching it to the children. A big executive from a publishing company that sold millions and millions of books to schools in America happened to visit New York and found all the kids there singing 'This Land Is Your Land.' He got permission to put it in one of his songbooks, and now the whole country found that children loved to sing it. This song was never sold in a single music store. It was never played on the radio. But kids in every state took the song home with them and sang it to their families. Twenty years later, everybody in America knew this song! It literally would have been unknown if it hadn't been for those kids. Kids made the song famous.

Woody liked to sing for kids, but as this disease took over his brain he wasn't able to do it as well as when he was younger. I remember once, in Canada, he couldn't quiet the children down, and I had to take over for him. It was humiliating for him. I was seven years younger than him, but I didn't have his terrible disease eating at my brain.

He made up most of his children's songs for his own children, especially little Cathy, who at age three was burned up in a terrible house fire. An electric fire set fire to some cloth and then it got onto her dress, and little Cathy ran around the room trying to put out the fire. When her mother got back from the store it was too late to save her and she died in the ambulance on the way to the hospital. I don't think he wrote many songs for Arlo, but he might have for Jody or Nora.

Woody did get out of the hospital one weekend when Arlo was about seven years old, and Arlo knew how to write, and Woody said, 'Arlo, the whole country is singing my song now, but they left out two of the best verses.' He said, 'Arlo, you got a pencil and paper? Write down those two verses, they are the most important verses of the song.'

One bright sunny morning, by the shadow of the steeple
By the relief office, I saw my people
As they stood there hungry I stood there whistling
This land was made for you and me

There was a great high wall there, tried to stop me
Was a great big sign there, said private property
But on the other side, it didn't say nothing
That side was made for you and me

Isn't that wonderful, to rhyme 'stop me' with 'property'?

And then he sang a third verse, one that none of us had ever heard before. Did he make it up in the hospital, or when?

Nobody living can ever stop me
As I go walking that freedom highway
Nobody living can make me turn back
This land was made for you and me

Those three verses were never lost to history, thanks to little Arlo knowing how to write things down.

THE LAST TIME I HEARD WOODY SING

In 1952, The Weavers had a job in Hollywood, and Will Geer said, 'There's going to be a little party out in Topanga, would you come out and join us?' I did, but The Weavers weren't with me. On my day off I went out to Topanga Canyon, and there was a little house party at the home of a man named Bob DeWitt, and by gosh there was Woody Guthrie. He'd come out there with one more girlfriend. The party was not very big—fifteen people, maybe— and we went around the circle. There was a tall black woman in the corner, and she astounded us all with the power of her voice. We never heard her before, but she said her name was Odetta. And finally it came Woody's turn, and he made up new verses to a famous old Irish tune called 'Acres Of Clams,' and he had a verse about the FBI visiting his house, and he said, '*I being so foolish, I let them in.*' Then his next verse, he sang:

He asked would I would fight for my country?
I answered the FBI, 'Yay.'
I said, 'I will point a gun for my country,
But I won't guarantee you which way.'

So, even though he was not at the peak of his powers, he was able to improvise that extraordinary little verse.

That was the last time I ever heard Woody sing.

• • •

At about forty-two, Woody was getting these dizzy spells, and more dizzy spells, and he got arrested, and the doctor said, 'You weren't just drunk. You have a disease that you probably inherited. Did one of your parents have any mental problems?'

'Oh, yeah. My mother, she burnt down the house, she burnt up my sister. She died in an insane asylum.'

'Well, Mr. Guthrie, she probably had the same disease you have. Did her father have it or her mother have it?'

'Oh, her father, I was told he fell off a horse when he was fording a stream. I don't know about him, but I don't think my mother knew her father very well.'

So now they examine him, and tell him, 'Yes, you have Huntington's chorea.'

That's what they called it back then. Nowadays it's called Huntington's disease. Woody's daughter, Nora Guthrie, has raised the money so they could investigate it, and now, thanks to the money she raised, they now can be sure that somebody has it or does not have it. If one of your parents have it, you have a fifty percent chance of getting it. Woody's first wife lost all her three children; however, Marjorie, Woody's second wife, not one of her three children got it.

When Woody had been in this hospital for a couple of weeks, two friends visited him. They said, 'Woody are they treating you okay? Is the food okay?'

And Woody said, 'Sure, sure. The food's great. Besides, this is the freest place in America.'

'What do you mean? There's bars on the windows.'

'Well, here,' says Woody, 'I can jump up on the table and say I'm a Communist and they just say, Oh he's crazy. You try that anywhere else in America and see what happens to you.'

In 1958, little *Sing Out* magazine decided to have a fundraising concert and they found they could get permission for Woody Guthrie to get out of the hospital and sit on the balcony to listen to it, even though he could not sing himself. It was in a medium-sized auditorium called the Pythian Temple, about a thousand seats on the west side of Manhattan. We sang song after song after song. Then we sang one of Woody's songs, and the people who had brought Woody from the hospital asked him to stand up, and the whole audience looked. He was in one of the boxes in the front of the balcony and the whole auditorium downstairs and upstairs could see him there, and he waved to us, and we sang 'This Land Is Your Land' over and over to him. It was a very moving thing. And the people there, old and young, knew that Woody knew that we all knew the words of his song. We didn't need to look at them in a book. We memorized them. We even harmonized on them. So Woody waved to us.

• • •

The last time I saw Woody, he was in the hospital, never to get out again. He could not speak at that time, but his wife, Marjorie, had written on two big sheets of cardboard, *YES* on one piece and *NO* on the other, and she had the two big pieces of cardboard spread out on his hospital bed. She spoke very slowly and very clearly, right into his ear, 'Woody, Pete has come to visit you. Do you recognize Pete?' And his hand waived around through the air, and finally slapped down on the *YES*, and that's the only way that I knew that he knew I was there.

Only a few months later, I was in Tokyo, Japan, when the news came that Woody Guthrie, the composer of 'This Land Is Your Land,' had passed on.

CHAPTER 05 SOME WEAVERS TALES

The Weavers represented a watershed moment in Pete's life and career. It was his first major commercial success and brought folk music onto the national airwaves to an extent never before witnessed. Pete tended to shun the trappings of success, but his disdain for such things was surely surpassed by his desire to communicate the ideals embodied in the music.

The Weavers first recognized their special blend when singing in November 1948, behind international folk dancers at a fundraiser for the *People's Songs Bulletin*. They began to practice each week using the repertoire from the magazine as a basis for their own sets. Without work, Pete approached Max Gordon at the Village Vanguard, offering to play for only $200 per week plus free hamburgers. Max extended their two-week engagement over and over as the crowds grew larger and larger until they were 'discovered' by Gordon Jenkins, a bandleader at Decca Records who surrounded their arrangements with horns and violins and put them on the radio.

The rise in The Weavers' popularity was nothing short of meteoric. Before being ruthlessly suppressed by the blacklist in 1951, the unlikely group of self-described 'ragtag folksingers' became the number-one singing group in the nation, playing at all the finest nightclubs and upscale hotels and selling more records than any other singing group. 'Goodnight Irene' topped the *Billboard* charts for the entire summer of 1950 and drifted out of every jukebox. As Pete put it, 'You couldn't get away from that song.'

A string of other hits followed, but allegations of alleged Communist leanings in the magazine *Counterattack* and the subsequent blacklisting of the group quickly took their toll. Radio stations and music venues dropped the group from their rosters as their fall from the national scene in 1951 became equally meteoric as their rise. By 1952, with insufficient work to sustain them, The Weavers broke up—or as their manager, Harold Leventhal, put it, 'took a sabbatical.'

In Pete's subsequent testimony before the House Committee On Un-American Activities, he bravely pleaded his First Amendment right of free speech instead of invoking the Fifth Amendment, as so many others had done. But this resulted in a threatening jail sentence for contempt that hovered over him for years and limited his ability to work or travel internationally.

Ultimately, there was a degree of resurrection and redemption. After three years apart, The Weavers reunited in 1955 for a Christmas Eve concert at Carnegie Hall. Vanguard Records recorded the concert, and the album not only became a bestseller but more importantly, documented an iconic moment in folk music history that elevated The Weavers to hero status for standing up to the blacklist. After that concert, offers poured in from colleges and concert halls. These were less commercial than their previous venues, but that meant they could ditch the tuxedos and be themselves. The Weavers continued touring in this fashion for several more years, first with Pete and later with Erik Darling and other banjo players.

This story is beautifully portrayed in a film called *Wasn't That A Time*, created by the documentary filmmaker Jim Brown. One thing the film makes clear is how The Weavers became a seminal inspiration for the larger folk movement that followed from the late 1950s into the 1960s and beyond. It can reasonably be said that without The Weavers there would not have been a Joan Baez or a Peter, Paul & Mary. Perhaps not even a Bob Dylan, or at least a very different Bob Dylan, because the Greenwich Village folk scene that Dylan developed and thrived in would not have been the same.

Many future folksingers, including Baez, personally attended the 1955 Carnegie Hall reunion, and others such as Harry Chapin and his brother Tom were inspired to continue their musical pursuits after hearing the record.

Whether they acknowledge it or not, many of today's singers and songwriters owe a debt to The Weavers for forging a path upon which so many others have now trod.

There is, however, a qualitative difference. As opposed to today's singer/songwriters, who populate much of the acoustic scene with 'original' songs, The Weavers by and large arranged and sang existing material from the folk lexicon. There were some notable exceptions: Leadbelly's 'Goodnight Irene'; Pete and Lee's 'If I Had A Hammer'; the anthem 'Wasn't That A Time,' co-written by Lee and his poet friend Walter Lowenfels; and of course Woody Guthrie's 'This Land Is Your Land.' For the most part, though, The Weavers' repertoire was mined from the different corners of America and from other lands, with their sets often including songs in several languages. This was all part of their nascent mission to honor the different communities that comprised the American workforce in a somewhat naïve but very earnest attempt to create a national singing labor movement.

The Weavers didn't really regard themselves as a 'folk act' but more as 'cultural workers.' This sense of mission, together with their individual talents, infused Weavers performances with an infectious energy that no other group from the folk boom ever really matched. This is probably why The Weavers became such a perceived threat to the blacklisters, who became quite alarmed to see how people all over the country—and especially young people—were embracing them.

The blacklist limited The Weavers' commercial opportunities—even after their successful reunion album, they remained unwelcome on radio or television—but never diminished the love and respect they had earned from their public. All of their reunion concerts were immediate sellouts: first in 1955; then in 1964, when Pete reunited with the group for a single Carnegie Hall event; again in 1980, for their final reunion as a foursome; and once again without Lee Hays in 2003 to honor their longtime manager, Harold Leventhal.

The story of The Weavers is worth remembering and retelling. I was fortunate to have had the opportunity to speak with and get the perspectives of three of the four Weavers.

• • •

Gordon Jenkins was a very, very decent honest guy. He was a little confused by us occasionally. I remember he once said, 'Lee, this world is sure getting more and more chaotic.' And Lee said, 'The more chaotic the better.' Gordon was just confused by that. He came to a dead stop.

At first, we had six members. Ronnie Gilbert had a roommate named Jackie Alpert now but Jackie Gibson back then—they'd known each other in Washington in World War II when they were both still in their teens, and Jackie loved to sing—and Boots Casetta's girlfriend, Greta. Then Greta and Jackie said, 'No, you want to be full-time singers, it's not practical for us, traveling and everything.' They backed out of the group. Then we tried getting an African American woman to be with us—I can't remember her name, but she was already on a different course musically. She wanted to work more classically and show off her voice, and we were in a sense working backward into the old folk style.

Fred Hellerman came up with our name. He read the German socialist play called *The Weavers* in translation by a man named Gerhart Hauptmann. We were looking for some kind of name that wouldn't imply that we were cowboys or something like that, nor a funny name. Although Lee would kid around and say, 'We're now The Weavers, I'm the warp and Pete's the woof,' or 'Pete's the warp and I'm the woof.'

In the beginning, I tried writing out every arrangement. I was into getting the right kind of harmony and the right kind of bass. I had a piece of music paper about fifteen feet long, folded like an accordion, and taped it up on my six-string guitar. But it pretty soon became obvious that what they call 'head arrangements' were the best of all. One person would say, 'I would like to sing this song and I think I could do it best with so-and-so to help me, it just needs two of us,' or 'I would like to sing this song and I think maybe this is all we need for the accompaniment, maybe just guitar or just banjo or both guitar and banjo,' or 'I would like to sing a song and I think it would take all four of us.' I think it would be comparably rare that we would take three of us and leave one out.

Fred and I were often thinking of arranging. Lee was thinking of words and continuity. He would stick to what he knew, hymns and new songs that were in the style of hymns. Lee knew when to be very solid and not try anything fancy. We'd just start singing, and somebody would say, 'Oh, that was a nice part, do that again.' 'When does Ronnie's alto come in?' 'Is Pete singing a falsetto here? He's above Ronnie!' Or Ronnie would say, 'I just can't sing it in that high key, can we modulate?' It's kind of an artificial cliché to modulate, but then we decided to try it with 'When The Saints Go Marching In,' and it worked perfectly.

It was hard for Ronnie and Fred in a way, because Lee and I had known each other for almost ten years already. I met Lee in 1940 and we started The Weavers in 1948, and then two years later is when we were singing professionally. So it was a little hard for them. In a way, they had to struggle for the right to be heard. Lee and I were sure we knew what to do.

At the Village Vanguard, we had one microphone. It was a very small place. I think one hundred and fifty people was the most allowed in there. Some were just four feet away from us and some were all of thirty feet away, so we got away with one mic. We moved closer in and out of it. It was a joke that Ronnie could be two feet from the mic and be heard above all three of us even when we were six inches from the mic, but we did not go in for two or three mics. Vanguard couldn't afford somebody to sit at the controls. I think we still kept the single mic until we started working with bass players.

When we traveled and sang in hotels, we had arrangements for an orchestra to go along with us, although we preferred just a bass player. That's when I knew Bill Lee. Our sets were usually a half-hour long, which meant six or eight songs, but Lee's spoken interludes became more and more important.

When we were at the Village Vanguard, Toshi says, 'If you all dress differently, you will be in continual disagreement with each other. Let me take you up to the clothing garage and get you some cheap suits that at least match each other and Ronnie can find some gowns that will blend in.' So we got yellowish-tan tuxedos for the three men, but we wore ordinary shirts with ordinary ties. When we had to work at the Palmer House or the Strand Theatre, they said, 'No, you have to wear a tux,' and I hated it.

'On Top Of Old Smokey' had another male singer. Somebody at Decca wanted to push the career of Terry Gilkyson. Poor Terry's been ashamed of it ever since. Decca said, 'We want The Weavers to help make a record. Terry Gilkyson is going to lead off the singing and you back him up.' And then they found I could give the words in advance, and Ronnie's voice sounded so great. Terry Gilkyson said, 'You don't need to use my voice so much. Use Ronnie's voice there.'

The Weavers' tempo was an important thing. 'Tzena, Tzena' was done at a breakneck speed. I think a quarter-note was 152, whereas marching tempo is 120, and most people if they're loafing along will do it much slower than 120. At the start, I might have done a three-rhythm on the banjo, but it comes out over four beats. You have to tap your feet right.

We were tempted occasionally to try some of John Jacob Niles's songs but for one reason or another decided not to. Niles had that beautiful melody of 'Venezuela,' and Ronnie used to sing it beautifully, and then when she became more class conscience she said, 'No, I'm not going to sing that song anymore, it's a song that degrades women.'

We really were quite different people, with different aims in mind and different lifestyles and so on. We were all lefties but we were very, very different. Lee with his Arkansas tradition and me with my New England traditions, and while Fred and Ronnie were both Jewish, they had very different outlooks on life, so we were four quite different people, drawn together by music.

Then you have the achievement of the music reaching far more people than we ever thought we would reach. We were disappointed we didn't reach the unions. The Cold War had split the labor movement apart. I am sure the blacklisters were saying, 'How did we let those so-and-sos slip through our fingers? We thought we had taken care of these guys.' And all of a sudden, there we were on every jukebox in the country, and they didn't know what to do about it.

The attacks on us happened that very summer of 1950. The whole country was humming 'Goodnight Irene,' and even those two comedians with the banjo and the mandolin, Homer & Jethro, had a song to 'Tzena, Tzena.' That very month, *Counterattack* comes out with a blast against us, and we lost a job. Milton Berle went ahead and had us in August or September. He said, 'What's these odd rumors about you? This is great music you're making, what are they after you for?'

We just hedged. 'They got politics on the brain.'

In spite of the fact that the blacklisters blasted us in the summer of 1950, we were still singing strong in the fall and in the winter of 1950, and making good records and getting great applause in Ciro's of Hollywood and the Palmer House in Chicago and so on. But by the summer of 1951, they chopped us down. We sang a little here and a little there, but the left was under such pressure they couldn't pay us anything. What the left wanted of us was 'fighting fascist' songs, and we were singing all folk songs.

I tend to lose track of where The Weavers left off and my own work continued because I just went to work singing in colleges—not at the very moment, but I guess a year later. Some kids that I sang to at Camp Woodland were in Oberlin College. I went there in 1953, and then to Antioch, and then I found a couple of other places and I realized that one college engagement led to another. I couldn't sing at the big state universities because they were too much under pressure of politics and the American Legion could complain and so on. It wasn't until the 1960s that I could sing at Ohio University. I could sing in Oberlin and Antioch every year, for bigger audiences each time. The first time I went to Oberlin it was two hundred, next year five hundred, next year a thousand, and then I got so busy I couldn't go there every year.

Vanguard recorded our 1955 reunion concert at Carnegie Hall. I remember a movie was made that shows someone outside waiting in line for tickets and hearing it's a sellout. I stayed about two years after that. That's when disagreements arose between us about exactly how we were going to keep living. So when we were offered a job to sing a commercial for L&M cigarettes, I didn't want to do it. But the other three said, 'We need the money, Pete. Maybe you can make a living some other way, but we can't make a living if we don't do this.' I said, 'Let's find another way to make a living then, that's safe.' But after the L&M commercial, I said, 'I think you can get along without me. Get Eric Darling to take my place.' He's a better singer than I am, and they made some wonderful records with Eric. I wanted to be able to sing the songs I wanted to sing without having to think, *Can we get away with this?*

Editor's note: Mario 'Boots' Casetta, mentioned above, was one of Woody Guthrie's buddies in the merchant marines during World War II, and he recorded some of The Weavers early music before their commercial success. Bill Lee, the filmmaker Spike Lee's father, was a very well-respected jazz bassist who played occasionally with The Weavers at their live shows.

FRED HELLERMAN *I was influenced early on by the popular music of the day, which was the big bands, Benny Goodman and all. Gordon Jenkins made us sound like part of a big band, and I loved it! He doesn't get nearly the kind of credit that he deserves. He'd be down at the Vanguard every night listening to us. If he didn't show up, we figured he was sick. And when he went back to California he would call the payphone and say, 'Leave the phone off the hook, I want to hear the show.' When it came to recording with us, Gordon never once asked us to change a single note of what we did. He wrote around us.*

As a teenager, I remember someone playing The Almanac Singers' 'Talking Union,' and it just knocked me out. This was not Benny Goodman stuff. And to suddenly discover that there were things other than unrequited love in fifty-seven varieties to sing about was an epiphany.

During World War II, I was aboard ship in the Coast Guard. There was a guitar there, and I sat down and figured out how to play it. After I got out of the service, I began to meet other guitar players, and I listened and learned and asked questions. I was playing here and there and going to Brooklyn College and People's Songs was just getting started. One day I got a postcard from Lee Hays who was the head of People's Songs at that time, and it said, 'There's a word going around that you're a pretty good singer. Why don't you drop by and let's get acquainted.' So that's how I got involved with People's Songs, and that's how I met Pete.

Ronnie Gilbert and I had met at camp Wo-Chi-Ca, which sounds like a good Indian name but it actually was the Workers Children's Camp—a left-wing camp run by the International Workers' Order. Ronnie and I were counselors and she and I began singing, and Ronnie was also around People's Songs.

We were having hootenannies, and at this particular Thanksgiving hootenanny they had folk dancers there, and they needed something to dance to, so Pete, Lee, Ronnie and I made some music for them. That's where we invented the medley of international dance tunes we called 'Around The World' that stood us in good stead all the time we were performing.

Originally, we got together just because we liked the sound we made once a week in Pete's basement on MacDougall Street. Then at one point, Ronnie was going to go out to California, and I was going to go out to the University of Chicago to do graduate work, but nobody was very happy about breaking up. So it was out of desperation that we said, 'Let's see if we can get a job together.'

If you think about it, it was really rather peculiar. The thinking was to get a job, so we can stay together, so that we can continue to sing on Wednesday afternoons.

Pete had worked down at the Village Vanguard as a single, so he suggested we try there. Max Gordon brought us in for two weeks, and then he had us stay on for another two weeks, and then another month, and it ended up being six months. That's where we did our rehearsing. We worked out things every night onstage. We found our parts, and little by little arrived at something that just got set by itself, and that was by far the most productive period. People's Songs gave us a repertoire. We were singing so much that we all knew the songs. Somehow, everything just fell into such a natural place. It happened very automatically.

I have to point something out. Sometimes, somebody would do a solo song and it would just bring down the house. I think there are a lot of groups where the other people are very jealous, and I'm really very pleased and very proud to say that never happened with The Weavers. Their victory was our victory. And that too came very naturally.

Pete wouldn't like it if you called him the boss, but he was the boss—not by declaration, but just by the sheer weight of his authority, the sheer weight of his talent. Pete and Lee also had the experience of the Almanacs that Ronnie and I didn't have. Some years later, a piece about The Weavers described Lee as the 'brains of the group.' Lee wrote to the author protesting that description: 'There are no brains in The Weavers.' When Pete left the group, I became more active. It just fell to me. Whoever's holding an instrument in their hands, they're boss! When Pete's around, banjo will out-noise a guitar anytime.

I don't think success really changed us. We all enjoyed it except Pete. Hal Leventhal would make sure that we were met at the airport by a limousine. Pete would go nuts! Lee, of course, adored it. Lee could afford room service anywhere he went. But by and large, we all looked at our big commercial success in the Decca period with a very bemused look. We all knew that this wasn't going to last very long. No one ever took it very seriously.

I never thought of myself as a very good guitar player. I go down to Washington Square and there's kids there playing rings around me. What I do bring to the table though, is a level of musicianship, and I think of myself as being a very superior accompanist. Within the framework of The Weavers, I could hear what's called for is just something a little solid in the background and not to muddle it up with all kinds of things.

My musical respect for Erik Darling is just immense. One of my favorite Weavers albums is the one we did at Carnegie Hall with Erik Darling and Frank Hamilton. There were seven of us up there. I listen to that album, and the driving force on that is Erik. I never felt like I was terribly good rhythmically. Erik Darling is the Rock of Gibraltar.

I also think of Erik as incredibly courageous. He took on a role that you had to be insane to take on. To try to fill in for Pete Seeger had to be the most thankless task ever. I'm reminded of the time when The Weavers were down in Galveston. We did a concert, and afterwards we went to some place where Lightnin' Hopkins was playing. It was in the black part of town, and somehow Erik got up to play some blues there. And he was so great! That took a lot of guts to do. He had to play the blues, and he delivered. When he came into The Weavers, he had to step into Pete's shoes, and he not only did that in spades, but he also brought some of his own stuff to bear.

One of the things that I'm very grateful for when I look back on The Weavers: Most of the time we did so well with audiences, but occasionally, you hit that bad night. When that happened, we never—with maybe one or two exceptions in our whole career—walked off and said, 'Gee what a lousy audience.' The first question is, 'Where did we fail to reach them?' It was a wonderful thing about The Weavers. There were no egos at work there. And it's something that really stood us in very good stead.

RONNIE GILBERT *My mother was Polish, and my dad was from the Ukraine, from an area where Jews were forbidden to have land. When they came to the United States, their dream was to have a farm. Somehow my father obtained some land in New Jersey and started a farm, but they just couldn't make a go of it, so they moved back into New York City. My mother was pregnant with me at the time.*

I was born in 1926, right before the big stock market crash. My mother worked as a factory worker and was active in the International Ladies Garment Workers Union, the ILGWU. I was brought up on strikes for a penny-a-garment. My mother sang in the union choruses. This was all part of the coming together of immigrants on the political left. In our piano bench, we had the old version of The Little Red Songbook.

I was eleven years old when the Spanish Civil War broke out. My first direct civil action was collecting money for Spanish war relief for the children. I learned Spanish Civil War songs from sheet music. I would sit at the piano and pick out the tunes.

I went to summer camp, Camp Wo-Chi-Ca, run by the International Workers' Order. The IWO was not an official offshoot of the Communist Party, but there were certainly many Communists who worked with the IWO. The organizations that were part of the Communist Party were usually labeled 'Communist,' such as the Young Communist League (YCL).

The Communists were some of the hardest-working and most concerned people, and they did a lot of the hardest work in these organizations to help people's lives. The IWO was a fraternal organization, and, among other things, it provided burial services to workers. My mother was a member of the Communist Party and a member of the union, and she attended a lot of meetings.

The Taft–Hartley Act had a terrible effect during the time when Communists were being persecuted during the blacklist because the law required any union leader who had an affiliation with the Communist Party to admit that affiliation, with the obvious result. I recommend reading the book by Howard Fast entitled Being Red if you want a full understanding of what it was like being a Communist back in those days.

My introduction to folk songs was at age sixteen in Washington DC. My mom was sick in the hospital, and I was the only breadwinner, so I went to DC and took a temporary job as a clerk. A group of singers met in the basement of the house where I was renting a room. They were called The Priority Ramblers, and their personnel included Bernie Aspell and Tom Glazier.

When I came back to New York the following summer, I was a counselor at Camp Wo-Chi-Ca, and that's where I met Fred Hellerman. I shared my songs from The Priority Ramblers, and they also sang songs by Richard Dyer Bennett and Burl Ives, who later named names in front of the Committee. Fred and I got involved in the New York folk scene, and Fred played for some folk-dance companies.

I met Pete Seeger at People's Songs. We went out caroling one night in Greenwich Village around Christmas. This may sound strange, but even with six to eight people, I could hear the four of us. Pete always wanted to sing with choruses, and he wanted one for a hootenanny. One of the first things The Weavers did as a quartet was a Bach chorale at a hootenanny with new words by Tom Glazier.

Singing with The Weavers was decades before I had feminist consciousness. I had a strong mother, and I too am a strong woman. I learned some strength from Betty Sanders, who I feel was an important woman singer. At one time, I started to play guitar and even joined the musician's union. Playing an instrument would have raised my stature. But I was the 'girl singer' in The Weavers, and that's what I wanted at the time, and I loved it.

The Weavers' arrangements were all head arrangements. That was my strong suit. I was very good at harmony. I had no formal voice training, but when my parents separated when I was age eleven, I was sent to Missouri for the summer to live with my mother's half-brother. Their daughter was a voice student in college and would vocalize and sing arias and art songs. I was mesmerized. I listened to her practice, and then when she was finished I'd sneak over to the piano and try it, and I would imitate what I heard. I learned about six of those songs, and I have never forgotten them.

Editor's note: *The Little Red Songbook* is a well-known, red-covered book of workers' rights songs published by the IWW (International Workers Of The World), who are often referred to as the Wobblies. They coined the popular slogan 'Workers of the world, unite!'

TOM CHAPIN *We first heard the recording The Weavers At Carnegie Hall when I was twelve and Harry was fourteen and Steve was eleven. That was the record that informed us and taught us and inspired us. And we started playing as The Chapin Brothers. Harry got a banjo. We call it the Harry Forbes banjo because it was my great uncle's banjo from about 1890.*

The first time I met Pete, I was eighteen or nineteen years old. My mother's first cousin Arthur died unexpectedly. It turned out that his wife Judy and Toshi had gone to school together at the Little Red Schoolhouse. They were friends, and they'd kept up. A week after Arthur's death, there was a Quaker-style gathering at their house, and who shows up but Pete and Toshi.

I remember we talked backstage, and I said, 'You know, this is the first time I've been to the funeral of somebody I really knew and loved. I don't know if I can sing.' And Toshi said, 'Of course you can. What you do is you sing, let them cry.' She was very supportive.

Pete had a twelve-string guitar. He got it out and tuned it, and then he sat down, and people talked. About forty-five minutes into it, there was a silence, and Pete reaches over and picks up his twelve-string and goes, Brummmm…'To every-thing, turn, turn, turn.' He didn't even say a word. He just sang that. And I remember thinking, as I've thought many times in the concerts we've done with him over the years, *This is a perfect song, and the perfect person, and the perfect moment for that song.* That impeccable sense of what is right for the moment, and how to make the moment larger than it was, and bring us all together, which of course was his vision.

The first concert I ever did with Pete was with my brother Harry at a benefit for World Hunger Year out on Long Island at Huntington High School. Before the show started, this young reporter came up to us, and he said, 'Mr. Seeger, I know you've done all these benefits over your entire life—has it ever made a difference?' And Pete goes, 'I don't know. But I do know I've met the good people with live hearts, live eyes, and live minds.'

That has stayed with me, and it stayed with Harry too, the wonderful way Pete deflected that question so that his answer was not about him changing the world but about what the world had given to him in having the opportunity to meet and work with great people who changed his life and who he learned from.

PETER YARROW *When I was growing up, Pete Seeger had a big voice in the world of the High School of Music and Art because everybody loved folk music. A lot of us learned about songs newly revealed or written by Pete by going to hootenannies with performers like Sonny Terry and Brownie McGhee. So early on, I was inspired by this music.*

But I was also there in 1955, as were many others, at Carnegie Hall, when that extraordinary concert with The Weavers just brought many of us to a place where we really understood how the passion of one's perspective in life can be united as an active force in making music and performing it. That was a definitive moment in my life. Mary Travers was at that concert, though I was not to meet her for five years.

In the early 60s, Pete and I worked together on the Newport Folk Festival board of directors, and that evolved into many shared performances. He would call upon me to appear at an event, or vice versa. Those events included the March on Washington in '69 for half a million people, which I had co-organized with Cora Weiss. In each case, it's almost with a certain degree of reverence that I watched Pete perform because there was an aspect to him that was so self-effacing that he was letting the song really tell the story that he felt needed to get out there. It was not a presentation that celebrated his persona or his gifts in the ways that other performers would dramatize the songs. There was a great purity to him.

The effect that he had on all of us was ironic. A lot of it sprang from his having been blacklisted, and having to eke out a living by singing at summer camps for part of the year where he proceeded to inspire a whole generation of activists. These were young people, unformed and idealistic. Pete Seeger had a massive influence on the generation that grew up receiving his messages, his passion, and following his path. This was certainly the case for Peter, Paul & Mary. Mary used to call us Seeger's Raiders, and rightly so.

I would attribute a lot of the folk renaissance to Pete, because it was not just about the music: it was about allowing the music to permeate your soul and give you a view of an honest, authentic sense of the past and your identity. That was an extraordinary gift. And I feel that there is no one more important as a source of inspiration and process in the world of folk music than Pete. I'm deeply proud to have shared my efforts with him, and to be able to call him a friend.

WORK O' THE WEAVERS

During the run-up to the war with Iraq in 2002, folksinger James Durst and I designed a program to honor The Weavers. We had both witnessed an almost eerie silencing of dissenting voices in the media and watched in dismay as those speaking out for moderation and peace were cut short, dismissed, and even called 'un-American' by television personalities who seemed to have no understanding of how loaded that term was, nor its connection to the blacklist.

We enlisted a great alto singer from Connecticut named Martha Sandefer, and the multi-talented Mark Murphy, the Hudson Valley's ubiquitous bass player. We didn't want to be just a tribute group, copying arrangements. Instead, we wanted to weave a spoken-word narrative into the program that would recount The Weavers' history as a cautionary tale for the present.

After roughing out the program, Pete sat with us by the fire at the Beacon Sloop Club and patiently helped us with corrections and suggestions. We workshopped it during the summer of 2003 at a club in Great Barrington, Massachusetts, and debuted that fall at the Walkabout Clearwater Coffeehouse in Katonah, New York. Fred Hellerman, who lived in nearby Weston, Connecticut, watched from the front row and graciously sang 'Goodnight Irene' with us at the end. He told the audience, 'I finally got to sit out front and enjoy a Weavers concert.'

Over the next ten years, Work O' The Weavers toured up and down the East Coast and westward to twenty-seven states, and to Canada and Israel, and put out two CDs containing Weavers material and more recent songs of a similar trajectory.

Although Work O' The Weavers was a success by most standards, we found that most of our audience were older people who had come to bathe in the nostalgia of a bygone era. I am reminded of a comment singer Happy Traum made at a recent performance, 'These days, I find myself singing to older people ... and their parents.' Although that statement brought the house down, the grain of truth is unescapable. In today's world of viral videos and internet culture, it's hard to generate young people's interest in the happenings of a fifty-year-old folk music group.

Despite these shortcomings, it was an honor to receive the kind words and generous assistance of Pete and Fred and Harold Leventhal, and a privilege to celebrate their contribution while they were still here to see it. When I look back on The Weavers and the generations of folksingers they inspired, I am reminded of the question my wife Mai often asks me after watching the evening news: 'Where are the protest singers of today?'

CHAPTER 06  SOME BOOKS

THE BOOK THAT ALMOST NEVER WAS

The first book I ever helped to write was not published until many years later. Woody Guthrie and I put together a songbook we called *Hard Hitting Songs For Hard-Hit People*. I thought of the title, and we put it together in about five weeks in the back room of the loft of a sculptor named Harold Ambellan and his girlfriend, Elizabeth Higgins.

In a sense, the book was started off by Alan Lomax, but he could not take credit for it back then. He had a job in the Library Of Congress, and putting out all these left-wing songs would not have been approved of. As a matter of fact, once some suspicious congressman came over to the Library and says, 'Is this where you put new words to old songs?'

Alan had, over five or six years, put together a big pile of old records and song sheets, and his father didn't want to put them in his folksong books. But Alan was a young leftie, and he wanted to see the songs reprinted somewhere. So he handed the whole pile to Woody and me and says, 'Why don't the two of you work this into a book?' And during the month of June 1940, that's what we did. Alan even recorded one or two of the songs with The Almanac Singers just before we left New York in late June.

We took the manuscript west with us with The Almanac Singers. Out there, we met Theodore Dreiser. In his old age, he'd become a member of the Communist Party, and he said, 'I'd like to look at the book.' He returned it the next day, saying, 'You've got a lot of work to do before this can be published.' And he was right. But, nevertheless, we kept on, even added a few songs like Woody's 'Why Do You Stand There In The Rain?'

Woody says, 'Oh there's lots better songs than this.'

I said, 'No, but this tells the story of this particular period of history.'

And then The Almanac Singers were back east, at Almanac House on West 10th Street, right next to the firehouse station. Millard Lampell, who had been rooming with Lee before we started the Almanacs, was living there, and he borrowed the book to look at it, taking it to his parents' home in New Jersey, and he left it in the bus station. Was Woody furious! We didn't have an extra copy. That was our only one. Woody put humorous and angry signs all over Almanac House, how writer Millard Lampell lost the *Songbagenorous*—a take-off on Carl Sandburg's *The American Songbag*, which had come out a few years before.

Millard went back to Paterson, and he went all over, and by gosh he found the manuscript. Somebody had picked it up and said, 'Well, this is obviously the manuscript for a book, and it looks like an interesting book.' And so they did not just throw it away. And Millard finally found the right person and he proved that he was the man that had left it there.

I guess Harold Ambellan and Elizabeth later got married, because Elizabeth lived the rest of her life with the name of Elizabeth Ambellan, and she became a professor at the University Of Connecticut at Storrs. It's thanks to her that the book finally came out, because during the days of *People's Songs*, we'd given up on the book and it was split up into little pieces. The textile workers' songs went into the 'textile' section of the library, and the miners' songs went into the 'miners' section, and the farmers' songs went into the 'farmers' section, and we didn't even have a table of contents to tell us how to put it back together when Elizabeth showed up with a carbon copy she'd saved way back in 1940.

The book finally got published in 1964. Alan Lomax was now able to claim credit as the editor, Woody got credit for writing the introductions to the songs, and I got credit for working on the music. I don't know exactly how many it sold, but it started with little Oak Publications, so it probably sold only a thousand or two thousand copies.

We'd met John Steinbeck, the author of *The Grapes Of Wrath*, the great book of 1939 and he had a wonderful description of Woody, saying, 'Woody is just Woody, with a voice like a tire iron hanging on a rusty rim.' We used the foreword that he had originally written for the book, and I added a little extroduction, putting in some of the rather humorous things.

The University Of Nebraska Press put it out again in 1999 but they only printed about a thousand copies and then it was out of print again. But I was delighted.

Now it's the year 2010, and I recently met with some people who are enthusiastic about putting the book out again, saying they could do for this book what we did with my songbook *Where Have All The Flowers Gone* and make it possible for people who want to listen to the music to hear it. Hopefully, sometime in the next year, the first book I ever worked on will be out again.

Editor's note: back in the 1960s, after Elizabeth Ambellan found the original table of contents, she gave it to John Cohen of The New Lost City Ramblers, who brought it to Pete. Pete then worked closely with Happy Traum and others to recreate the original book that he and Woody had first cobbled together back in 1940. *Hard Hitting Songs For Hard-Hit People* was republished again by the University Of Nebraska Press in 2012 and remains available. On December 3, 2017, a celebration of the new edition was held at the Towne Crier Café in Beacon, New York. Happy Traum and John Cohen both came and sang.

• • •

In February of 1940, over six thousand members of the American Youth Congress demonstrated in front of the White House for peace and jobs. They stood there in a soaking rain while President Roosevelt gave them a half-hour speech saying that they were just young and foolish.

Woody Guthrie made up a hilarious song about it. He took an old tune and put new words to it and wrote a bunch of satirical verses about the president, and then each chorus said, '*Why do you stand there in the rain?*' In his written introduction to the song, Woody dedicated it 'to them six thousand kids, and about 130 million others in this country that got soaked the same day.'

Roosevelt gave the students a tongue-lashing. He said, 'You are all wet behind the ears, you don't know what is going on in the world, and you got to help the people who are fighting Hitler.' Actually, the president was right. But it's a shame that they've put up the concrete barriers down in Washington DC so that people can't march as close to the White House as they used to. Whenever there are large demonstrations down there in front of leaders who don't always want to listen, I think of this song.

WHY DO YOU STAND THERE IN THE RAIN? *Woody Guthrie*

It was raining mighty hard on that old Capitol yard
When the young folks gathered at the White House gate
And the President raised his head and to the young folks said:
Tell me why do you stand there in the rain?

Why do you stand there in the rain?
Why do you stand there in the rain?
These are strange carryin's on, on the White House Capitol lawn
Tell me why do you stand there in the rain?

Well they tell me they've got lands where they will not let you stand
In the rain and ask for jobs upon the lawn,
Thank God in the U.S.A. you can stand there every day,
But I would not guarantee they'd take you on.

Why do you stand there in the rain…

HOW TO PLAY THE 5-STRING BANJO

When I was still in the US Army, I remember my father writing me a letter saying, 'Peter, have you ever thought of writing a manual about how to play the banjo? You have the experience of learning it, of teaching yourself.' So I started sketching out how to do it. One day, somebody had a camera, and in my fatigues, as they called them—which is not your uniform but what you put on when you're doing some dirty job—I had them film a 'roll.' That's when you let your little finger go first and your index finger last—*bddddump.* The picture is in my banjo book. But I didn't get around to writing the book until around 1948. That's when I finished my first edition.

I didn't know a darn thing about writing an instruction book, but I figured if I took a few students, maybe I'd learn. One of the students was Eric Weissberg, and I had a couple of other adults. I think I had four or five students, and in the late summer of 1948, in between other things, I would teach banjo.

Henry Wallace was running for president and I was trying to help him, so I'd make a date to teach my class and then I'd have to call all five of them up and say, 'I'm sorry, there's a Wallace rally that I have to go sing at,' and I'd have to postpone it. Finally, I went on tour with Wallace, and I took a typewriter and some mimeograph stencils along, and in the hotel, I'd have a few extra hours, and I'd type a few pages of this manual. By then, I'd been teaching students for three or four months.

By the following winter, I had about forty pages, and I got a little company down near Union Square to mimeograph about a hundred copies. Whenever people would ask me, 'How do you play the banjo?' I'd say, 'Well I got a little mimeograph book on it.'

In three years they were sold. So now I had five hundred copies mimeographed, and they sold in four years. I thought that was a big sale. Five hundred copies in four years!

Now I rented an Electromatic typewriter. The barn was built in Beacon then, and upstairs I typed the whole book over again. Now it was up to about sixty pages. I put that lovely painting in there called *The Banjo Lesson* by Henry Tanner. He was a black painter, and this was his most famous painting. It's a great painting of a father or an uncle or a grandfather showing an eight- or ten-year-old boy how to play the banjo, lit by the light from a fireplace or lamp in a little cabin. It was painted in the 1890s, and it's on the wall of a famous institute down in Norfolk, Virginia.

Well, the sixty-page version sold in four years. I think it was around fifteen hundred copies and was printed by photo offset.

Now I got ambitious. I thought, *If this book is going to sell this many copies, let me really do it right.* I think I took not a few months but half a year. I got my son Danny and my daughter Mika to help me lay out the copies and proofread for me. You could see it was built out of the earlier book, but it was a real attempt to write a good book. It started with a chapter on the history of the instrument. Then the second chapter was about how to hold it and where to put your fingers, and the third chapter showed what that fifth string, the thumb string, does. That's where I invented the phrase *bump-ditty, bump-ditty, bump-ditty.* There were chapters on 'hammering on' and 'pulling off' and double-thumbing and so on.

After those six months, the book was printed, and now I even contacted some people who might like to sell it—*Sing Out* magazine or Oak Publications. But I laugh. I tell people, 'That's been my bestseller.' It sold a hundred thousand copies in the last fifty years.

• • •

I'm sure there've been tens of thousands of copies made of Henry Tanner's painting. With the fame he got from this painting, Tanner went over to Paris. Like not a few others, he felt, *Here's a country that didn't discriminate.* He was an African American, and he could eat anywhere in any restaurant he wanted, stay in any hotel he wanted, buy a house anywhere he wanted. So Tanner never came home. He made a living as a painter, though none of his paintings in Europe got as famous as *The Banjo Lesson.*

It's amusing that only three months after I gave him a few lessons, Eric Weissberg was playing rings around me. He's such a talented performer. His father was a photographer, and one of his jobs was in the Waldorf Astoria Hotel. Two years later, when 'Goodnight Irene' was out, I met the photographer and he said, 'I know you because my son learned banjo from you.'

One thing I'm a little proud of is that two little phrases I invented when I first mimeographed my banjo book are now known worldwide: 'hammering on' and 'pulling off.' They're used around the world, and if someone is playing guitar and says, 'I'm hammering on,' or 'I'm pulling off,' other musicians know what they mean.

Editor's note: thousands of banjo players around the country started with Pete's little banjo book, including well-known performers such as Dave Guard of The Kingston Trio and the renowned Tony Trishka.

CHAPTER 07 SOME SONGS

Pete's songwriting process often involved taking inspiration from unusual sources and borrowing from here and there. For instance, 'Where Have All The Flowers Gone?'—synonymous with peace movements throughout the world—is one of his best-known songs, but it would be hard to simply say that he 'wrote it.' The words are based on the text of a Russian novel, and the melody is largely from an old Irish farming song. Pete was an expert at cobbling together different ingredients and then adding something of his own to get something completely new. That's why Pete would sometimes say, 'I put this song together when ...'

Pete was also a great collaborator, sometimes with his contemporaries and sometimes across the centuries. 'Turn! Turn! Turn!' is based upon the biblical words of Ecclesiastes. Pete tells us they were set in a poetic writing style of repeating phrases called *anaphora* that was brought to the Middle East when the Greeks charged through there on their way to Egypt about two thousand years ago. Pete wrote his version in the 1950s, but the song wasn't popular until 1969, when The Byrds changed the melody of the last line and put it to a rock beat.

'We Shall Overcome' came from an old gospel song called 'I'll Be Alright,' filtered through the slow meter style of Lucille Simmons on a tobacco worker's picket line in 1940, and then through the sensibilities of Zilphia Horton and Guy Carawan at the Highlander school in Tennessee, and then through folksinger Frank Hamilton's penchant for the 12/8 gospel meter, and finally through Pete's

'WASPish' sensibilities, which may have turned '*I will*' into '*We shall*.'

Pete also adapted material from many cultures. Songs such as 'Wimoweh' and 'Guantanamera' became widely known in this country largely because Pete adapted them, recorded them, and played them at concerts.

What follows are just a few songs Pete helped 'put together.'

WHERE HAVE ALL THE FLOWERS GONE?

I got the idea for the song 'Where Have All The Flowers Gone' from a famous novel by Mikhail Sholokhov, a Soviet writer from the mid-1930s. It was printed in this country and called *And Quiet Flows The Don*—the Don River—and it tells the story of the Don Cossacks galloping off to join the army of the czar over a hundred years ago, singing. Then in small type, it gave three lines of their song:

Where are the flowers? The girls have plucked them
Where are the girls? They're all married
Where are the men? They're all in the army

I said to myself, 'That sounds like an interesting song. I should look it up,' so I copied down those three lines. But I never got around to looking it up.

Meanwhile, about four or five years later, I was in an airplane on my way to sing at Oberlin College, and I pulled out my little pocket notebook, and all of a sudden, a tune comes to me. I didn't realize that it was an old Irish tune:

Johnson says he'll load more hay
Says he'll load ten times a day…

Then I noticed a line I had also written down '*long time passing*,' and I said to myself, 'That line would sing well.' Twenty minutes later, I'd put it all together and had three verses. I sang it slowly:

Where have all the flowers gone?
Long time passing
Where have all the flowers gone?
Long time ago

Where have all the flowers gone?
Girls have picked them every one.
Oh, when will we ever learn?
Oh, when will we ever learn?

That last line is the intellectual's perennial complaint!

Well, I got the three verses, and I stuck them onto a microphone at Oberlin College and sang them, and they liked it, after a fashion. I put it with two or three other very short songs. One was a little whistling song I called 'The Goofing Off Suite.' When I was back in New York, I recorded it along with a batch of very short songs. Just those three verses.

But one of the Oberlin College students, Joe Hickerson by name, bought a copy of the record. And he got a job at a summer camp in the Catskills—a wonderful little summer camp called Camp Woodland, the first interracial camp in the Catskill Mountains—and he was making up extra verses. He also gave it rhythm, because he was singing to kids and the kids wanted some rhythm to the song.

Joe had a verse like '*Where have all the counselors gone? Broken curfew every one,*' but by the end of the summer, he had '*Where have all the soldiers gone? Gone to graveyards . . .*' and then '*Where have all the graveyards gone? Covered with flowers,*' taking you back to the beginning. The kids liked that.

When they got back to New York City, some of them were in Greenwich Village, where Peter, Paul & Mary were singing at a little nightspot called the Bitter End. They heard it from the kids, and they thought it was an old folk song that the kids had picked up in camp. And The Kingston Trio got it from Peter, Paul & Mary, with Joe Hickerson's rhythm and the two extra verses.

About three years later—I think probably 1958 or '59—I got a telephone call from my manager, the late Harold Leventhal.

He says, 'Pete, didn't you write a song called Where Have All The Flowers Gone?'

I said, 'Yeah, about three or four years ago, I think.'

He says, 'Did you ever copyright it?'

'No, I don't guess I did.'

He said, 'Well, The Kingston Trio just recorded it.'

Well, I knew Dave Guard well. I'd sold him a copy of my mimeographed book *How To Play The 5-String Banjo*, one dollar and fifty-nine cents, and a year later I got a nice letter from him saying, 'Pete, I've been putting that book to hard use. I and two others have a group we call The Kingston Trio.'

So, I had his phone number and I called him up. He said, 'Oh, Pete, we didn't know it was your song. We'll take our name off it.' It was very nice of him, because legally, I had, as they say, 'abandoned copyright,' and I didn't have a legal claim to the song. But he took their name off the copyright, and Harold Leventhal copyrighted it. You know, that song pays my taxes for me nowadays. It's been translated into languages all over the world.

Marlene Dietrich is the one who really took it around the world. Her daughter said, 'Mother, there's a record by The Kingston Trio I think you'd be interested in.' And she heard the song and got a German translation made, which sings better than the English.

Sag' mir, wo die Blumen sind?
Wo sind sie gebliebben?
Sag' mir, wo die Blumen sind?
Was ist Geschehn?
Sag' mir, wo die Blumen sind?
Mädchen pflüuckten sie geschwind
Wann wird man je verstehn?
Wann wird man je verstehn?

Marlene Dietrich had a one-woman show she took around the world the last ten years of her life. And if she was singing in an English-speaking country, like Australia or England or Canada, she'd sing my English words, but anywhere else in the world, she'd sing the German verses.

Editor's note: Pete did eventually locate the original Cossack song after *Sing Out* magazine offered a prize for anyone who could find it. The song is entitled 'Koloda Duda,' and it can be heard on the CD that comes with Pete's republished songbook *Where Have All The Flowers Gone—A Singalong Memoir*.

Here are the last two verses of the Russian:

A ee-dye-zh devki?	*And where are the girls?*
Devki zamuzh ushli	*The girls have gotten married and gone away*

A ee-dye-zh kazaki?	*And where are the Cossacks?*
Na vionu poshli	*They've gone to war*

GUANTANAMERA

I remember singing 'Guantanamera' with The Weavers at our 1963 reunion concert, and many times since. Over the years, that song has become more and more important to me.

I'm convinced that if José Martí hadn't been killed, he would have gone on to write more poetry, and the world would think of him along with Pushkin, Shakespeare, and Dante as one of the world's greatest poets. He was only forty-two when he died. He was born in 1853 and killed in '95. Although he was born in Cuba, I found out that he wrote the words to 'Guantanamera' only thirteen miles from where I learned the song, at Camp Woodland in Phoenicia, New York.

Back in 1890, there were trains that went from Kingston up to Phoenicia, and then the tracks turned at right angles and went north up to Haines Falls and Tannersville. That's where José Martí rented a room for the summer and wrote over a hundred-and-fifty little stanzas. A year later, his friends said, 'You must publish these,' so it came out in 1891 as *Versos sencillos*, which means 'simple verses.'

Martí had been banished from Cuba at age seventeen because he supported independence from Spain. In 1891, he was temporarily in New York, making a living as a journalist, as he had all his life, but on the side writing novels, plays, and poems. He was sick with indecision:

I want independence for Cuba, but I don't want to hurt Spain. Spain is the mother country. And if we do get independence, how do we keep Cuba out of the claws of the great Eagle of the North?

He didn't have the answer to that, and it was putting him into great indecision. His doctor said, 'José, you're making yourself sick with studying and thinking. Go up to the country. Go walking in the woods. Get your health back—that's most important.'

So, Martí rented a room for the summer in Haines Falls, thirteen miles north of Phoenicia, and he wrote all these subtle and philosophic verses summing up life. He was thirty-nine years old at the time. He returned to Cuba in 1895 and was killed in an abortive uprising.

Over a hundred years later, the Cuban composer Julián Orbón found that Martí's stanzas fit the well-known melody of 'Guantanamera,' a song that had been made up to satirize the women who went out with American sailors. A local satirist named Joseíto (José Fernández Diaz) had written it in the 1920s, and he would sing it every afternoon on the radio, writing new verses from the newest scandals in the daily newspaper. Orbón added a new energy to the song by starting the chorus off on the sixth note of the scale, backed by the harmony of the 'four' chord.

In 1950, a young man named Héctor Angulo was one of Orbón's students. Ten years later he was studying at The Manhattan School of Music and he took a summer job up in the Catskill Mountains at Camp Woodland. Angulo was able to select just the right stanzas out of almost two hundred to teach to the children at the camp.

I visited the camp that year to sing to the kids, but at the end they wanted to teach me 'the great new song we learned from our counselor.' They brought me to Angulo, who taught me the song. Martí's philosophic verses ennobled the old melody, and I have sung 'Guantenamera' ever since. I've performed it in thirty-five countries on four continents, and it rings true in every one.

When I speak with people about 'Guantanamera,' I urge them not to try and translate it when they sing it. The verses flow so poetically in the original Spanish. Instead, I pause during the song and speak the following rough translation, then finish the song in Spanish.

I am a simple man from the land of palm trees,
Before I die, I want to share these verses of my soul.

My verses are of a clear green, and of flaming red.
My verses are like a wounded fawn that seeks refuge in the mountain.

I cultivate a white rose, in June and also in January,
for my sincere friend who holds out to me his honest hands

And as for the cruel ones who would cut out the heart with which I live,
I cultivate not thistles nor nettles. I cultivate a white rose.

With the poor people of this earth that I want to cast my lot.
The little stream in the mountain pleases me as much as the sea.

Editor's note: the complex history of 'Guantanamera' is only partly accounted for in the following attribution: 'Original lyrics and music by José Fernández Diaz (Joseíto Fernández). Music arranged and adapted by Julián Orbón, Héctor Angulo, and Pete Seeger. Words (verses) by José Martí, lyrics adapted by Julián Orbón (1949). © 1963, 1965 (renewed) by Fall River Music Inc.'

KISSES SWEETER THAN WINE

As I remember, I first played 'Kisses Sweeter Than Wine' in the key of A because Leadbelly played the tune on a twelve-string guitar. His twelve-string guitar was very low, and he had a very high voice. We were singing it low, but I wanted to play the same notes. He sang in A minor but he played an A major chord, singing a blues note—basically an astonishing combination of African and Irish traditions.

It wasn't originally called 'Kisses Sweeter Than Wine.' It was an Irish ballad, a lament for poor Drimmer the cow, sung to a lugubrious old melody:

If it wasn't a Drimmer, I'll tell you right now
About an old man, he had but one cow
He took it to the field, to be fed,
And all of a sudden poor Drimmer dropped dead
Oh oh, mush is sweeter than thou.

It was a comic song, and the humor of it was the exaggerated slowness of it:

I have no butter, to butter my bread,
Poor Drimmer is dead.

Leadbelly liked the melody, but instead of playing in the minor, he gave it an A major and played the melody on the bass strings. He garbled up the words as well as changing the melody, so we had completely new words.

About a half-year after Leadbelly had died, I guess it was in the spring of 1950, I was remembering this Irish song, but I couldn't remember the words at all. All I remembered was something about a dead cow. But I remembered the new chorus, '*Oh kisses sweeter than wine*,' and I thought, *Gee that's a nice chorus*, and I jotted it down on a piece of paper, and it went into a folder of 'Song Ideas 1950.' I've got folders of these—thousands of ideas that I jot on pieces of paper and never do anything about.

Nine months later, The Weavers had a job in a nightclub, and we get a letter from Pete Cameron, our manager, saying, 'Decca wants to record some more songs. Get busy rehearsing them. We'll probably record in Chicago.' The Weavers read Pete Cameron's letter, and Lee says, 'Pete, look through your folder of song ideas and see what you got. Maybe we can make up a new song.' When he came to this chorus he said, 'Hold on, let me try working on it,' and the next day he'd written seven verses. As I remember, we pared them down to five, and we were happy enough, and we started singing it in our nightclub engagement. We didn't know what would happen to it, but we were willing to try recording it up in the hotel room.

In The Weavers' recording with my six-string guitar, we sang in D minor, but I was in A position, five frets up; and then, after that, the orchestra took over.

Leadbelly had learned the song from an Irish singer named Sam Kennedy, who had come to New York in 1940. They met at a party, and Leadbelly liked the song so much that he took Sam into the bathroom to learn it. The song was an unaccompanied lament, but Leadbelly gave it both chords and rhythm.

Later, at a gathering at the apartment of the activist Henrietta Yurchenko, Pete and Leadbelly emerged from the bathroom and said, 'We got a new song' and sang the chorus, '*Kisses sweeter than wine*,' to the same melody. I guess you could say it took two bathrooms to write the song.

The precursor to 'Kisses Sweeter Than Wine' wasn't the only thing Sam Kennedy brought with him to New York. He also brought a design for paper doves that Pete always kept and distributed widely. You just cut the paper to the pattern, fold it, put the tab on one side into the slit on the other, and you have a beautiful dove. For years, they were hung at the Beacon Sloop Club during the holidays.

IF I HAD A HAMMER

Lee Hayes wrote the words in January 1949 and mailed them to me and said, 'Pete, do you think you can make up a tune for this?' Lee wrote it without any particular things in mind. It was like a hymn as far as he was concerned. I sat down on the piano and *plunk, plunk, plunk* made up a tune. The Weavers liked it, and we sang it at a meeting to raise money for the victims of the Smith Act. In 1949, we made a recording for a tiny little company called Charter Records. You can now get it from the box set put out by the Bear Family Record Company in Germany.

It wasn't a bad tune, but it wasn't as good as what most people know now, because Peter, Paul & Mary started singing it years later, and they had made a number of quite important changes in my melody. Mary Travers and Peter Yarrow and Paul Stookey worked out this fantastic, wonderful arrangement, and it became a hit record, and it's been covered by hundreds of different recordings all over the world. Sometimes they would mess up the words. In Italy, they had a record, '*If I had a hammer, I would hit you on the head, because you stole my man you so-and-so ...*'

Our manager would not allow us to sing this song in 1950. He says, 'I'm trying to get the blacklisters off your back. This just encourages them.'

For the musicians among us, the most important change Peter, Paul & Mary made to the melody was in the last line of the verses. In the original version, '*love between, all of my brothers*' goes down to the low tonic note of the key, and then down to the dominant fifth below that. This is a very low note indeed—one that only a fine bass singer like Lee Hays could reach with authority. But when Peter, Paul & Mary sang '*love between my brothers and my sisters,*' they went up to the fifth and sixth notes of the scale above the tonic, almost a full octave higher than the original melody Their new, inclusive words not only broadened the message but also placed the powerful part of the chorus in a vocal range where all of America could sing it. Ever the uniter, Pete quickly devised a chord structure that could accommodate both melodies simultaneously, so that both generations could sing it together when he played the song at concerts.

TZENA, TZENA AND ISSACHAR MIRON

In the fall of 2007, a man with a thick Israeli accent called me and asked, 'Is this the David Bernz who has a new recording of Pete Seeger singing Tzena, Tzena, Tzena?' The man's name was Issachar Miron, and he was the original composer of the song back in the 1940s.

Almost eighty years of age at the time, Issachar was looking for a copy of a recording of Pete singing the song at the Walkabout Clearwater Coffeehouse a few weeks earlier. But Pete, who was also approaching eighty at that point, had only sung the first few lines and then let the chorus sing the rest of it. That wouldn't do for Issachar, because this version of 'Tzena' had a new set of Arabic words, and he wanted them to be heard clearly.

Pete and Issachar had been working together to create a three-language version of the song to transform it into a song of peace. At the concert, Pete introduced it as follows:

Back in 1939, a man wrote a song for the regiment he was in. It was a Jewish regiment from what is now Israel, but then it was part of the British army. The song was so popular they sang it across North Africa, they sang it in the Normandy beachhead, they sang it through Germany and into the holocaust camps.

In 1950, the great bandleader Gordon Jenkins made up English words to it and the Weavers sang it to the top of the hit parade. Now, in the twenty-first century, the man who originally created the music, Issachar Miron, he and I think that it might have a new career. We have not only an English translation but a translation in Arabic. And all these parts harmonize with each other.

The original Hebrew lyrics by Yehiel Haggiz spoke of soldiers calling girls out to dance with them. In 1950, Gordon Jenkins added an English verse for The Weavers, calling friends out to dance with 'people from every nation.' Now, decades later, Issachar and Pete enlisted the help of Palestinian poet Salman Natour. Using the word 'Zaina,' an Arabic word that refers to a pretty girl, Salman crafted an Arabic verse that brings up the specter of an Arab boy asking a pretty Israeli girl to dance both the Hora and the Dabkeh, with a subtext of not being afraid to be seen together enjoying dances from both cultures.

TZENA TZENA *Arabic verse by Salman Natour*

Zeina zeina zeina zeina	*Zeina, Zeina, lovely girl*
Ma-hkad yuw kaf bei'-nil	*None shall separate us tonight*
Bei'-na b'lei let t'aw-ad na.	*One from the other*
Yal-la ma-a-na, ma-a-na yal-a	*Come to me, I'll come to you*
Nyd'-bek Dabke, nur-kus Hora ma	*Dance the Dabke, hop the Hora*
As-ad na	*Be happy! Loosen your shoe!*
Zeina zeina	*Zeina, Zeina,*
Yal-la ghran-nu ma-a-na	*Let's welcome our friends*
Ah-lan bi-kom ya as-khab	*Come where all our friends will find us*
Zeina zeina	*Zeina, Zeina,*
Yal-la rud-du ma-a-na	*It's the night*
Yal-la ya kul leil akh-bab.	*Of our friendship*
Zeina zeina nur-kus Hora,	*Zeina, Zeina, hop the Hora*
Nyd-bek' Dabke yal-la	*Dance the Dabke*
'Khu-bi ad u-ma ba-ad-na'	*None shall make us afraid*
Zeina zeina, ghran-nu ma-a-na,	*Zeina Zeina Zeina, lets sing*
Ghran-nu ma-a-na ghran-nu	*Let's dance with*
Zeina zeina zeina!	*Zeina Zeina Zeina!*

As the existing Walkabout recording was not usable, Issachar scheduled a recording session at one of the renovated piers in New York City with Pete and the chorus and other singers. It was the first time I met Issachar in person, and he was a pleasure to work with.

Issachar and I became friends, and over the next few years he asked me down to New York to work with him on several projects. On these visits, it was always a pleasure to see his wife, Tsipora. She and Issachar navigated their upper West Side apartment, filled with pictures and memorabilia, like two denizens of a lair that seemed part cave, part palace.

On one visit, Tsipora approached me and said with a bit of pride, 'You know, Issachar also writes rock'n'roll.' When I asked how so, she said, 'Many years ago, Issachar was working with an oboe player who was a friend of Mick Jagger, and the next thing we knew, Issachar's melody was all over the radio.' Then she hummed a few notes, and I realized that it was the melody to 'Paint It Black.'

I asked Tsipora if Issachar ever tried to get his royalties and she said, 'No, he never sues anybody.' I understood. Issachar had always been a man of peace, and conflict just didn't seem to be in his repertoire.

ISSACHAR MIRON *I remember an article was written about me by the foreign editor of the Reader's Digest, and it evoked really extraordinary interest around the globe. The whole thing originated from one single educational concept. I became the 'officer in chief' in charge of education and special events within the Israeli army, with an idea to bring closer the diverse groups that had come to Israel from practically seventy countries around the world.*

They had different cultures. How do you bring together and mold them into a loving cooperating group? I had the idea of bringing people together by singing, and it was very effective. I came to the conclusion that possibly it could help to bring Arabs and Israelis closer together. I discussed the idea of a Palestinian songbook with my friend Mayor, who was a friend of the prime minister of Israel, and the prime minister said that his office would publish the book.

Then I spoke to some friends who were Arab educators, and they sent me the material. I agreed to help make the book under the condition that there would be a board comprised of prominent Arabic educators and musicians. This was the beginning of Garlands Of Melodies, the first Palestinian songbook ever published by Israel, and the only music book ever published by the prime minister's office. It was published and distributed in the late 1950s. So unknowingly, I performed the task of extending a hand of musical friendship between the Israelis and Arabs.

Adding Arabic words to 'Tzena, Tzena' was an idea of Pete Seeger. He had heard about my interest in Arabic songs, and he knew the story of my book. I embraced it, and I thought, Who could write the text that will be singable and happily fitting into the concept of Yehiel Haggiz's original lyrics? I knew Arabic, and 'Zaina' was the closest thing to 'Tzena' that you can say. 'Tzena' in Hebrew means 'come out girls,' and 'Zaina' in Arabic means 'you're beautiful.' So 'Tzena' embraced 'Zaina.'

We added these new words in the 1990s. I found the poet Salman Natour through my contacts in Israel. I approached my collaborator friend, the greatest poet of Israeli songs, Haim Hefer, and consulted with him, and he said, 'Absolutely, Salman Natour is the best.'

SOME SONG INTRODUCTIONS

It has become stereotypical for folk musicians to talk between songs. It's sometimes referred to as 'stage patter,' but that word implies that it is somehow unimportant, whereas with Pete the song introductions were an integral part of his presentation.

Some of Pete's introductions were detailed and others surprisingly short, and sometimes Pete would launch into a song with no introduction at all, as he often did with 'The Hammer Song.' Where appropriate, though, Pete presented introductions that contextualized the song for his listeners. Delivered with his trademark lilt and conveying his underlying respect for all people, these words from the stage and the music that followed were a potent combination that transformed many of Pete's concerts into true community events as Pete succeeded in uniting audience after audience with hope for the human race.

Although it's difficult to catch the exact flavor of a live performance in writing, I felt that any book that attempts to portray Pete's use of the spoken word ought to include at least some material spoken from the concert stage. What follows are just a few examples of perhaps thousands of such introductions Pete offered up over the years, largely taken from a live concert at the Walkabout Clearwater Coffeehouse in 1997.

VISIONS OF CHILDREN

I put new words to a two-part melody written by Ludwig Van Beethoven way back, two centuries ago. The year was 1997, and Mayor Giuliani, mayor of New York City, was going to auction off one hundred and sixteen beautiful community gardens. And an organization called the Green Guerillas organized a rally at Sixth Avenue and 42nd Street, with busy traffic pouring by, and I got three altos and three sopranos to sing this song, and Beethoven's Seventh Symphony floated out across the traffic...

We'll work together, even though we work differently
When we consider, all the many great dangers
Visions of children, asking us to save them
Building their gardens, all through the world.

IF IT CAN'T BE REDUCED

In the winter of 2007, the following words were put down by the Zero Waste Commission of the city of Berkeley, California: 'If it can't be reduced, reused, repaired, rebuilt, refurbished, refinished, resold, recycled or composted, then it should be restricted, redesigned or removed from production.' Those twenty-four words were given to me by a woman at a little peace demonstration who said, 'Can you make a song out of it?' Well, I laughed. But I had a bad cold the following week. I couldn't speak. For four days I was in bed, and I stuck the twenty-four words up on the wall. By gosh, at the end of four days I had a song.

If it can't be reduced   Audience: *If It can't be reduced*
Reused, repaired   Audience: *Reused, repaired*
Rebuilt, refurbished, refinished,
Resold, recycled, or composted
Then it should be   Audience: *Then it should be*
Restricted, redesigned   Audience: *Restricted, redesigned*
Or removed!   Audience: *Removed!*
From production

Here's to the city of Berkeley
Here's to the city of Berkeley
Here's to the city of Berkeley
And its Zero Waste Commission
Here's to the city of Berkeley
That beau-ti-ful city of Berkeley
Here's to the city of Berkeley
And its Zero Waste Commission

THE CHANUKAH CHASE

My niece, Kate Seeger, found a song that is one of the best holiday songs in the world, I think. Every holiday season now, when the sun looks like it's going to leave the world, people in the northern hemisphere always had songs. This particular song was written by Judith Kaplan Eisenstein, the daughter of the man who started the Jewish reconstruction movement. My niece calls it 'The Chanukah Chase' because halfway through it becomes a kind of cannon. You listen to the way the women start, and the men come in a few moments later:

From my window where you can see the glow
From my menorah on newly fallen snow
Where I will set you one little candle
On this the first night of Chanukah...

ON THE LAST MONTH OF THE YEAR

Way back in the year of 1939, the folklore collector Alan Lomax visited Parchment State Prison in Mississippi. And some of the women prisoners sang this song. My stepmother, Ruth, put this song in her book *American Folk Songs For Christmas*. Never got picked up much, though, and I think it should be. It's one of my favorite Christmas songs.

What month was my Jesus born in?
On the last month of the year
What month was my Jesus born in?
On the last month of the year
Oh, January, February, Ma, ah, ah, ah arch
(Oh Lordy) April, May, and June
You got July, August, September
October Lordy November
On the twenty-fifth day of December
On the last month of the year...

STEP BY STEP

This is an unusual day. All around the country, people are taking petitions to ask people who run the country to do something about the fact that there's products being made around the world in sweatshops where people work for pennies. And these kinds of conditions, we thought were done forever. And they shouldn't go on. It's not going to be an easy thing to solve. Countries need jobs somehow. There ought to be things like the Minimum Wage Act for the whole world! The poverty-stricken little countries are saying, 'They're asking forty cents an hour, we'll work for thirty cents an hour.' So, we're going to end off with a couple or three union songs. One was written—I don't know who wrote it—it was in the preamble to the constitution of the Amalgamated Mine Workers in 1860 in Pennsylvania.

Step by step, the longest march, can be won, can be won
Many stones can form an arch, singly none, singly none
And by union what we will, can be accomplished still
Drops of water turn a mill, singly none, singly none …

HOW CAN I KEEP FROM SINGING?

Sitting in a train, I found myself playing a song I haven't sung for years. It's an astonishing Christian hymn when it started out. Ann Warner was the writer of this song. She wrote a lot of hymns. She and her sister lived on a little island in the Hudson, right across from West Point. But I didn't know that when I first heard it.

The song was taught to me by a woman from North Carolina, a friend of my mother-in-law's who'd come north and said, 'This is my grandmother's favorite song.' She says, 'Way back before the Civil War, it was made up and it was a comfort to people like us who were Quakers and were against slavery in North Carolina.'

I didn't know then that the third verse was not the original third verse but what was made up by my friend Doris Plenn. About four years ago, a wonderful singer in India made a record that sold six million copies in Europe. I couldn't get a penny of royalty for my friend Doris. I printed it in *Sing Out* magazine with no copyright.

My life goes on in endless song above earth's lamentation
I hear the real, though far-off hymn, that hail's a new creation
Through all the tumult and the strife, I hear that music ringing
It sounds an echo in my soul. How can I keep from singing?

LITTLE BOXES

Malvina Reynolds was riding with her husband south of San Francisco and passed a place called Daley City. She looked up and says, 'Bud, take the wheel. I feel a song coming on.' When she got down to where she was singing for the PTA somewhere, she had this song finished:

Little boxes, on the hillside,
Little boxes made of ticky tacky,
Little boxes, little boxes,
Little boxes all the same.
There's a green one, and a pink one
And a blue one and a yellow one,
And they're all made out of ticky-tacky,
And they all look just the same.

BLUE SKIES

Irving Berlin was raised on the Lower East Side. At age eight, he was shaking a can for a blind beggar. His parents were so broke, they didn't let him go to school. As a teenager, he got a job in a restaurant and was always making up satirical verses about the other waiters. And in his early twenties, he had a hit record—not record, they didn't have much records in those days—'Alexander's Ragtime Band,' around 1910. And he went on to write some of America's most famous songs.

Around 1920, he met Victor Herbert, the famous composer of operettas. He says, 'Mr. Herbert you know, I don't know a thing about music. I just play by ear. Do you think I should go study it?'

And Mr. Herbert was very sensible. He says, 'You got a talent for words and music. I think it would cramp your style.'

So, Berlin never learned. He played the piano only in the key of G flat—the black notes. And he was rich enough to have a special piano built. You turn a crank and all the notes go up or down, so it'll be a piano capo. Here's one I think is his greatest song.

THE BALLAD OF HARRY SIMMS

I was a teenager when I first met a family from Kentucky that was living in New York City. Jim Garland had met a young union organizer from the north. Harry Simms from Springfield, Massachusetts. He'd come down to help organize coal miners. He made up a song for his friend after his friend had been murdered. They shot him in the stomach as he was walking down the tracks one day. They took him to a hospital. It was a company hospital. They said, 'No, you can't take him in unless you have money.'

Two hours he sat, holding his guts in his hand and bleeding to death. Well, his friends—Jim and others—raised some money, and they took him in. He died on the operating table. Since then, I've become acquainted with Harry Simms's brother, who became a union organizer in Springfield and still works there.

Come and listen to my story, come and listen to my song
I'll tell you of a hero, who is now dead and gone
I will tell you of a young boy, his age was nineteen
He was the bravest union man, that I have ever seen…

FEEL LIKE I'M FIXIN' TO DIE RAG

We sang this song (by Country Joe McDonald) in countries where you'd never think it would ever go. We sang it in Paraguay, Brazil, and Argentina two years ago; one year ago in India. And I tell people very frankly, in my opinion, it was a great victory for the American people to get out of Vietnam…

Come on all you big strong men
Uncle Sam needs your help again…

CHAPTER 08 SOME POLITICS

THE PEEKSKILL RIOTS

Pete's relationship with the city of Peekskill in northern Westchester County, New York, changed a lot over time. In 1949, just as he was relocating his family to the nearby city of Beacon, Pete participated in an infamous concert there to support the Civil Rights Congress that came to be known as the Peekskill Riots. When Pete shared his thoughts and memories of those dark events, one thing that shone through was his abiding faith in the fairness and decency of people, including the majority of the people of Peekskill.

When one is inoculated against smallpox, your arm swells up, but the rest of your body is alerted to the danger, and now your body does not get smallpox. In a way, that's what happened in Peekskill, New York, on September 4th, 1949. The fascists led by J. Edgar Hoover were determined that America would put twelve thousand people behind barbed wire that he was sure were communists. I was probably one of them. But what happened at Peekskill looked so ugly. All America saw on television or in pictures in papers these hate-filled faces shouting, 'Go back to Russia!' 'Kikes!' 'Nigger-lovers!' And it was not a pretty picture, and Hoover was never able to do that.

The first concert was a week before. That never took place. It was supposed to be an evening concert, but a mob came to beat up the people who were setting up chairs. Howard Fast, the writer, was head of the committee that organized the concert. They set up one thousand rented chairs and they bolted together a small stage—big enough to hold a piano, maybe twelve feet square, and not very high, maybe twenty inches high off the ground. And the mob attacked them.

First Howard Fast and the others beat them off. There were just a few of them. But then more came. Howard and the others retreated to the stage, and they were singing 'We Shall Not Be Moved' but not knowing exactly what to do, because it got to be a bigger mob. Now, the mob started a bonfire with the paper. There was a lot of paper to be distributed for the Civil Rights Congress—which was a lefty group—and they started a fire. They threw into the fire all the chairs, one thousand chairs. It made a huge fire!

And now they advanced on the stage, at which point a policeman suddenly realized that he'd been watching the whole thing and not stopped it. There are people going to be killed, and he'd be in court and be asked, 'Why didn't you do something earlier!' And so he shouted, 'EVERYBODY GO HOME!'

Howard Fast and the others got into their bus and were fortunate to be still alive, and they drove back to New York. And the mob, after they set fire to the stage, broke up the PA system with hammers. This was four or five o'clock in the afternoon. Now, at six o'clock, I drove my mother down because I was supposed to sing two or three songs at the beginning, and there was a traffic jam. We couldn't get through. But I saw a tall policeman with a broad hat, and I shouted, 'Officer, can you get me through, I'm singing here tonight.' And he gave me a strange look and simply said, 'There's not going to be any concert,' and he strode off. Well, we waited a little longer, but I said to my mother, 'I guess he's right,' and we turned around on the grass and drove home, and the next day found out what had happened.

Well, Robeson got on the air, and he said, 'It's America. I've got a right to sing. I am going to sing!' And I went to a meeting at the Audubon Ballroom in Harlem. I think there were at least five thousand people there, and a thousand or two thousand members of Local 65—it was a left-wing union—and they said, 'We'll stand all around the edges of the field to see that no one gets in who doesn't have a ticket.'

Now it was going to be an afternoon concert, and they got there in the morning and people stood literally arm-in-arm all around the field.

My mother had gone back to her home, but I said to Toshi and the kids, 'I'm sure they can't do what they did last week, not after all this publicity.' Toshi's father said, 'Are you sure you should take those babies? I'm coming along too.' And Boots Casetta and his girlfriend were there, so there were seven of us in the car.

And I was right. They didn't do what they did last week. They did something different.

The week before, they had invaded the field and set things on fire. This time, the concert took place. Sylvia Kahn sang 'The Star-Spangled Banner,' Leonid Hambro played some Prokofiev and other classical music, and I sang three songs. One of them we had just written, 'If I Had A Hammer.' I think I sang 'T For Texas' too. Woody Guthrie had taught it to me.

And then Robeson sang for about one hour. About five other men stood in back of him and on each side of him, to the right and left, because there could be sharpshooters in the woods—and there were, actually. In the front, there were people looking all around to make sure there wasn't anybody lifting a rifle.

He sang for an hour and then, after the applause, he went down and he got into a car. I didn't notice this, but it seems he went out the other side of the car and into a van, and maybe went from that van into another van, so people who would want to stop him didn't know which one to stop. And he got down on the floor. He couldn't be seen—people were above him. So he got out okay, but the people following him all had stones thrown at them.

At the end of the concert it was very slow getting out because there was only one narrow dirt road leading out of the field. I remember at the gate coming in, there was a small crowd, and they were the ones I heard shout, 'Go back to Russia!' 'Kikes!' 'Nigger-lovers!' I remember those phrases. But they were behind barricades, and the police didn't let them in. But now there was no crowd, and I said to the policeman, 'My home's to the north, I'm turning left,' and he says, 'No, all cars go to the right.' And that's where the stones were. We turned to the right, a winding road for about a mile and a half, and now there were stones. The people next to the piles of stones were mostly young people. I didn't know it then, but there were some adults sitting behind the teenagers in the bushes so that if any car stopped and grabbed a teenager, they had extra people there.

There were seven of us in the Jeep station wagon. We hadn't gone more than a few feet when I see glass in the road. I say to the family, 'Uh oh,' because around the corner was a pile of stones each about as big as a tennis ball or a baseball, and a young man heaving them with all his force at every single car that came by. So it was *crash!* and then around the corner was another pile of stones and another *crash!*

We had three windows on each side and a divided windshield, and they were all broken, not once but several times, so I think there must have been between fifteen and twenty piles of stones. They must have been covered up with canvas or something so we didn't notice them when we drove in. Mika was only one year old, Danny was three years old. He can remember it. He can remember being shoved to the floor and his grandfather's body being right on top of him. And I was driving, and I kept my eyes as high as I could. Glass flew around, but none of it got into my eye. There was a policeman standing about fifty feet from somebody throwing stones. And I stopped the car and tried to roll the window down, but it was so splintered I only got it about an inch down, and I shouted, 'Officer aren't you going to do something!' He just shouted, 'Move on, move on.'

Now the interesting thing—and this is the important part of the story— signs went up in Peekskill. These were bumper-sticker-type signs about five inches high and two feet wide, saying, 'Wake Up America, Peekskill Did.' About five weeks later, they *all* came down. They were on bumpers, they were in windows, in stores, in gas stations. There must have been thousands of them in Peekskill. The signs disappeared. They were all taken off. Why? It seems in Europe, they were horrified. They said, 'Those are the same signs that went up in Germany after Kristallnacht when Hitler said, *Wake up Germany, Munich did—throw stones at all the Jewish storekeepers.*' And they said, Is America going fascist?' Well, a lot of people thought we were, but I was not convinced. I said, 'There's a stronger tradition of freedom of speech in this country than you would believe.' And I was right.

At the time of the Peekskill Riots, Pete was in the midst of building his cabin on twenty acres of hillside just outside of Beacon, New York. When Pete and the family got home, they had to clean the glass and stones from their car. The fireplace in the cabin was only partially complete, so Pete took a round river stone from the floor of the car and cemented it into the fireplace as a reminder. It still rests there, looking quite out of place next to the other mountain-type stones.

The events at Peekskill had a profound effect on Pete. It was a mixed bag of sorts. The left claimed victory because they had held their concert, but they were also smarting from the beating they took. Howard Fast, Lee Hayes, and others answered artistically with a ten-inch LP entitled *The Peekskill Story*, featuring Fast's narration heard over the actual sounds of the crowd shouting epithets at the concertgoers. It also contained Lee's song 'Hold The Line,' which described the events in ballad form, with each verse followed by an optimistic chorus:

Hold the line, hold the line
As we held the line in Peekskill we will hold it everywhere
Hold the line, hold the line
We will hold the line forever till there's freedom everywhere.

Not everyone was so optimistic, however. Pete began to ponder about how such an event could have been prevented, and his artistic response came in the form of a play.

AUNT ROSA'S VICTORY

I wrote a play about this. If I say so myself, it was a good play, but I wasn't a good playwright. It was about an Italian American family. The play was called *Aunt Rosa's Victory*.

Auntie Rosa's husband has died, and her brother says, 'Well, Rosa, you can live with us. You can get free board and room, but you have to help out with the housework.' So they got a free servant by giving her board and lodging. She was helping to make beds and sweep floors and so on.

Well, she is out in the garden, picking up stones, and says, 'Stones, stones. Why'd God make so many stones?'

And her nephew says, 'Ah, Auntie Rosa, give 'em to me, I know what to do with them.'

She says, 'What you going to do with 'em?'

'Oh, you'll find out.'

And then she hears the talk, and she realizes what's going to happen. But she's scared to speak up, because then where's she going to go? She doesn't have a penny to her name. And her brother, who's all for the stone-throwing, says, 'That Robeson, they should lynch him. They should kill him.'

Her nephew is one of the stone throwers. After the attack, she gets together with her black neighbor, who also knew that stones were going to be thrown, and they're both embarrassed that neither of them spoke up. They say, 'Maybe we could have stopped it if we'd spoken up—if we could've gotten on the radio and said something.'

And then they go see a white minister, a protestant minister, and he's embarrassed that he didn't speak up.

And then Rosa's Catholic priest says, 'I should have spoken up too, I knew what was going to happen.'

All three of them go to the mayor, and the mayor says, 'You're speaking up for those commie bastards? Get out of my office!'

Well, the three of them go to get a cup of coffee, and they say, 'We've got to do something.'

They drive up to Albany, and they speak to Governor Dewey, and they said, 'If you don't do something, we think we're going down to Washington to speak. It's not fair to Peekskill that Peekskill should have this terrible reputation. A lot of people in Peekskill didn't like what happened, but they were scared to speak up like we were scared to speak up.'

Next, the governor is talking to Washington, and Washington gets back to the mayor of Peekskill. 'Get those signs down.'

'But we just put them up just a couple of weeks ago.'

'GET THOSE SIGNS DOWN!'

Slam goes the receiver.

So, the mayor calls in the police to get those signs down.

'But Mr. Mayor, we just put them up a little while ago.'

'Get those signs down!'

And so the signs came down. And now, Rosa's talking to her dead husband, and his picture is on her wall, saying, 'Tony, we didn't really do what we should, but at least those signs came down.'

That was Auntie Rosa's victory.

Oh, the last thing. She gets together with her niece. She says her nephew didn't really know what bad things he was doing,

'We can't change your father's opinion, but we can change your brother's opinion. Let's make the best pesto we've ever made—we're going to change his opinion with food.'

That's how it ends: the sister and the aunt have got a long-term conspiracy. They're going to get to the brother through food.

PEEKSKILL REVISITED

Pete did not appear in Peekskill for a long time after the events of 1949, but sometime in the early 1990s, a local healthcare organization invited him to perform a fundraising concert at the Peekskill waterfront. Thousands of people attended, and he was very well received. Afterwards, someone approached Pete and admitted they had been among the rock-throwers.

Well, they decided to run a waterfront fundraiser. And from way up in Poughkeepsie, they rented one of these big trucks that becomes a stage, and they had several thousand people down there at the waterfront, listening to me give a one-hour concert. I did it for two or three years. And then I realized that the people who threw stones were not the majority of people in Peekskill. The majority of Peekskill were ashamed of that, and they've tried to forget it as if it never happened. That's like somebody writing a history of America that doesn't write about lynchings.

Pete appeared often in Peekskill after that concert, and in 1994, some of us helped organize Clearwater's twenty-fifth-anniversary celebration at the Paramount Theatre, located right in the center of town, where Pete and others sang to a packed house. Not long after that, Pete and I appeared at the Dane's Lumber Fest about a block from the waterfront. The Dane family's lumberyard was a local fixture for decades.

As 1999 approached, I proposed to Pete that we mark the fiftieth anniversary of the difficult events in 1949 by holding a big community concert in Peekskill, but I didn't feel his support for the idea. Pete was probably right that healing can be more useful than guilt, and a large concert with a bunch of left-wing singers might only deepen divides. Besides, Pete often preferred multiple small things over one large one. So instead, Pete opted to participate in a press conference and a small church gathering...

Now this was an achievement of Paul Robeson Jr. He set up a kind of legal support group called the Paul Robeson Foundation, and they approached the county executive of Westchester and said, 'We are planning not a rally, but a press conference, and not more than a few hundred people, but we would like you to speak at it. It will be held only by invitation.'

They had chairs and a small speaker's stand and a small sound system, just enough for two hundred people, and it was right where the stones started to be thrown. It was on the opposite side of the street from the gate to the concert field. The gate to the concert field is now grown up with trees. Back then, they were small trees. And what used to be a big field is now full of houses. The county executive had his police chief, a black man, standing out there seeing that cars did not stop.

And that was where a man in his sixties said, 'I was a teenager then back in 1949, and I and some friends were talking on the sidewalk right in the center of town when a truck pulls up and a policeman gets out and said, You all get in the truck. We're going to go down to Ossining Beach and pick up stones to throw at the commies.'

There's a pebble beach down there in Ossining. You need to have a rather steep beach and the sand gets washed away and the pebbles don't. And these were not just pebbles but small stones, two or three inches in size. The kind that can break a window. So it wasn't very much of a secret what was going to happen. The sixty-year-old didn't just say it to me. He was one of the people speaking, and he said this in his speech.

And it came out also—somebody from the American Legion, I think, said, 'About a month before, maybe two months before, a high official in the Truman Administration came to Peekskill and said, This man Robeson loves Russia. He hates America! He's coming here to sing, to give a concert. I'm sure you know what to do.

And he went back to Washington. In other words, he gave them the green light to do whatever they wanted to do.

There were members of the Ku Klux Klan up and down the river who then got involved. I had a friend whose father was in the fire department, Bob Gibson. I knew him when he was sixteen. He came up to my house after I got to know him better, and he says, 'You know, Pete, I know all about that 1949 attack on you at the Robeson concert.'

I said, 'Really, well tell me, how was it organized?'

He says, 'The Ku Klux Klan had members in the police force, and they actually organized the whole thing.'

I said, 'How do you know that?'

Bob says, 'You know, they had the whole concert area surrounded with walkie-talkies, just like a battlefield. You guys didn't have a chance.'

They had people in the woods. Woods surrounded three sides of the field and some very small trees were on the fourth side, and that's where people entered. Now, they weren't able to assassinate Robeson at the field, but maybe they thought they could in the two miles leaving the concert, because that's where the damage was done.

After the press conference, we did go into Peekskill in the late afternoon or evening. There must have been another two hundred people, and these were local black people, and that's where I sang a whole batch of songs. I must have sung for half an hour down there.

Pete and some others traveled to a local Peekskill church in the late afternoon after the press conference. In addition to the audience, some choruses were there, including a children's chorus from one of the black churches. Pete stood at the center of the room and had to turn in different directions to face everybody on different sides of the room. We sang several songs there, and by the end Pete had everyone singing together on a rousing version of 'This Land Is Your Land.'

BEIRUT

In 1963, my wife and I took our three children on a trip around the world. Our youngest child was only eight, and the older two were fifteen and seventeen. We sang for our supper in about thirty countries, went across the Pacific, stopped off at American Samoa and native Samoa, went to Australia, went up to Indonesia, and then to Japan, where Toshi's father joined us. It was the first time Takashi had been back seeing his family in fifty years.

On that trip, we also stopped in and sang in Israel. We stopped at a left-wing kibbutz, and they got along well with the Palestinians—in fact, some of them married Palestinians, but we didn't realize that they didn't represent all of Israel. Four years later, in 1967, I was asked by Israel if I would come back and sing 'Tzena Tzena' at a huge rally in Tel Aviv with about twenty thousand people. And I told my manager that I wanted to visit an Arab country too, so he arranged for me to get a ticket from Rome to Lebanon. Back then, you could not go directly from Lebanon to Israel, so I had to go back to Rome and then from Rome to Israel.

I went to Beirut, the big city in Lebanon, and got a room in a cheap hotel and went walking down the street like any other sightseer. I remember seeing a beautiful brass tray for sale with lovely Arabic script, and I said, 'How much is this?'

And he said, 'Twenty-nine dollars.'

And I said, 'I think I can afford that.' I gave him the twenty-nine dollars. I suppose he could have just kept the money, but when we got home, this brass tray was there. We still use it. It's absolutely beautiful.

Then, about a block later, I heard a voice calling, 'Pete Seeger, is that you?' I turned and there was a young man with a white shirt with the sleeves rolled up. He was a young doctor. And he said, 'What are you doing here?'

And I said, 'Well, I've never been to an Arab country. I wanted to see what one is like.'

He says, 'Well, let me show you around. I'm here for a week. I have a job in a hospital on the Persian Gulf, but I have a week's vacation. I came back to see my family, but I'll tell my family I can see them another time. Let me show you around.'

This young man, who I called Sharif, took me up to the Roman ruins in the far northeast of Lebanon, where they had huge music festivals where the great Egyptian singer Oum Kalthoum would sing for tens of thousands, and where they had music from different countries.

He took me to visit a Bedouin camp where they have lots of goats, and he says, 'You know, these goats are the villains. That's why there are no more cedars in Lebanon. They eat every young cedar they can find, and now the only cedars of Lebanon are the ones in a hundred-acre park where they have a tall fence so no goat can possibly leap over and get in.'

We get to the Bedouin camp, and the only person there was an eagle-eyed woman in her sixties or seventies, but she wasn't scared at speaking to two strange white men. She offered us some coffee. She wanted to get to know us a little before showing us around. She gave us the strongest coffee I'd ever tasted, and I sipped a little of it to be polite. And she wanted to give me more. The way you say you don't need any more, you tip your glass a little, and that says you don't need any more.

'Yes,' she says, 'they've gone on to find a new place for the goats to graze, but my goat just had a kid and I couldn't travel with it, so they'll come and pick me up tomorrow.'

And then she invited us into the tent where she lived. The tent was about thirty feet long and only about five feet high. She was short. At one end was the mama goat and the kid just born. In the middle part was a hole dug in the ground, maybe eight inches deep and two feet wide, and this is where she cooked the meals. This was the dining room for her and her family. And in the far end was the harem—the bedroom.

And then she said, 'Feel this cloth. I spun every thread as a child. And when I was married, the rule is I must have enough cloth to make a tent for us to live in.' And she was very, very proud that the entire tent had been from cloth that she wove from thread that she had spun as a child. Probably when she was three years old, she was learning to spin thread out of goat's hair. And so it's a tremendous achievement for a young woman. She'd made that whole tent.

She showed us around the camp and showed us where the other tents had been, and she said, 'Tomorrow some of them will come and then we'll take my tent down, and we'll take the goat and the kid to the new location.'

Sharif also took me to a restaurant about fifty feet into the Mediterranean from a very steep hillside, almost like a cliff coming down from the mountains of Lebanon, north of the city of Beirut a few miles. You could look down forty feet and they had a light down there so you could see the fish swimming around. It was literally as clear as glass, and the reason is that these were waters that had seeped down the cracks in the mountains of Lebanon and then welled up offshore.

I had been scheduled to do a program at the University in Beirut, but before we went there, Sharif took me to meet his friends at the United Nations School, and at one point Sharif says to me, 'Pete, if you're going to Israel next week, do not mention it when you are here in Lebanon. You will probably never get to Israel. You can't imagine how bitter the feeling is. They feel that their homeland has been stolen from them, and they will not give up till they get it back! There is going to be war, sooner or later, again.

There was one war in 1948, and that's why I'm here. I was twelve years old, living in the little town of Aka, just north of Tel Aviv, and the radio says, 'Leave your home. Go up to Lebanon where it's safe. When we have driven the Jews into the sea, then you can come back.'

And, of course, the Jews won the war of 1948, and he never got back to his home.

'I went to the United Nations School. There's no playing hooky there. That's a passport to the future. I got good marks, and I was able to get scholarships to American universities. That's why I'm a doctor.'

And I kind of laughed. Thinking it was a joke, I said, 'Well, now, if you can be an American citizen, you can go back to Aka if you want it.'

And one of Sharif's friends says, 'Oh, don't! It would break your heart! You'd walk down the street where you used to live. No Arabs there. All Jews.'

And he really meant it would break your heart to see where you used to live.

They took me to the university in Beirut and I sang a program there, just a few different songs, and they sang along with me, and I told them that this was the first time I've visited an Arab country and how interested I was in everything there.

One of the songs I sang was 'Guantanamera,' and when I introduced it, I said, 'Whenever I sing this song, I think of the man who led most of his life in exile from Cuba. José Martí was a great poet—one of the greatest poets the world ever knew—and I'm sure you know great poets in the Arab world, but he led all but a few months of his life in exile. He went back to Cuba once or twice but couldn't stay there and had to leave again. So I dedicate this song to exiles of nineteen years and exiles of two thousand years.'

Afterwards, some of the men said, 'We hope you will come back and visit us again. We would love to have you sing for us some more.'

And I said, 'I'm sorry, I don't think I can come back. I can't stay even one day longer. I've been silent for a week, but now I can't be silent anymore. Twenty-four hours from now, I'll be singing in Tel Aviv for twenty thousand people. But I promise you, I will introduce that song the same way.'

And there was a silence. And they said, 'Will you tell them in Israel that you have been here in Lebanon?'

I said, 'Of course.' And they were silent. They realized there was more freedom of speech in Israel than they had in Lebanon.

When I got to Israel, I did sing for twenty thousand people in a huge outdoor amphitheater. And when I sang 'Guantanamera,' I told them, 'Whenever I sing this song, I give it this introduction: I dedicate it to exiles of two thousand years and exiles of nineteen years.'

Afterwards, in my dressing room, an Israeli man said, 'Mr. Seeger, you're very brave.'

I said, 'What's so brave?'

He said, 'You don't know how serious the feelings are.'

But no one tried to assassinate me, at least. That might have happened if I had spoken to a large group in Lebanon and said I'm going to be in Israel tomorrow night.

Because I had a week or more to spend in Israel, I had the time to speak with Rashad Hussein, the extraordinary Arab journalist who was the only Arab writing for a Jewish newspaper. 'Down in Egypt,' he said, 'they called me a collaborationist, but I asked the Egyptians, Where in this world do you think a Jew should live? And they couldn't answer.'

Incidentally, Oum Khaltoum was a fantastic singer. As a young woman, as a middle-aged woman, even as an old woman, she was still singing, and people would come from thousands of miles to hear her. She was an Egyptian singer, and as a young woman she would sing sexy love songs and so on. As an older woman, I'm not sure if she still sang the love songs, but she had such a fantastic voice people would come to hear anything she sang.

• • •

In 2010, I was asked to participate in a worldwide broadcast sponsored by the Israeli organization known as ARAVA, which is supported by the Jewish National Fund. I was misled a little bit. The Jewish National Fund may have said they were trying to bring Palestinians and Jews together, but in a way the Palestinians were giving way to the Jews, because the Jewish National Fund actually wants to get more Jews living in the far south and taking land away that Bedouins had been living in. So I'm a little sorry I appeared on the broadcast. But there was one Palestinian invited onto the program who knew what the Jewish National Fund was doing and still decided, 'But they will let me on, and they will let me speak,' and he was speaking out so Jews had to listen to him.

He says, 'What you've done, especially in what they call the settlements, you are taking our land away from us. Now, there are six million Jews in Israel and there's only a few thousand Palestinians left. They've left. Fourteen thousand Palestinians living in London, for example, and they've come to America. They would like to go back to their homeland, but it's all occupied by Jews now.'

And exactly what to do, nobody knows. All I know is, if the human race comes to an end, it's liable to start with a war in the Near East. Old as I am, I think it would be worth going to Israel if I could persuade Israelis that if there is going to be a human race here in a hundred years, Palestinians and Jews must be talking with each other. I'll tell them what happened in Ireland with Tommy Sands, and how he got leaders from the north and the south to sing together at a songfest. I wonder, how can we get a songfest together where Arabs and Jews will say, 'We want to forget politics for the moment and just sing'?

If they do, perhaps one of the songs they can sing together is 'Ghannu Ma'i.' I learned this song because a Lebanese woman in California by the name of Lina Maccach went to Ronnie Gilbert and says, 'Ronnie, I hear you and Pete and others sing songs in German or French or other languages, but no one ever sings anything in Arabic. Arabic is a beautiful language. That's why I'm going back to my home. My father was a journalist and he got assassinated and I fled to this country with my children. But I want them to be raised as Arabs, so I'm going back to Lebanon, and I think, if I'm careful, we will not get assassinated.'

And Ronnie says, 'Teach me a song that's not too difficult.'

Ronnie and I actually sang this together at a concert at the University Of California with Arlo Guthrie and Holly Near. It was called HARP (Holly, Arlo, Ronnie, Pete). They wanted us to do some more concerts because it sold out, and we could have done one concert after another out there, but I'd been away from Toshi too long already, so I said I couldn't. But that's how I learned the song and learned how it was made up as part of a children's play.

In Lebanon, there was a young engineer named Abido Bosha who liked to work with children, and he had a children's theater group. They had a play called *The Vegetarian Fox* and they wanted a song, so he wrote the words of this song, and he got quite a well-known Lebanese musician, Paul Matar, to do the music. Nowadays, when I sing this song, I explain to the audience that at first the song asks us to *'sing to her so she will come closer,'* and you think the 'her' refers to a woman, but by the end you realize that it is freedom that we are calling to. I then get the audience singing on two of the important Arabic phrases: *'U-wa-h' la, u-sa-h' la,'* which means 'welcome'—something like the Spanish *'mi casa, su casa,'* which literally means 'my house is your house.' And then, at the end, I ask the audience to repeat the phrase *'bi-ba-h' ri-ki-ya-huh-ri, ya-huh-ri,'* which means 'in your ocean, oh freedom.'

On the HARP album, we called this 'Ghannu Ma'i.'

Phonetically:	Translation:
Rha-nnu ma'i, rhann-la	*Sing out with me, sing out to her,*
U-wa-h' la, u-sa-h' la, u-lu-la	*And 'welcome' say to her*
Win ka-net ma-rra b' ai-di	*And if she was once far away,*
Bet' arr'b bass-en da hu-la	*She will come closer, but call to her*
Ma bekh' zhal, ma bekh-i hams	*I am not ashamed, I don't talk in whispers*
Dowl am-ar, u nuri shams	*Light of the moon, and light of the sun,*
B'l-da n'l karra-t'l khams,	*The countries of the continents five*
Ne'ta-z' ri-ri, ne' tau bas	*Are a drop, small, a drop only*
Bi- ba-h' ri-ki- ya-	*In your ocean,*
Huh-ri, ya- huh- ri	*Oh freedom, oh freedom*
Bi- ba-h' ri-ki- ya-	*In your ocean,*
Huh-ri, ya- huh- ri	*Oh freedom, oh freedom*

FIRE ON THE MOUNTAIN

Toshi and I have gone under the assumption that our phones have been tapped here, at least during the 1950s. Who knows but what now?

I'm sure it's come up occasionally with the local militia-type people,

'Why don't we get that guy Seeger! We can do anything we want up there.' But the nearest they came to it was this guy who started a forest fire about a quarter mile away at the edge of our property, and then about two hundred yards at the edge of our property the following week. Our friends in the local fire department probably got to them, saying, 'Trying to burn the mountain down 'cause you don't like Seeger?'

That was in 1967. The headline in the *New York Times* said, 'Pete Seeger Sings Anti-American Song In Moscow.' It was not true. I'd sung a lament for somebody killed in Vietnam, but it wasn't anti-American. I wrote to Turner Catledge, and he said, 'You're right. We changed the headline in future editions.' But the damage was done.

Two weeks later, I was scheduled to sing in the high school. Armed with this headline, people went up and down Main Street and got seven hundred signatures saying that I should not be allowed to sing. We had a friend—a doctor in Beacon, a wonderful man—who said, 'You know this is fascism. You should cancel the concert. You're going to be run out of town.' But we figured that it was worth making a stand on.

It turned out we were right. Because, at the end of the two weeks, some local people stood up for us, and the whole situation turned upside-down. There was a hardware merchant that I went to regularly. He was a conservative. He voted for Goldwater. He said, 'I don't know what your politics are, but it's America. You got a right to your opinion.'

There was a woman running a little convenience store where we'd pick up the newspaper, and they said to her, 'If you don't sign this petition, you're not going to get a lot of business,' and she said, 'Well, so be it. Pete and Toshi have always paid their bills with me.' There were people like her, and the high school kids stuck up for me.

So I was able to sing. But Toshi and I realized that we had been using Beacon like a bedroom community, and we decided we should get to know people better.

Editor's note: it was after this incident that Pete and Toshi both became more involved in local organizations such as the PTA and the VFW. A few years later, Clearwater launched, and they started the Beacon Sloop Club. From then on, both Pete and Toshi were more visible and for the most part accepted in Beacon.

MIKA IN MEXICO

I've got several adventurous children. My daughter Mika was going to UCLA and got fascinated with Latin-American culture, and she decided to leave UCLA and go to Mexico, where she would learn Spanish and discuss politics and learn what's going on down there. She happened to arrive on a hateful, terrible day in 1968, when the government of Mexico, prodded probably by the Cold War people in the United States, decided that the students had to be taught a lesson. There was a big student demonstration, and Mika was on the sidewalk, looking at it, when police arrived and opened up with machine guns and killed a whole batch of students. Mika's friends on the sidewalk said, 'You better get out of here. You're not a citizen.'

She went back to her hotel, and they were already waiting for her with a warrant for her arrest. She was charged with the same thing all the students were charged with—assault and battery and phony things like that. She was taken to a temporary jail, which was not a happy place, but very soon she was transferred to a woman's jail, and that was not so bad. She ended up getting to do exactly what she wanted to do. She learned Spanish, in a hurry, and discussed politics, because her fellow students were also in jail. They actually had very good food because the jail allowed them to run a little vegetable garden outside the prison walls, so they had good vegetables to eat and didn't have to depend on the terrible official food.

As soon as we found out about it—she must have gotten a letter to us— Toshi went down there. She told me, 'Don't you go down there. It's you they're after.' So I stayed up here while she telephoned me occasionally and let me know how things were going. Toshi found a rather well-to-do conservative lawyer who hadn't participated in liberal things, but he was so outraged with what had happened to the students that he took on Mika's case.

It wasn't easy for Toshi. At one time, there was an earthquake down there, and Toshi had the sense to stand under an arched doorway at the entrance to the hotel so she wouldn't be killed by falling bricks or anything else.

At another time, she realized that she was being followed. She thinks it was by the American FBI and not the Mexican people, because the lawyer said, 'Yes, you're quite right. It's your husband that they're after, and he should not come down here.'

Toshi and I knew a few people in Mexico, but the moment they found out we were involved with the student demonstration, they said, 'Oh, please don't call us again,' and hung up the phone, because anybody connected with these students was going to be deported from Mexico, and some of them had houses down there. But one woman, a sculptor, risked her life and her career and her home down there to help Toshi find a place to stay that wasn't as expensive as the hotel, and she helped Toshi find the lawyer.

After about two or three months, the lawyer said, 'I think you can go back. I'll get in touch with you. I think I'm on the track of how we can get your daughter out, and I'll let you know.' Toshi had only been back about three or four weeks when she gets a telephone call from Mika in Houston Texas, and here's what happened.

Mika was doing everything the lawyer said to do, *Don't write this letter but do write that one* and so on. He may have bribed somebody. Whatever it was, he was visiting with Mika, and he says, 'I think I can get you out of here fairly soon.' And he left the prison, and then, within five minutes, guards came in and said, 'Come with us.'

And Mika said, 'Where am I going?'

They said, 'You'll find out.'

She didn't have time to pick up any papers or passport or any money or anything or ask any questions. She was just put in a car and taken and put on a plane. When she got on the plane and the plane took off, she asked the stewardess, 'Where is this plane going?'

And the stewardess said, 'Don't you know?'

'No, I don't have the faintest idea where it's going.' The stewardess was confused. She went into the pilot's cabin and came out rather embarrassed and said, 'We're landing in Houston in five minutes.'

What would have happened to me if I had gone down to Mexico? In 1968, I was *persona non grata* with a number of important people.

A SPY AMONG US

The *Clearwater* first came to Beacon in 1969, and I think it was that very first year that they allowed a local hitchhiker to sail up here on the boat. We had no strict rules then, and the captain said, 'Sure, we have room,' and let this hitchhiker on. However, the captain saw him drinking wine, and he was very happy to let him off in Beacon.

At that time, we didn't have the sloop club at the riverfront. We paid a hundred dollars a month rent for a former store on Main Street maybe twenty feet wide and forty feet deep. This hitchhiker, when asked his name, said, 'Oh, I'm just Ritchie,' and he said, 'Let me help you.'

He helped sweep up the store and reinstalled the lock. Richie said, 'Can I sleep here?'

And we said, 'No, Richie, we're renting this place as a store, and we're not allowed to have people sleep in here. It's summertime. Go up and sleep in one of the cabins on the mountain. They're free.'

And then I was home and got a telephone call from John Vassulo, another teenager in the club, and he said, 'Pete you better come down here. I was hanging a picture on the wall and Richie was drinking wine and sitting just about fifteen feet in back of me, and he said, *You know I could put a knife between your ribs, couldn't I, any time*, kind of talking to himself.'

So I went down with a couple of others. We said, 'Richie, we can't let you in anymore. You can't be trusted.'

He said, 'Where am I going to go?'

I said, 'Richie, go sleep up on the mountain, but you can't come 'round to this club anymore.' And we changed the lock in front of his eyes because we didn't know if he had an extra key to the old lock.

That was the last I saw of him. But I heard from a member of the sloop club who was over in Newburgh about a week later. There was a drug bust in a bar, and there was a whole semicircle of police cars and other officers, and there was Richie with a machine gun. He was part of the drug bust, working with the other agents there. And the sloop club member just went near enough to say, 'Rich you son of a bitch,' and then walked on.

About one week after that, I was driving down Main Street in Beacon in my pickup truck and a man burst out of a bar and waved his hand and said, 'Pete, stop!'

He came up to the window and held up a card, and I looked at it and it said 'Treasury.' It was a US Treasury Agent's card. And he said, 'Pete, have you seen Richie?'

And I said, 'I haven't seen him, and I hope I never see him again.'

He said, 'Well, we ain't seen him in a week, and we think one of your guys may have done him in.'

I said, 'Oh, don't be ridiculous!' and I just moved ahead.

I saw this same man about a year later. He was no longer working for the Treasury. He looked like he might be a bum. I said, 'You still working for the Treasury?' And he just said, 'No, no.'

All I can guess is they might have had some kind of plan to leave some kind of stash of some kind of drug in the back of the sloop club, and now we will go in and discover it—that kind of thing.

AM I A COMMUNIST?

The word 'Communist' is a very loaded term, historically speaking, and the question that forms the title of this section sparks uneasy memories of a time when many people, including Pete, fought against being forced to answer it. When considering that question, it would be good to recall that the vast majority of people calling themselves Communists back in the 1930s and '40s had no desire for Russia to take over the US. They were decent, caring people with a vision for a better future, toiling in the political trenches to better the lives of working people.

The various organizations on the American left provided all sorts of services to their members, such as social events, summer camps, sports leagues, and even burial plots. They supported union rights and safe working conditions, and they opposed racial discrimination. During the Depression, they volunteered for benefit programs, fought unjust evictions, and called for peace between nations. One of the great ironies of history is that most of what they supported back then is official government policy now.

While the right-wing stereotype of the bearded, bomb-throwing revolutionary was never a reality, it is true that, for a short time, the American Communist Party followed the lead of its counterpart in Russia on a number of issues. One example was the initial opposition to a war against Germany after Hitler and Stalin entered into their non-aggression pact in August of 1939. Put in context, however, this temporary alignment preceded Hitler's atrocities. It also predated the Cold War tensions by more than a decade. At the time, Russia was not considered our enemy but instead became an important ally of the United States for the duration of World War II.

In any event, people like Pete Seeger and Woody Guthrie were never considered reliable party members. They had no desire to sit in meetings and endlessly argue small points of policy. For the most part, the American left considered them 'the entertainment.' By 1951, Pete had drifted away from the party, and in 1956, when the atrocities of Joseph Stalin became exposed, most other people also left the Communist Party, and it never held significant power or influence after that time.

But labels die hard. American corporate television, born of the 1950s, had no stomach for the likes of Pete Seeger. With few exceptions, Pete wasn't invited on any of the major networks for almost twenty years. In 1963, ABC television aired a show called *Hootenanny* to capitalize on the growing interest in folk music that had been largely sparked by Pete and The Weavers, but they refused to have Pete on. In 1967, Pete was invited on *The Smothers Brothers Comedy Hour* in the midst of the Vietnam War, and a controversy erupted over his choice to sing 'Waist Deep In The Big Muddy.' Eventually, Pete was able to perform the song on the air but not long after, the Smothers Brothers' show was canceled by the CBS network brass.

Pete once interviewed with Harry Reasoner and asked him backstage if he had been officially blacklisted, and Harry told him point-blank that he had. If it had not been for Pete's own PBS television show, *Rainbow Quest*, which Toshi helped produce, and which aired in the mid-1960s, most of the country would not have seen him. Rainbow Quest was a lovely, informal show where Pete interacted with some of the country's best folk musicians, and where some fair-minded mainstream musicians such as Johnny Cash also appeared.

There is no question that Pete, who served in the US army, and who helped this country in so many other ways, was a true patriot. But there are still many who can't seem to see beyond the word 'Communist.' And if that term is loaded, then so is the word 'revolution.' It should be noted that when Pete talks of revolution, he is generally not referring to violent and deadly upheavals but a softer kind of revolution—a revolution in the way people relate to each other, and to their planet. The following was taken from several of our conversations.

I tell people that the Communists I knew were the bravest people I ever met. Of course, discipline and courage are not all you need—you need wisdom too. Did you ever hear of an anarchist named Ammon Hennacy? I quote him in my book. He ran the Joe Hill House in Salt Lake City for the last ten years of his life. Ammon Hennacy says, 'Courage alone is foolhardiness, as in the average soldier. Love alone is sentimentality, as in the average churchgoer. Wisdom alone is cowardice as in the average intellectual. You need all three.' If there is a revolution, I may not live to see it through, but I am going to give all I have to see that it succeeds.

I wonder what thoughts went through his mind when Stalin purged the Central Committee of all his rivals. I think this probably happens every time there is an oligarchy. One member of the oligarchy says, 'I want to be the chief oligarch' and finds a way to get rid of his competitors. Saddam Hussein did the same thing in his country. There was no evidence that any of these people had actually done anything wrong. All they had were confessions, confessions, confessions. They probably said, 'Look, you confess, or we'll get your wife and your children.'

'Don't touch them! I will say whatever you want me to, please don't touch them.'

So, Stalin got rid of his competitors, and the world only found out about it with the Khrushchev revelations in 1956, at which time the membership of Communist parties all around the world plummeted. There had been a hundred thousand members in this county. There probably were ten thousand members the next month. Howard Fast, the great writer, resigned. Lester Rodney, the sports writer, resigned. I had already drifted out of the party. I didn't like being a member of a secret organization.

I still thought of myself as a Communist. Funny thing is, I still think of myself as a Communist in the broadest sense of the word. At age seven, I was deeply up to my ears in love with the whole idea of the American Indians. I read the books of Ernest Thompson Seaton, who held up American Indians as role models. He said they were brave, they were honest; there were no rich, no poor. If there was food, everybody in the tribe ate. If there was hunger, everybody in the tribe, including the chief and his wife and children, was hungry. There was no thought that one person would have a full stomach and next door there would be somebody with an empty stomach. And that, to me, is the way people should live. I would like to see a world without millionaires.

On the other hand, it is not easy. How do you do it when one person is a brilliant inventor and invents something new? Do you tell him, 'No you have to give all those profits to the government?' To do what?

The best coffee ice cream in the world I tasted last year, and whenever I can get it, I buy it, even though it comes from Starbucks, which puts out of business a whole lot of nice little restaurants.

Of course, anthropologists who study human history know that tribal communism was the way all of our ancestors lived for a couple million years. And then we discovered agriculture. There's good and bad about everything. People ate a little better, but now kings and queens ran the world, and everybody else had to do what they said. Then, when people back two hundred years ago said we should have a revolution and get rid of kings and queens, they called it socialism at first. And they were Christian Socialists. It was a Christian Socialist named Edward Bellamy who said that we should have a few words that could be recited by everyone. He was the younger brother of Ralph Bellamy, who wrote a famous socialist novel called *Looking Backward*. And Edward Bellamy invented the Pledge Of Allegiance.

So, what happened during the 1950s, in the age of McCarthy? It has been going on for ten thousand years in some places, and in other places only five thousand years or less. It still goes on.

In a sense, lefties have been blacklisted all of the time. Way back in 1940, The Almanac Singers got on the radio for one nationwide broadcast called *This Is War*, and we sang:

Round and round on Hitler's grave
He won't get up no more

The next day, the *World-Telegram* says, 'Commie Folksingers Try To Infiltrate Radio,' and that was the last job we got.

You can assume that if you have songs the establishment does not approve of, you will not get welcomed to mass media. When I am asked about the blacklist, I always point out that the establishment has been careful to control as much as they can of the music that people hear. They cannot do much about the old folksongs sung by the peasants in their homes, but they can control what gets composed for the operas. They can control popular music.

Figure this: at one time in history, back when our ancestors lived in small tribes like the American Indians, there was one kind of music that everyone knew. The chief and the men knew the same hunting songs. The chief's wife and the women knew the same lullabies. Now, somebody invents modern agriculture, and you have fields growing grain and herds of cattle, and these are owned by a class of rich people and a class of poor people do the work.

The beginning of class society came with the agricultural revolution. Plato is supposed to have said, 'It is very dangerous to allow the wrong kind of music in the republic.' And there is an old Arab proverb, 'When the king puts the poet on his payroll, he cuts off the tongue of the poet.'

• • •

Way back in the 1940s, the Communist Party was one of the few parties that really put right at the top of their agenda to get rid of Jim Crow and give rights for workers to organize unions. Right near the top of their agenda! They didn't like to see war. That is when I became a Communist. I was in college. And Litvinoff stood up in the League Of Nations, saying, 'All aggressors should be quarantined.'

He was talking about the Japanese in Manchuria, and Italy and Ethiopia, and Hitler and Mussolini trying to help Franco take over Spain. I joined the Young Communist League way back in 1937. I backed away from it when I moved up to the country in 1949. I never liked the idea of being a member of a secret organization. And, of course, after 1956, after Khrushchev made his speech revealing Stalin's terrible atrocities, I saw the weakness of an oligarchy like never before. Still, lots of good things went on in Communist countries. Also, a lot of bad things went on.

I will apologize for thinking Stalin was simply a hard driver and not a supremely cruel misleader. And, twenty years later, I was writing my autobiography, a singalong memoir entitled *Where Have All The Flowers Gone?*, and I go on to say, 'Perhaps white people in the United States should apologize for stealing land from Indians and enslaving Africans. And Mongolians could apologize for Ganges Kahn.'

My favorite Communist leader of all time was Ho Chi Min. I never met him, but I was in North Vietnam just three years after he died, and they told all sorts of stories about him. In one story, he goes to review some troops and he sticks his head through a door of a tent and sees all the officers in the front rows, and behind them the non-commissioned officers, the sergeants, and corporals, and then in the back the privates. He didn't enter the tent. He walked around to the other end of the tent, and from the back of the crowd he hollers, 'About face!' And now, with the privates right close to him, and behind them the sergeants, and behind them the lieutenants and the coronels, he says, 'The most important part of this army is the rank and file. The most important parts of the counties of the world are the rank and file of people, not the powerful people, not the rich people.'

By his own example, Ho Chi Min showed that the best officers were the ones that could inspire the rank and file to do their best. He never dressed up in fancy clothes. He went around with sandals made out of old automobile tires. That was what poor people wore in Vietnam. You cut up the tire for soles, and the inner tubing you cut up for straps to hold the sandal on your foot. When my wife and I were visiting Vietnam, I got some of those and started wearing them, and people laughed and said, 'You have sandals like Uncle Ho.'

I have been to Cuba also. I went to Eastern Europe. I went all the way out to Siberia. There was an article in the *New Yorker* by a man named Marshall Goldman, who was the head of Russian studies at Harvard, and it was so anti-Soviet. He said that Lake Baikal—a huge lake, four hundred miles long, one mile deep, fifty miles wide—is going to be polluted because they built a factory on the shores, and, because of the dictatorial Soviet system, Lake Baikal will be lost to the world. It would be polluted.

I felt this couldn't be a complete story. Well, I decided to see for myself with my son. I paid for it by doing some concerts in Moscow and Leningrad, but we flew all the way out to Lake Baikal and sang in the city of Irkutsk. I found that a limnologist—a man who studies freshwaters—named Dr. Galasy had an Institute Of Limnology right overlooking Lake Baikal. And he saved it.

Of course, scientists there are like priests, and they couldn't shut him up. He said, 'We are going to lose Lake Baikal if we are not careful.'

Kosygin, the minister of industry, flew all the way out and said, 'Dr. Galacy, why are you holding up progress? Don't you know we must have this rayon, and this clear lake is the best place to make rayon.'

Dr. Galacy was ready with all of the statistics. He said, 'You're right. Right now, the pure water of this lake can make very good rayon very cheaply. But in thirty years, you will have polluted it, and you will not be able to make rayon any better here than anywhere else. Furthermore, you will have polluted this lake for five hundred thousand years. Lakes do not clean themselves out quickly the way a river can clean itself out, and you will have gone down in history as the person who could have saved it.'

'Well,' Kosygin said, 'you tell us what we can do and what we can't do,' and he went back to Moscow.

That's like telling the *Clearwater*, 'You're in charge of cleaning up the Hudson.'

So, Dr. Galacy said, 'You will not build any more rayon plants. If you clean up the pollution from this one factory, perhaps you can keep it, but I'm going to test the waters every day, and we'll send all the effluent from this factory to a tunnel through the mountains into a neighboring river, but not into the lake.'

So, when I was interviewed by a young television interviewer in Irkutsk, a city right near Baikal, he said, 'Oh, Dr. Galacy is our hero. He refused to be silenced.'

In other words, the average person could have been silenced, but Dr. Galacy was able to make his point. Now that free enterprise has taken over, we'll see what happens to Lake Baikal.

• • •

'Socialism' is a word people don't agree on. Did you ever realize the Post Office is a socialist organization? The government pays for it. Hopefully it does a job for everybody. On the other hand, I tell my socialist friends, 'How is it not a single post office department in the world—east, west, north, south—invented Federal Express?' It took one ambitious guy in Memphis to dream up the whole scheme.

DAR WILLIAMS *Having been Pete's neighbor, two miles down the road, for so long, and having worked with him for years before that, I have my own vision of Pete's legacy. The thing that's the most overarching in terms of his legacy is that I would call him a 'Communitarian' more than a Communist. He really looked at all* *of the ways that we could connect with each other within our human community via music, but also festivals and food and stories in a way that ultimately could have a lot of power in terms of how we govern ourselves and how we stay civilized. I think there's this narrative of how we keep democracy ahead of capitalism, which is just an economic system, and we don't know that language of how we assemble democratically, and organize democratically, and lead democratically, unless we can find one another in the commons, and have that evidence of where, working in harmony—in Pete's case, literally in harmony—is beneficial to us, as opposed to living in zero-sum games with paranoia and distrust.*

When I was on the Conan O'Brien show with him in 1999, Pete had to leave right after our performance to go to a sloop club meeting where they were planning the Strawberry Shortcake Festival. And he described to me as he was leaving the NBC offices how, on the day of the festival, one person gets the piece of shortcake, and then the next person puts the whipped cream on, and then Toshi puts the strawberries on, and they hand this fresh strawberry shortcake celebrating the season in our beloved Hudson Valley to this person attending the festival.

He understood how these things that are special to us where we live—our strawberries, our river, our mountains, our boats, our history—are civilizing factors. So, yes, music is certainly an example—a potent example—of how creating various vibrations and rhythms and melodies side by side can help us find each other, and find our way as a society. But Pete also understood the way all of these other different things within our specific communities can make our conversations more participatory and positive as opposed to just partisan. And I think he was prescient in looking for ways we could find one another, because distrust is very de rigueur and very politically advantageous to people who want us to opt out of our democratic system.

So it always rankles me that Pete was called a Communist, even though he identified with that party for a long time. I think that the Communist Party has a certain meaning that, after 1950, we could have called Communitarianism, where we just find our decentralized community voices through food, music, nature, and history, and find our way as a democracy.

CHAPTER 09 SOME PHILOSOPHY

THE BRAINS GOD GAVE US

Alfred North Whitehead was a friend of the famous mathematician Bertrand Russell, and he wrote a little essay in a book called *The Aims Of Education And Other Essays*, which is famous in the academic world. Whitehead says:

> When one considers in its length and in its breadth the importance of this question of the education of a nation's young, the broken lives, the defeated hopes, the national failures which result from the frivolous inertia with which it is treated, it is difficult to restrain within oneself a savage rage.
>
> In the condition of modern life, the rule is absolute; the nation that does not value trained intelligence is doomed. Not all your wit, not all your social charm, not all your victories on land and sea can turn back the finger of fate. Today we maintain ourselves; tomorrow, science has moved forward another step, and there will be no appeal from the judgment of history upon the uneducated.
>
> We can be content with no less than the old summary of an educational ideal which has been current at any time from the dawn of our civilization. The essence of education is that it be religious...

At which point most people say, '*Religious?* I thought he was talking about science.'

> A religious education is an education which inculcates duty and reverence. Duty arises from the potential control over the course of events. Where attainable knowledge could have changed the issue, ignorance has the guilt of vice ...

In other words, if there's something that needs to be done, we ought to do it.

> And the foundation of reverence is this perception: that the present holds within itself the complete sum of existence, backwards and forwards, that whole amplitude of time, which is eternity.

I usually follow it with a few words of my own. I tell people that you clap your hands, and that's cause and effect for all eternity. It disturbs molecules, which disturb other molecules, which disturb other molecules, for all eternity to come.

Of course, I think it was Einstein who once said, 'There are two infinite things, one is the universe and the other is human stupidity.' And then he adds, 'I'm not sure about the universe.'

Einstein was part of it, though. If he had never invented that great little equation $e=mc^2$, they never could have made the atom bomb.

Well, who knows? But I tell people, when you come to a curb at the edge of a street, do you look up in the sky and say, 'God, it's dangerous crossing streets, will you please save me?' No, you don't do that. You look to the left, you look to the right, you use the brains God gave you, and if there's no car coming, you cross. It's the same way with the future. You don't just look up in the sky and say, 'God, won't you save the world.' You get busy thinking of what needs to be done to save the world, and you get people to do it.

We've got a new song about it. A friend of mine wrote two of *Clearwater's* favorite songs, including 'Sailing Up, Sailing Down.' It's been sung for forty-one years now. The songwriter's name is Lorre Wyatt. He had a stroke about fifteen years ago, but he fought his way back, so now he can talk again and walk again and drive again, and he called me up and said, 'Pete, I've got some song ideas, but I haven't been able to finish them as much as I like. Could I come visit you?' And we spent two days just tossing around ideas for this and that, and all of a sudden, we had one of the better songs I ever helped put together.

GOD'S COUNTING ON ME, GOD'S COUNTING ON YOU
Pete Seeger, Lorre Wyatt

When we look and we see
Things are not what they should be
God's countin' on me,
God's countin' on you

Refrain: *Hoping we'll all pull through*
Hoping we'll all pull through
Hoping we'll all pull through
Me and you

It's time to turn things around
Trickle up, not trickle down

And when 'drill baby drill'
Leads to 'spill baby spill'

We've got problems to be solved
Let's get eh-everyone involved

Don't give up, don't give in
Working together, we all can win!

What we do, you and me
Will affect eternity

When we sing with other folks
We can never give up hope

Lately, I've begun asking people, 'What do you think the chances are there'll be a human race here in the next two hundred years?' I must admit, I've become more optimistic. I think we've got at least a fifty percent chance. And if we do survive, I think it'll be because of many small things—many small organizations made up of people who find they have something in common. Maybe they like to sing songs, or share recipes, or stand at a vigil.

When people ask me about these things, I often say the following words, which have become a kind of mantra:

The agricultural revolution took thousands of years. The industrial revolution took hundreds of years. Now, the information revolution is only taking decades. But, if we use the brains God gave us, we will have the revolution that must come if there's going to be a human race here next century. I call it the non-violent revolution. Some may call it the love revolution, or the willingness to communicate revolution. Who knows? If we learn to grow—not in size, but grow in generosity, or grow in a sense of humor, or grow in the ability to talk with people we disagree with—we will still have great-grandchildren here by the time the twenty-second century comes along.

A MILLION LITTLE THINGS

Pete didn't always like or trust big things. If someone suggested raising $100,000 with a big concert, he might say, 'I think we should convince one hundred people to each have a house party where they could raise one thousand dollars.' Pete often pointed out that a small thing like Rosa Parks not giving up her seat on a bus sparked the whole civil rights movement. This excerpt is from an interview where Pete was asked about the progressive labor leader Harry Bridges. After speaking of Harry for a time, his mind wandered onto this:

I'm now convinced if there is a human race here in a hundred years, it's not going to be because of any one big revolution bringing peace on earth and all. It's going to be tens of millions of little things. It may be a group of women and children who start a community garden in a big city. It may be some little business, or some little discoveries being made. It may be the internet bringing people together who would otherwise never would have been able to get together.

But the establishment is so powerful they can break up any one thing they want to. They've got so much money. They can attack it from the outside. They can corrupt it from the inside. They can co-opt it and mislead it. But what are they going to do about ten million little things? They destroy one of them and two more like them spring up.

So, I am actually more confident now of the future than I was sixty years ago, when the bomb dropped on Hiroshima. I thought surely within twenty or thirty years, some fool would drop a bomb and others would drop others, and if we weren't killed, we would be poisoned by the fallout.

However, General Eisenhower's people would not let General Curtis Lemay start World War III. He tried his best and they slapped him down. He was playing chicken with the Russians. He had a hundred planes in the air during the Bay Of Pigs and sent messages to a hundred pilots saying, 'Communication with Washington may be cut off, and if it is, take your orders directly from me.' When Kennedy's people found he had done that, they told him to never do that again. When he retired, he ran as vice president with George Wallace of Alabama. He died in 1990, still grumbling we would have been better off if we had World War III.

A Frenchman once defined an expert as somebody who avoids all the little mistakes on the way to the big fallacy. Well, I am now more optimistic than I was because I see not just a few experts but millions of people realizing that we have either got to learn to talk with each other or we are going to kill each other. This lesson is going to have to be learned in Washington, in spite of the powerful people there. It is going to be very interesting. I wish I could live another twenty years, because there are going to be some fantastic things happening, win, lose, or draw. But if we learn the lessons that Harry Bridges teaches us, this is going to be one of the millions of things.

• • •

Imagine a big seesaw. One end of the seesaw is on the ground because it has a big basket half full of rocks in it. The other end of the seesaw is up in the air because it's got a basket one-quarter full of sand. Some of us have teaspoons, and we are trying to fill it up. Most people are scoffing at us. They say, 'People like you have been trying for thousands of years, but it is leaking out of that basket as fast as you are putting it in.' Our answer is that we are getting more people with teaspoons every day. And we believe that one of these days, that basket of sand is going to be so full that you are going to see that whole seesaw going zoop! in the other direction. Then people are going to say, 'Gee, how did it happen so suddenly?' And we answer, 'Us and our little teaspoons over thousands of years.'

WHEN WORDS FAIL

The hope of the human race is communication, and words are good, but they can fool you. I would say there is probably no word under the sun that means exactly the same to two different people, even the word yes or no. There is a song I do these days 'English Is Crazy.' Josh White Jr. made a rap after reading a book called *Crazy English* by a man named Richard Lederer, who taught English for twenty or thirty years and wrote down all the funny contradictions in the English language. Josh put into rhyme and meter:

In what other language do you drive in a parkway
And park in a driveway
Recite at a play but play at a recital
Ship by truck but send cargo by ship
Have noses that run and feet that smell
English is crazy.

You have to marvel at the lunacy of the language in which
Your house can burn down when it burns up.
Your alarm clock goes off when it goes on.
You fill out a form when you fill it in
If a vegetarian eats vegetables, what does a humanitarian eat?
English is crazy.

Anyway, what do we do when words fail? We can use pictures for one. Great pictures sometimes have changed the course of history, like the picture of the little girl running naked down a Vietnamese street with her body on fire from napalm. Millions of people saw that picture and changed their minds about the war in Vietnam.

I think melodies have sometimes changed history—nobody knows for sure—like that great melody 'Glory Glory Halleluiah' may have helped win the Civil War. I have to admit words were important there. When Lincoln met Harriet Beecher Stowe, who wrote the book *Uncle Tom's Cabin*, he said, 'So you are the little woman who started this war?'

I'd say all the arts should be used. If we are going to save the human race, we should use all the arts we have, whether they're pictures or melodies, words, poetry, or dancing, or food. Cooking is one of the greatest arts in the world. We use it as an organizing tool up and down the Hudson. I called a meeting for the Beacon Clearwater Club and only three people showed up. My wife said, 'Don't call it a meeting, call it a pot-luck supper.' Thirty people showed up. We meet once a month now on the waterfront of our hometown.

You might consider that sports are a great medium too. It is not generally known but it was a Communist sportswriter, Lester Rodney, who actually broke the color ban in baseball. He was the son of a Republican businessman who lost every penny he had in the crash of 1929, and Lester was a teenager who got jobs anywhere he could, pumping gas and mowing lawns. But he was a reader, and one day he read a copy of the Communist newspaper the *Daily Worker*, and he was outraged they didn't have a sports department.

In New York, he walked to the office and knocked on the door of the editor and asked, 'How come you don't have a sports department?'

And the editor said, 'There are more important things to write down. That's more read in circuses.'

'It is not read in circuses. This is like opera for the Italians or great novels for the French or the Russians. This is life for the working people of this country. If you don't have a sports department, you're not a working-class newspaper, you're just a bunch of intellectuals.'

Lester Rodney started working in the mid-30s, and every time he interviewed a player or a manager or occasionally an owner, he'd say, 'When are you going to take up Satchel Paige on his annual challenge?' Because every year, after the World Series was over, Satchel Paige would say, 'I want to challenge the winner,' and they would never take him up on his challenge.

Lester kept talking it up, and they'd answer, 'Quit harping on it. It will never happen, it will never happen, it will never happen.' But for ten years he kept asking, 'When are you going to take him up on his challenge,' because everybody knew he'd win. He was the best baseball pitcher in the country. Joe DiMaggio once faced him in an exhibition game and said that Paige was the toughest pitcher he ever faced, and he faced a lot of them.

Finally, it was Branch Rickey who decided, 'Let's gamble on it. Truman integrated the armed forces, let's do it with baseball.' He selected a good guy to do it, a tough fellow who wouldn't give in, no matter what names he was called—Jackie Robinson.

MUSIC AND THE MOVEMENT

There was never such a singing movement as the civil rights movement, not even the Wobblies. Music was so important. Children sang, old folks sang. There was a wide range of songs, some funny, some deeply tragic, and some a mixture of all. But the civil rights movement literally wouldn't have existed if it hadn't been for music. They were singing in jail.

There is a song I've written about Dr. King, which I sing everywhere I go these days:

Down in Alabama, 1955
Not many of us here tonight were then alive;
A young Baptist preacher led a bus boycott
He led the way for a brand new day without firing a shot

Don't say it can't be done,
The battle's just begun
Take it from Dr. King
You too can learn to sing
So drop the gun…

Well, I have been working at it for seventy-eight years. I was given a ukulele at age eight, so about seventy-eight years ago I started getting people around me joining in. At an early age, I was quite aware that the powers that be wanted us to sing light, happy songs, even while there was this thing on called the Depression and a lot of people were in a real bad way.

The exception proves the rule. Yip Harburg had a hit with 'Brother, Can You Spare A Dime?' On the other hand, I have to admit some of these pop songs were awful good songs. I still sing Irving Berlin's 'Blue Skies,' and I get a whole crowd singing it, but I confess I also sing Slim Slams' scat version. We have *Clearwater* words to that, and I get a whole crowd of people singing the *Clearwater* words.

I would say that my audiences today are not quite as full of illusions as maybe many of us were back in the late 1940s and early 50s. They've seen what Stalin did, what Mao did. They realize that socialists can make mistakes, commit crimes, as well as anybody else. But they have not necessarily given up hope. So I tell people there is hope for this world if we keep in mind to think globally but act locally.

I am often singing for little local things here and there. Just yesterday, I sang in the little town of New Paltz. It's a college town, and they got a green mayor. Jason West is his name, and he wrote a wonderful book called *Hope For The Future*. He says we just need to straighten out the way of voting. To have somebody with a mere plurality be the winner to take all doesn't make sense. You should have instant runoff voting.

I really believe that whether it was the old songs, or the new songs, or mostly combinations—they put new words to their old songs—I don't think Dr. King, with all his great power of oratory, could have won all the things they won without music. The children sang when they were marching. The teenagers sang. Some of these people are now world famous, like Bernice Reagon, who started a group called Sweet Honey In The Rock and got a McArthur fellowship.

One of the disadvantages of much music is that people simply become listeners. In 1910, John Phillip Sousa, the famous bandleader who wrote 'Stars And Stripes Forever,' said, 'What will happen to the American voice now that the phonograph has been invented?'

It is perfectly true—people don't sing like they used to. How many mothers sing lullabies to their kids? *Oh, put the kid in front of the tube. He will fall asleep soon.* How many men sing while they are at a bar? There is a TV going on at the bar, and it silences anybody who wants to sing a song. Families don't sit around the table after eating supper singing with each other like they used to. Not every family did, but often there were singing families whose favorite recreation was singing.

I urge people to make up songs that the audience will want to sing themselves. Don't make it so difficult for a rank-and-file person. Admittedly, they got away with it with 'The Star Spangled Banner.' It was first sung by an actor standing on a stool in a Baltimore tavern. And he sang all four verses to the tune of a well-known drinking song. Women were not supposed to listen to it, but everybody knew the tune, or at least all men knew it. And a printer the next day printed up the four verses and sold it in the streets of Baltimore. And stage coaches took copies down to Richmond and points south and up to Philadelphia and Boston in the north. It was the hit song of 1814. It was probably sung faster.

When people want to make things official, they want to make them impressive and slow them down. And sometimes that's good.

'We Shall Overcome' was first sung as a fast gospel song:

I'll overcome
I'll overcome
I'll overcome someday...

And unions first made it into a union song:

We will overcome
We will overcome someday...

I've seen a copy of the *United Mineworkers Journal*—it's an interracial union in Alabama—and a letter on the front page says, 'At our strike last year, every meeting started with a prayer and that good old song, We Will Overcome.'

But in 1946, a group of tobacco workers—three hundred women, mostly Afro Americans—were on strike in Charleston, South Carolina, and one of the members, Lucille Simmons, liked to lead this on the picket line very slow. A friend of mine, Guy Carawan, gave it a slow rhythm in what they call 12/8 time. Each beat is divided up into three little beats. That's the way he introduced it to the founding convention of SNCC in 1960, and a month later this was not *a* song, it was *the* song all around, from Texas to Florida to Virginia to Arkansas. Guy Carawan is the man who should really get credit for spreading that song. I just recorded it in 1963, three years later, and played it the way Guy taught it to me.

It might have been me who changed *will* to *shall*. It opens up the mouth better. But a woman named Septima Clark was the education director at the Highland Folk School, where Rosa Parks had studied. She always liked *shall* rather than *will*. It could have been her.

My father, who was an old musicologist, says, 'Don't argue if it's a folk song or what. Just know that the folk process has been going on for thousands of years. People take old songs and add to them. It happens in every field of culture.'

WORK SONGS

I hope some of the songs I sing deal with things that happen to ordinary working people in their lives. I can't prove a darn thing, though. I've sung 'John Henry' for sixty-five years now, since I learned it from the painter Tom Benton. And I made up a song called 'Waist Deep In The Big Muddy,' showing what it was like to be a rank-and-file soldier, doing what you are told. Some people call these protest songs, but beware of oversimplifications—after all, isn't the fella singing an unrequited love song protesting unrequition?

I don't think that the term 'blue collar' can be applied to specific kinds of music—maybe once upon a time but not now. There are a few songs, like 'Sixteen Tons' or 'Take This Job And Shove It,' which are obviously blue-collar songs, but I doubt there's more than a few people who can remember the old songs that were sung when people did manual labor, shoveling, digging, rounding up the horses in a cowboy camp, yodeling. Even in the prisons of the Southern states of America, they no longer have black prisoners singing while they're chopping. That went out many years ago. I doubt they have men hauling on ropes and singing anymore, except maybe on the *Clearwater*, that beautiful boat on the Hudson River where we take fifty children out at a time and teach them what makes a river dirty and what's got to be done to clean it up.

Face it, the TV age has stopped people singing while they're working— with one exception. There's a work song that may go on through the centuries until somebody invents an automatic mother. There's really no substitute for mothers singing lullabies to a kid that needs comforting. That's a work song.

There are still artists that describe what it is like to be a working man or woman in their songs. There are too many to list—not dozens, not hundreds, but thousands of people making up songs about their work—they just don't necessarily sing these songs while they're working.

Cisco Houston and Woody Guthrie sang songs about working people. They were friends, but they were quite different. One came from Oklahoma and the other came from California. They had different backgrounds and sang differently, but they liked to sing songs about work.

Joe Hill was a Swedish immigrant, but he fell in love with ragtime music and liked to tinkle the ivories in the union hall. He put new words to any pop song of the day, or put new words to an old hymn, or new words to anything. His songs were printed up in the little union songbook of the Industrial Workers Of The World, the IWW, over ninety years ago. The Wobblies were started in 1905, and after World War I they were beaten out of existence by the US Government and the employers. Some of them were lynched and killed. Others were jailed. They never really grew to their former strength, but they were a singing union.

There was another union that tried to do the same thing. In the late 1930s, when the CIO unions were going strong, there was a warehouse union in New York City, and they also printed a little songbook. You could put it in your back pocket, and when you were drinking a cup of coffee with a friend in the union, you might pull it out and say, 'Hey, let's wake up this joint.' And they'd start singing some new union verses to old tunes. There was an old Jewish folk tune, and they put new words to it:

One day while walkin' down forty-fifth street
I ran into a guy who looked dead on his feet
He had no green button or smile on his face
Kept pushin' a truck round, kept getting' no place

He's a fool (he's a fool)
He's a fool (he's a fool)
He's a fool for not joining the union

They'd get a whole crowd of people singing that. It had several verses about how he finally wises up and he joins the union. The last chorus was:

He's no fool (he's no fool)
For he up and he joined with the union.

I learned that song around 1941, when Woody Guthrie and Lee Hays and Millard Lampell and me and some others formed a group called The Almanac Singers, and we'd sing that song around.

My younger half-sister, Peggy Seeger, sings songs about work. Like me, she came out of a very academic background, her father a musicologist and mother a composer of avant-garde string quartets, but then she hitched up with Ewan McCall. In my opinion, she's one of the more talented songwriters of this century. Her song 'I'm Gonna Be An Engineer' is known all around the English-speaking world now.

She's written a lot of other good songs too, and she's written songs about work, and I'm sure she's sung lullabies to her kids, so she's sung work songs. But I'm curious. I guess I got to ask Peggy, 'Did you ever think of writing a song to make dishwashing easier, or scrubbing the floor easier?' I've washed dishes and I've scrubbed floors, and I have to confess I've never made up a song for it.

Editor's note: Peggy Seeger's 'I'm Gonna Be An Engineer' is a long ballad about a woman who felt trapped into being a wife and then a mother and a housekeeper and an underpaid typist, but it ends, *'I'll fight them as an engineer!'*

I also think we need some shorter songs. Maybe something you could sing while waiting for an elevator. One person could start:

We been waiting here too long,
I think we should use the stairway.

The next person could say:

No the stairway is dark,
It's dangerous, don't use it.

And the third person joins in:

Hey, if we all go together,
Perhaps it's safe to use the stairway.

They can all end on the word 'stairway.' Or maybe have a song for waiting on the bus:

Just us, waitin' for the bus
Oh driver, won't you please come soon.

The work songs in America start off from where we came from. There were English and Scottish and Irish origins to work songs in the early days, and a lot of the best nineteenth-century railroad songs were Irish:

Drill ye tarriers drill
Drill ye tarriers drill
It's work all say for the sugar in your Tay (tea)
Down beyond the railway
So drill ye tarriers drill, and blast, and fire

There were great canal songs:

Oh the Erie was a rising,
And the gin was gettin' low
And I scarcely think we'll get a drink
'Til we get to Buffalo

And factory songs:

Workin' in a weave room fightin' for my life,
Tryin' to make a livin' for my children and my wife,
Some are needin' clothing, some are needin' shoes,
But I'm getting nothin' but the weave room blues.

That song was written by Dorsey Dixon of North Carolina, way back in the 1920s or early 30s.

Then of course you have the African influences. African people have some of the most wonderful musical traditions in the world, especially in rhythm, and especially in 'answerback.' That's where one voice starts off and another voice answers it. The song isn't just a solo, it's a group thing.

The slaves torn away from their homes and put in chains found themselves in the fields having to learn a new language. And they learned a new religion: 'You mean to say this religion was not originally yours? That this book was originally in another language? You say Hebrew, Greek. This is extraordinary!' And they latched on to this revolutionary new religion that said God was going to see that the world was put to right—that this world full of sin was going to become better, and that prayer that says, 'On Earth as it is in Heaven.' This was something new! And while they were picking cotton in the fields they were making up songs—slow songs and fast songs. After the American Civil War, one of the first books that came out was called *Slave Songs*, and some of these songs were in it, and more came out later.

The Lomaxes carried on the tradition of collecting African American work songs. They also ran into one of the world's greatest singers—a man named Huddle Ledbetter, better known as Leadbelly, King Of The Twelve-String Guitar.

Leadbelly taught all of us some of the world's greatest songs. Not just 'Irene Goodnight' but:

The Rock Island line, it is a mighty good road
The Rock Island Line, it is the road to ride
The Rock Island Line, it is a mighty good road
And if you want to ride
You got to ride it like you find it
Get your ticket at the station for the Rock Island Line…

He had a song about working in a hot field:

Bring me little water Sylvie
Bring me little water now
Bring me little water Sylvie
Every little once in a while…

There are many different types of work songs from many different types of origins—European, African, Native American origins, or Asiatic origins, Latin origins. They're all tangled up, and I leave it up to the musicologists to untangle it.

I can't give you a perfect example of a work song. All I know is that the prison song 'The Midnight Special' is about trying to escape from prison, but it's also a work song. Whenever Arlo Guthrie and I sing together, we always start a concert with it and when my grandson Tao Rodríguez and I sing a program, we also start with it.

Let the midnight special
Shine it's light on me
Oh let the midnight special
Shine its ever-loving light on me…

Of course, I'll have different favorite songs at different times, but when you ask me, 'What is your favorite?' I say that's like asking a mother, 'Which is your favorite child?'

THE MONEY DIFFERENTIAL

Nobody knows what to do about the pressure of the power of money. I've got one idea. I think one of the best laws ever passed by the government was one saying that you should print on the outside of a food package what's in that food, so you can see what chemicals for example are in it, or how much sugar or salt are in it. And if you're on a diet, you know to avoid that particular kind of food.

Likewise, I think it would be a good idea to print on the outside of anything manufactured a little acronym, like the letter *M* for 'money' and the letter *D* for 'differential.' It would give the difference in pay between what the executives get and what the people who work on the line get.

Now, in some companies—especially family-owned businesses, where the whole family's working hard and they're hiring a few extra people— maybe the boss makes two or three times as much as the worker or the clerk who tends the counter of the store or the person who answers the telephone, but we all know very well that that's the exception. The bigger the company gets, the higher paid the executives are. Often, in some of the biggest companies—like companies that make clothing that's manufactured in Asia and sold in New York for high prices—the people are being paid pennies over there and the executives here are paid thousands of dollars. So it could be a little one over three, or one over a hundred, or one over a thousand, or one over ten thousand. And if you go to buy this article, you'd say, 'Gee, that company's not being very fair, are they?' And you might decide not to buy it. If you have a choice, you'd pick another article which might be about as good, but which has a better money differential.

Needless to say, a law like this would be very hard to pass, because money controls the legislatures of most of the world now. However, I think it could be started if some companies would start doing this, like the companies who listed that 'this milk comes from cows with no growth hormones.' It's been fought by parts of the dairy industry, but other parts of the dairy industry said, 'Hey, that's a logical thing; we'll support it.' So, let's take advantage of the arguments between the various people who control the industries and find out if we can't get some of them to do some better things.

And, little by little, things spread. Things like this are happening all over the world already now. You take advantage of the fact that no two people in the world agree, and quite often some very good things are done unexpectedly. Little things, bigger things.

CHAPTER 10 SOME FANTASY

Although he spent most of his life singing and advocating for real-world issues, Pete always understood the importance of fiction, or perhaps I should say of make-believe. This is most evident in the great song stories on his children's records, but Pete always seemed to understand that adults were just children who had gotten older.

The material in this section is partly drawn from a time when Pete was working with the writer Paul Dubois Jacobs on a lovely volume entitled *Pete Seeger's Storytelling Book*. Published by Harcourt in 2000, the book encouraged parents to tell stories to children. However, some of the material Pete dictated for that project dealt with issues more suitable for adults and were not included. The few examples set forth here are essentially works in progress.

Pete's fiction deals with certain repeating themes. Among them is the ephemeral nature of art—understandable coming from a person whose art often vanished the moment he struck the last note of a song onstage.

Another repeating theme is the unintended consequences of science and technology. As an environmentalist in a world of ever-increasing chemical and nuclear intrusion, Pete's concerns are well placed. His solution is to be very careful—to resist the assumption that all new knowledge and new inventions are inherently good. Having been branded a 'lefty' by so many of his detractors, Pete was actually fond of calling himself a 'conservative' in this regard.

Although dealing with serious topics, Pete relates these tales in his usual whimsical manner, so this section could have just as aptly been entitled 'Fables For Adults.'

THE WORLD'S GREATEST PAINT

James Penchick graduated from MIT, and he got a job as a chemist with a big paint company. They said, 'Mr. Penchick, your job is to try and discover some less toxic paints. Everybody's landing on us now, these environmentalists, saying your paints have lead in them and lead is poisonous, and your paints have cadmium in them and your paints have uranium in them. Cadmium yellow and cadmium orange are wonderful colors, but we can't use them anymore. Uranium red is one of the most brilliant reds we ever had, but they won't allow us to make it anymore. Your job is to invent some non-toxic paints.'

Well, Jimmy Penchick worked late, and he came home tired from working in his laboratory, but after several years, he had really gotten a fine lot of paints. Not only that, they were water-based. They didn't have to use oil, so they could be used for painting on concrete and brick and other masonry like acrylic paints. Some acrylic paints are not always as safe as we would like, but Jimmy's were completely non-toxic, made out of soybeans.

The company was delighted: 'Oh, these are the most brilliant colors we've ever seen, and non-toxic. We have to test them, though.'

And they tried them out. They put layers of these paints on the wall of their factory. They tested in different places. They had a factory in a very damp climate, and a place to test in a very hot climate, and they tested in a very cold climate.

But guess what? A year later, they said, 'Mr. Penchick, your paints might be possible in the tropics, but they cannot be used as far north as even Florida. Because occasionally Florida gets a cold snap and it will go below freezing—as you know, the orange groves occasionally have to battle a few hours of freezing weather—and they certainly will not do up north in New York or any other cold place, because do you know what happens, Mr. Penchick, to your paints? When it goes below thirty-two degrees Fahrenheit, your paint changes. It powders away, and over the course of the next few weeks and months, winds and rains leave the building so completely bare you wouldn't have known there was any paint there at all. Go back to your laboratory, Mr. Penchick.'

When he brought this news back to his family at suppertime, he was disconsolate. 'I thought I'd invented the world's greatest paint—non-toxic, inexpensive—and now I find it's only useful in a few very hot parts of the globe. But the parts of the globe that have got money also have cold weather occasionally. And according to what they report, a few months after the freezing weather has come, the wind and the rain have blown it all off the side of the building or whatever else it's on.'

'Well,' Jim Penchick's wife says, 'darling, don't feel bad. Do you realize you've got a more valuable paint than you know? In many ways, the world doesn't need more permanent things, it needs more continual creativity. Did you ever stop to think one reason I like cooking is because every meal is a brand-new thing? No one ever comes up to me and says, Your lamb stew isn't as good as the lamb stew you made ten years ago. But they come up to Louis Armstrong and say, Why aren't your new jazz records as good as the records you made in 1926? Or they come up to some composer like Verdi and say, Can't you make another *Rigoletto*? And he'll say, No, I can make another *Aida*, but I'll never make another *Rigoletto*. But no one ever scoffs at me, a cook. Cooks are the luckiest artists.

'But now, you've made a paint that can disappear. This can be one of the most useful things. We were thinking of putting a mural on the side of the building, but there was a big argument. People said, *No, don't put a mural. What if it's ugly? We'll have to live with it for decades*. But now, the mural will be gone in eight months. If we paint it on in the spring, by the following January or February, it will all be gone. Get me some of those paints. As a matter of fact, this weekend, I'm going to speak to some of the other mothers.'

They set up a committee, and they decided to let the children up to age twelve actually design what to put on the end of the building. They did this because someone in their meeting said, 'Kids over twelve are a little insecure, and they tend to get rather imitative. Sometimes they come from a family that encourages them to be creative, but the average teenager wants to wear their clothing or their hair the same way all their peers do. They don't want to stand out from the gang. That's dangerous!'

Not everyone agreed, but they thought, *Why not? Kids draw nice pictures. Let's have the kids under twelve draw pictures which they think would look nice. Maybe a busy, busy picture with lots of things in it. Maybe a very simple thing like a bird in flight, or a portrait of just one person who's a very important person.* Besides, they had other ideas for how the teenagers might help out.

Like so many other apartment buildings, their building had balconies along both sides, but at the end of the building was just a blank wall about forty feet wide and about a hundred feet tall. They took a picture of that blank wall and then drew a line drawing of it and made copies and gave a copy to each of the kids in the building.

In the middle of winter, they got together and chose a few dozen of the best pictures and put them up in the lobby. Below, they had a piece of paper that said, 'Folks, we'd like to put a mural on the end of our building. Which one of these pictures do you think would be nice? One thing we can guarantee you is that eight months later, the paint will turn to dust and be blown away by the winds and washed away by the rains so the wall will be perfectly blank again next spring. We guarantee that.'

For about a month, people in the apartment talked with one another, saying, 'What do you think of this picture?' or 'This would be nice if you maybe toned down the colors a little bit,' or 'This would be good but you don't need that figure in the lower corner.' Finally, they got a few leading ones, and then all they voted, and the picture was picked out. It showed a young man and woman on trapezes flying through the air, and down below, faces of the crowd on the surface admiring them, and there were all sorts of faces down below.

Next, they called on the teenagers in the building. Teenagers are not always such good artists—only a few, like Picasso, are so self-confident that they paint good pictures when they're teenagers. But teenagers like to do dangerous things, and, working together, they could do a good job of putting the picture on the little piece of paper in the lobby onto the whole side of the building.

They didn't ask them to figure out how to go up and paint. They said, 'We're going to get some professional people who paint billboards and put signs on the sides of buildings to show us how to rig a platform and how to have a safety belt so even if you lose your balance up there you won't fall.

And It'll be braced so that even if a wind comes along, even a strong wind, it will still be safe.'

The materials cost a little money, but no more than about a thousand dollars. And Mr. Penchick went to his boss and said, 'I know it's too expensive to make a lot of it, but can I have whatever samples you have left over?' And he was able to get enough of his paint for the job.

And so the teenagers transferred the picture from a little piece of paper just eight and a half by eleven inches to the side of this building, forty feet wide and a hundred feet high. For blocks around, people said, 'Have you seen that nice mural? I like to see kids' drawings.' And soon, other apartment houses were asking if they could do the same thing, and they asked Mr. Penchick, 'Can you get us some of those paints too?'

So Mr. Penchick persuaded the boss of the company to come down and see the mural. He came and said, 'I can't believe it! You mean to say we can sell a paint that is not permanent?'

They had to invent some special words to sell it. 'This paint is not permanent. It's beautiful! It's brilliant! It's non-toxic! But if there's any chance your weather is going to give it temperatures below thirty-two degrees Fahrenheit, this paint will disappear over the winter.'

This is what led to a situation where, all around the world, people were painting apartment houses with murals like never before. It became something for the kids. Instead of making graffiti, they became involved with making murals on the sides of their buildings.

• • •

Lee Hays, who sang bass in The Weavers, taught me a good deal of what I know about storytelling. He said, 'Keep in mind, every story need a beginning, a muddle, and an end.'

One reason certain ancient stories have lasted so long is because they can be appreciated on several levels. First time you hear it, you hear one thing. Then later on you hear the story again and you perceive something in it that you hadn't understood earlier. I compare a good story—or a good song, for that matter—to a basketball backboard, and you bounce the experiences of your life against it, and it bounces back new meanings. And that's the reason that some stories have lasted literally for hundreds and thousands of years.

A ROUND TUIT

At long last we have a sufficient quantity for each of you to have your own. Guard it with your life! These tuits have been hard to come by. Especially These round ones. This is an indispensable item. It will help you become a much more efficient worker. For years we have heard people say, "I'll do this as soon as I get a round tuit". Now that you have a round tuit of your very own, many things that have been needing to be accomplished will get done

— ✪ —

ABOVE 'A Round Tuit': one year, Pete sent out this handwritten message on round paper to many friends and acquaintances. *Author's collection.*

RIGHT In 1940, visiting Irish singer Sam Kennedy brought with him the precursor to the song 'Kisses Sweeter Than Wine' and this outline for a folding dove that Pete shared with many others over the years. *Author's collection.*
BELOW A fundraising letter from Pete to members and friends of the Clearwater organization. *Author's collection.*

OPPOSITE PAGE An early version of Pete's song 'Take It From Dr. King,' which at the time was known as 'Don't Say It Can't Be Done.' *Author's collection.*

Dear members and friends of Clearwater,

65 years ago I was a member of an organization with about 100,000 members. Most of them were working people, lucky if they could feed their family. But they raised a million dollars a year for their organization. How? They'd invite 10 or more friends in for a good supper and charge each one a few dollars which would go to the organization. I think that if all of us Clearwater members would do this, or just send a donation, we'd get the funds we really need, and could keep our precious sloop repaired.

Happy Hull-idays!

old Pete

Don't Say It Can't Be Done
(a song for solo and audience)

w & m Pete Seeger
Nov 13 2001
written in G - capo up as needed

① I'm trying to write a new song now
You may think it's right or wrong now
But Try repeating this line by line
I think I can Teach it to you
In a short time

(L) Don't say it can't be done. Repeat that:
(A) "   " " "   "   "
(L) the Battle's just begun. Repeat that:
(A) "   "   "   "   " (L) from The beginning now:
(A) Don't say it can't be done; The battle's just begun.
(L) Take it from Doctor King. Repeat
(A) "   " " "   "   " (L) from The beginning:
(A) Don't say it can't be done; the battle's just begun.

Tune of
verses

(A) Take it from Dr. King (L) you, too, can learn To sing
(A) You too can learn to sing (L) from the beginning
(A) Don't say it can't be done; the battle's just begun
(A) Take it from Doctor King, you too can learn To sing
(L) So drop the gun! (A) So drop the gun (L) that's it now,
(L) from the beginning!

A = audience
L = leader

Cho: Don't say it can't be done; the battle's just begun.
Take it from Doctor King — you, too, can learn to sing
So drop the gun !

Tune of
The
chorus
xx = some
percussion

② Of course; we need some more verses
They may be better or worses
But Doctor King showed us, we can win.
            when perceive
If we can see it's a brand new kind
Of light that we're in: Don't say it can't be done,
                    the battle's just begun.
            Take it from Dr. King, you, too, can learn to sing
                So drop the Gun !

in the Dispatch next week

Oct. 24, 2006

Dear Editor:

The eastern end of Main Street has a beautiful view of *is in a family that likes to sing*
Mt. Beacon. If any reader of this letter/likes to sing,
come there at 6 PM on Sat. Nov. 11 and Sat. Dec. 9. It
will be a holiday songfest for all ages and all kinds of
folks, singing old songs mainly, of many, many different
kinds, but good for singing together.
Dress warm! One hour, 6-7 PM.

The songfest committee: Michelle Marcus, Chris Ruhe,
Dorothy Medley, Pete Seeger, Dan Einbender,
Rafael Figueroa, Sue Altkin, Dave Bernz, Ellen Gersh

Dave
I'm sending this to every church
in town also !
Pete

YOU ARE HERE

ABOVE Pete sent out this letter
when he was trying to bring
attention to the much-neglected
east end of Beacon's Main Street
by holding a weekly singalong
there. *Author's collection.*
RIGHT One of Pete's favorite
postcards. *Author's collection.*

ABOVE Another of Pete's favorite postcards, which he would use to send out short messages. *Author's collection.*

Portraits of some of the guest contributors to this book.
TOP ROW Bruce Taylor, Connie Hogarth, Dan Einbender.
SECOND ROW Josiah and Tink Longo, Dar Williams, Michael D'Antuono. **THIRD ROW** Guy Davis, Pat Humphries and Sandy Opatow, Jim Brown. **FOURTH ROW** David Amram, Jim Musselman, Jeff Haynes.

TOP ROW Issachar and Tsipora Miron, Sharlene Stout, Tom Chapin. **SECOND ROW** Peter Yarrow, Ronnie Gilbert, Fred Hellerman. **THIRD ROW** Sarah Underhill, R.J. Storm, Steve Earle. **FOURTH ROW** Rick and Donna Nestler, Travis Jeffrey.

ABOVE The very first Martin Luther King Day Parade in Beacon, January 2014. Started by Pete and others at the Springfield Baptist Church, the parade is now an annual event. *Author's collection.*

THE PAINTING CONCERT

I was in Lee's Art Shop on 57th Street, buying some paintbrushes, when a man near me, about my age, looks at me questioningly.

'Pete?'

And I looked at him and said, 'I'm sorry, I don't remember you, but you do look familiar.'

He says, 'Tom Bremsen. We were right down the hall.'

'Good gosh! You were the skinny kid in my class at college.'

'Yes, and you were the tall skinny kid. You had hair on the top of your head then.'

'Well, we both changed, haven't we?' And we both laughed.

I said to him, 'I was going down the street to Carnegie Hall to hear a symphony concert, one of my favorite symphonies, but it doesn't start for another hour and a half. Are you in a great rush? Let's get a bite to eat and talk over what's happened to us.'

So pretty soon, we found ourselves in a little fast-food place, catching up on almost sixty years.

I asked, 'What were you in the art store for?'

He said, 'Well, you'll laugh, but a friend of mine likes to paint these pictures, you know, where they give you this piece of canvas that's got little faint lines on it, and areas, so the number three area gets the following kind of paint, and the number four area gets another kind of paint, and after you've filled in some dozens of areas, I don't know, maybe over a hundred, you have a picture. She likes mountains with snowy peaks especially. And the funny thing is, she actually does a pretty good job.'

I said, 'But really, couldn't you persuade her to paint pictures on her own.'

'Well, maybe she will someday. At the moment, she really enjoys painting, and I came to the conclusion that painting by the numbers isn't necessarily something to be frowned at.'

'Oh, how can you say that?' I said.

He said, 'Well, it so happens that I've seen it done very well. I mean, extraordinarily well. You got a half an hour still?'

'Oh, more than that.'

He said, 'Then I'll tell you…'

Way back right after World War II, I had a job with the American embassy in India. American money had helped build a tunnel through the mountains in the northeast and opened up a little mountain kingdom to the outside world. I had to go up there to say a few nice words at the dedication. I went to Kathmandu, got a car and a driver, and wound back and forth, zigzagging up the side of this huge, huge mountain. Then we went into a sleek modern tunnel right through the mountain and emerged into a valley.

Well, it was like Shangri-La! Flowers all over the mountainsides. Little terraces where they grew vegetables. And at the end of the little valley was a small town. There was a palace, and the young king came out to greet me.

He said to me, 'This is most fortunate that this occurs at this time of year because tonight we're having our annual painting concert.'

I asked, 'What's that?'

He said, 'Well, you'll see. It's after dinner tonight.'

After a sumptuous meal, I went with some fifty or a hundred guests into a large room. It must have been fifty feet square. And one wall was completely blank, with no decorations on it. But on that wall, they had hung a huge piece of cloth, and on the cloth were some very faint dotted lines. The whole room was lighted by some kind of lamp. What kind, I couldn't say. I don't think they had kerosene in those days.

When everybody was seated facing this blank wall, there was the sound of booming gongs, and a reedy instrument played some high melody, and out came about twenty people, men and women, dressed in rather simple robes, but with no color on them. They weren't black, they weren't white, just medium grey or brown robes. And the leader of them bowed to the audience and then turned to the rest, just like the leader of an orchestra.

Each one of them had in their hand some kind of a tray. And they also brought in bamboo stepladders. Some were short, three or four feet, but a couple were quite tall, twelve feet or more. Now they started painting, all two dozen of them, painting at the same time, with occasional gongs and other musical instruments. You couldn't say it was a musical performance, but music was part of it.

They were painting a huge picture. And, down below, some were painting what looked like green grass. But the funny thing is, they weren't all painting. Some had brushes and daubed on colors like brown and grey, but many of them would paint on something else, and then they would pick up a handful of pigment of some sort and blow—whew!—into their palm. Down near the bottom, they were blowing what looked like some green dust. And the pigment seemed to stick to the wall in certain places.

I leaned over to the king and said, 'How do they get that pigment to stick?'

'Oh,' he said, 'they paint honey in certain places, and when they blow the pigment on, the pigment sticks to the honey.'

'Well, well, that's extraordinary,' I said.

And, sure enough, there was a woman on the highest stepladder of all, and she would paint broad horizontal strokes with a big broad brush. And then she would blow some kind of blue pigment, and that whole area where she painted was suddenly blue like the sky.

Sometimes, there'd be something that would capture everybody's attention. Two women were working together painting a group of white flowers. It was difficult because they wanted to get the right pigment in the right place, and that seemed to have a special melody on a special instrument accompany that.

Then, finally, came the figure of a goddess. And now it all made sense. The goddess of spring was scattering flowers on the side of the mountain. And now the master painter had a few specialists who, with regular paint and small brushes, came in and put in black or grey lines in certain places. They were the only colors that seemed to be used with small brushes.

Well, I was so amazed. There, within an hour, they had created this enormous painting. It must have been twenty-five feet wide and fifteen feet high.

Finally, to great drumrolls and gongs, the music came to an end. All the painters moved their ladders to the side, and they bowed to the audience, which applauded, and they all took their leave.

Then it was time to discuss the painting, and I learned more about the culture of this tiny country, and the king said, 'Yes, we do this every year. Isn't it wonderful? Tomorrow, the painting will be hung on the outside balcony of my palace so that the rest of the town can admire it. And, of course, in a few days it will all be brown, and the piece of cloth will be washed.'

I said, 'What do you mean?'

He said, 'Well, all those pigments are made from powdered-up leaves of flowers. They're chopped actually. Finely chopped. And they had to be done just a few minutes before, so there were some thirty or forty women that you didn't see who were busy chopping leaves of different flowers. And the green down bottom was fresh green grass chopped very finely. Only the black lines are paint, which of course we made from lamp black.'

And I said, 'Could I speak to the man who designed it? Who is it?'

'Oh, it's the man who directed it. He does this every year.'

'Well, this is fascinating!'

Pretty soon, through an interpreter, I was talking to the conductor of the orchestra—really, the conductor of the whole thing. I found that he spends the whole year designing it.

'It's true,' he said, 'every year, it's my main job to think of what next year's painting should be. And of course, the whole town looks forward to it. And they discuss it. Oh, me! Often, I wished I could save them. Every now and then I get some inspiration, but all I can do is remember it. Now I understand you have things called cameras, and maybe I can photograph this. But wouldn't it be nice if I could save the whole painting itself?'

I said, 'Do you realize, in our country we have paints that are brilliantly colored paints, just as bright as these, that do not fade? Yes, I'll be going home soon. I'll send you some. See what you think of them.'

Well, I found myself at the same art store. This was, as I say, almost fifty years ago. And I got some government money and sent them a great big box of Windsor Newton oil paints, and extra brushes and so forth. Funny thing, I never heard from him.

'You never heard from him?' says I. 'Tom, that's impossible, did you try?'

He said, 'No, I even wrote a second time, *Did you get my paints?* but I never heard from him. Only just last year, I was in India again on business, I no longer work for the government—in fact, I'm retired from most business—but I was curious to see what had happened to that little country...

This time, I just rented a car. And I drove up the zig-zaggy road. Now it had advertisements along the road just like American highways do. 'Stay at this hotel.' 'Stay at that hotel.' 'Golf.' 'Tennis.' All sports. I guess tourism is the main industry out there now. And I went through the tunnel through the mountain.

Well, the little kingdom is still there, but I'm afraid it's a little different. The terraces on the hillside are mostly weeds now. And there were advertisements along the side where there used to be vineyards and orchards. But the little town at the end of the valley was still there. And when I parked my car I found the same man was still king. He was now an old man. And he said, 'Oh yes, you were the man who came here when the tunnel was built. Well, maybe it's clear to you now there are pros and cons to everything in this world. My country is not quite what it used to be. It's true, we have medical assistance we didn't have then. It's true, we have more education. But I'm not sure if we haven't forgotten things too.'

I said, 'Do you still have painting concerts?'

'Oh no,' he said, 'we haven't had them for many, many years. Forty-five years ago was the last one. The head painter killed himself.'

'Oh,' said I, 'maybe that's why I never heard from him.'

'What? Why did you expect to hear from him?'

'Well, I sent him a whole big box of oil paints.'

'You were the man that sent the paints?'

The king didn't say anything more. He closed his eyes slightly, and then opened them just enough so he could walk away from me, and walked out of the room.

I asked the attendant, 'Did I say something wrong?'

'I don't know, sir, but I guess the king is through talking to you.'

'Well, I wanted to see the man who was the painter.'

'Oh, that man died long ago, sir.'

'Is there any of his family still living?'

'Oh yes, his son is well known in town. I can take you to his house.'

The servant led me about a block and a half away and a man came to the door of a building, and I spoke with him.

'Yes, can I help you? Yes, I am the son of the man. It's true, he did commit suicide. What? You're the man that sent him the paints! Well, all I can say is that at first my father was so happy to have those paints. But now anybody could paint. And now, things have become competitive in a way that they never had been before. People said, Well your painting is not as good as that other person's painting, or This year's painting is not as good as last year's painting. And the change was too much for my father. I like to paint too, but I mainly work in the advertising business. I'm afraid that's all I have to say.'

'Well, I drove back to the airport,' said Tom, 'thinking, as I told you, of the pros and cons of everything in this world.'

Then Tom looked at me and exclaimed, 'And here you are, going down to a concert to hear some people play by the numbers?'

I said, 'What do you mean?'

He said, 'Well, are those people really playing what they think, the way a painter is supposed to? No, they've had the notes written out for them. They can play them a little louder or a little softer, and the conductor tells them when to play them a little slower or a little faster, but essentially, they're playing music by the numbers. So don't denigrate painting by the numbers. It can be done well.'

· · ·

Well, at age eighty-seven I tend to agree with my father. Scientists have the most dangerous religion in the world. When he was my age, he told me, 'Peter, I can't persuade scientists that they have the most dangerous religion. They think that an infinite increase in empirical information is a good thing. Can they prove it? They keep on inventing new weapons—new ways to wipe each other off the face of the earth.' My father said to me with a wry smile, 'Of course, if I am right, perhaps the committee that told Galileo to shut up was correct.'

However, if he was alive, I would argue with him. Remember Hagel says, 'There is thesis, there is anti-thesis, and there is synthesis.' That's in the song 'Turn, Turn, Turn.' There is a time for this and a time for that. And it is true that once upon a time, your ancestors and mine were all good killers. The ones who were not good killers did not have descendants. But you and I all descended from good killers, and probably in our genes is an urge to go whack! I like to chop trees. Others like to play golf or baseball or cricket. If we realize the contradictions of life—because you can't argue with people without recognizing the contradictions in life—then the human race may survive.

THE HEXAGONS

Let me ask you a question. I have been unable to make up a song about it, but if you could make up a song, this is what your song could be.

When you think about the contradictions in this world, you have to laugh if you don't cry. The good and bad are all tangled up. It's great when you get a job, but when jobs are most plentiful, it's mainly when the economy is growing.

A local politician in my hometown of Beacon, a very nice guy, said, 'Pete if you don't grow, you die.' At one o'clock in the morning, I woke up in bed and said, 'I know what I should have asked him. Doesn't it follow that the quicker you grow, the sooner you die?' The faster you grow, the faster you use things up. The world is only so big. Perhaps the solution is to slow down slowly.

I made up a story. Sometime in the future, decades from now, an elementary school teacher speaks to her class…

Children, now that you're in the fourth grade, it's time you learned about the Hexagons, or learn more about them. Maybe you didn't know that it was the Pentagon—I'm talking about the old military Pentagon—that helped us discover the Hexagons.

You see, the Pentagon wanted to go to the moon because they had laser weapons they wanted to put there that could control the whole world very cheaply. There was a treaty that said you should not use the moon for military purposes. But they said, 'Don't you want to go to Mars? We can only do it from the moon because the moon is the best jumping-off place. It's impossible to explore Mars from the earth. We have to go to the moon first and reorganize our equipment, and then we can explore Mars.'

People were so eager to explore Mars that we let them go to the moon and get their laser weapons in place. But people said, 'You're going on to Mars, aren't you?' And so the Pentagon says, 'Okay, we will.'

Up on Mars, they found that four hundred million years ago, on Mars, there was a technological society. We called them the Hexagons, because they had four arms and two legs and 360-degree vision, and most of their houses looked like geodesic domes. But, like us, they had languages and mathematics. It was a very advanced technological society.

However, in their early days, the Hexagons discovered that on Mars, five million years before that, there had been a rectangular society. We are a rectangular society, as you know. Our books, our panes of glass, our city buildings, and so on, are all rectangular. But that rectangular society on Mars only lasted about two thousand years and *BOOM!* It was all over.

Then, digging still deeper on Mars, they discovered that five million years before that, there was another technological society, and it was another rectangular society. It only lasted two hundred years.

BOOM!

The Hexagons came to the conclusion that all technological societies tend to self-destruct. They studied these two earlier technological societies and said, 'Oh, look, they both made this mistake. Look what happened. Let's not repeat those mistakes.'

And the Hexagons became very, very conservative. One thing is that they did things very slowly. Nothing was invented, or certainly not mass-produced, unless there was literally Mars-wide consensus that it was a good thing. Pure majority vote didn't get it.

You had to have literal worldwide consensus that there'd be no bad side effects. It was a good thing to have a new discovery acted upon, but even people who wanted to discover things worked in tandem with many others every step of the way.

And one of the first things they did was to level off their population, which had been rising. It took them hundreds of years until, by consensus, all of Mars agreed that they should not get any more numerous. Then it took literally thousands of years before they could figure how to gradually reduce their numbers.

And, sure enough, the Hexagons lasted not for tens of thousands of years or hundreds of thousands of years but millions of years, until Mars had no more air and couldn't support life anymore.

They sent spaceships out to the rest of the solar system, but at that time it was impossible to live on the Earth. The oldest life we've found on Earth is about 353 million years old, and that was just bacteria. The earth was being bombarded by asteroids and dust of all sorts.

The Hexagons gradually reduced their number until they built one big spaceship that could take all of them, and they set off for outer space, and we haven't heard from them since.

However, children, all ten of you will be going down to the wonderful Pentagon Festival. As you know, they have to reserve places in advance, or it would be too crowded. But next March 13 we are scheduled, our whole class, and I'll be with you. We'll go down to the Pentagon Festival in Washington, and from all five sides of the Pentagon there'll be wonderful exhibits and dancing and music and food from all around the world. It's the country's greatest festival, of course.

And now, I should let you ask you some questions, because children, you probably should learn if you haven't learned it already, the most important thing in the world is to find the right questions to ask.

What? Oh, what were their schools like? Yes, that's one of the first things we learned. My mother taught in the same school where we are now, but she had thirty students in her class, and one of the first things we learned from the Hexagons was to have smaller classes in our schools.

Oh, how did they make new Hexagons? Well, that's a very interesting question. First thing is, it took three Hexagons to make one new one. Well, we'll learn more as we go …

• • •

If we do discover Mars, and if we do discover the Hexagons, I think we'll find out the reason the Hexagons lasted so long is, they became very, very conservative. They loved, they laughed, but they did things pretty much the same. The kind of surprises they had were relatively inconsequential surprises. They weren't the kind of surprises Einstein had to face up to when he said, 'The atom bomb has changed everything except our way of thinking.'

How about making a song along this line? There is a *New Yorker* cartoon showing two insects glaring at each other, the caption reading, 'Insects will take over after mankind goes. But which insect?'

LETTER TO THE EDITOR

November 3, 2010

Dear Editor,

I am a musician by trade, but I have been a subscriber to your magazine for over half a century and write to ask if any branch of science is studying what things are most important to discover in these dangerous times. I come from a family of teachers; my older brother, John, felt that one can cure bullies who gained pleasure hitting weaker children, if you have about eleven years to do it. Could science find out how to identify bullies as soon as they are born, when curing them of their disease might be easier?

I'm told that Einstein, in his old age, said, 'Ach, mankind is not ready for it!' thinking probably of e=mc². Are there other things we are not ready for?

Two hundred years ago, John Adams and Thomas Jefferson corresponded; each was pessimistic:

How can one have prosperity without commerce?
How can one have commerce without luxury?
How can one have luxury without corruption?
How can one have corruption without the end of the Republic?

Now: how can one have a technological society without research? How can one have research without researching dangerous areas? How can one research dangerous areas without uncovering dangerous information? How can we have dangerous information without it falling into the hands of insane power-hungry people like Hitler who will use it to destroy the human race?

Looking forward to hearing from you.

Sincerely,

Pete Seeger

THE GREAT COLD CREAM EXPLOSIVE

Pete told me this story several times in different ways. In some renditions, actual conversations were lined out, and in others he had specific names and cultural and ethnic backgrounds for each the main characters. But perhaps it's best that it remains unfinished. Like a blurry TV picture, our mind can fill in the details. So, here's what is essentially a synopsis of a larger story, the way Pete told it one particular day.

If you read books much, you'll find there are lots of books about how the world comes to an end. It's almost standard today that you either have comedy or tragedy. Comedy is when it all ends happily, but real truth ends with everybody dying. *Hamlet* ends with a stage full of dead people. *Macbeth* ends with Macbeth and his wife being killed. Well, I decided that's too easy. Here's a story about how the world is saved.

What did it have to be saved from? Two brilliant young scientists, Nancy and Jim, invent a new kind of epoxy glue. It's completely non-toxic and very cheap. It's just made out of simple sand and clay. It does use a huge amount of heat to manufacture. Either oil or coal or something else has to be used. But this new epoxy glue hardens right when you want it to, either in forty minutes, or forty hours, or forty days, if you want to mix it to harden slowly. And now the little company that makes it is becoming a big company. Wonder Glue is on sale throughout the world. And the company says to the two young scientists, 'What will you invent for us next?'

Well, using the same time hook, they invent a skin cream. It's got some very powerful ingredients, but it gets rid of pimples. Forty minutes after a teenager spreads it on their face, the pimples are gone, but the time hook in the same forty minutes breaks down the powerful ingredients to harmless components so it doesn't hurt the body. And now Acne Off is on sale in every drugstore in the world. And the little company is just delighted and they're growing bigger and bigger. And they ask the two young scientists, 'What will you invent for us next?'

About three years later, to their horror Nancy and Jim discover that if you mix a half-cupful of Acne Off and Wonder Glue in a zip-lock bag, it looks like cold cream but can explode with the force of one barrel of dynamite, in forty minutes, or forty hours, or forty days, depending how you mix it. They look at each other in horror: 'We've discovered the end of the world. Any terrorist, any angry person can control the world with this knowledge. You could put a little bit of it in a pencil and an airplane would come apart. You could put some of it in the heel of a shoe and a house would come down. You could put it in a cement block that goes in a building, and forty days later the building comes down. There's no safety in the world anymore.'

They tried to get the company to withdraw the products. But the executive—his name is J.J., which stands for James Justice—he's a fat fellow, a cheerful fellow, but he says, 'Oh, we can't withdraw these products. People wouldn't understand.' And it ends in a shouting match. And they said, 'Well, let's meet tomorrow, and we'll discuss it when we're not so angry.'

At one o'clock in the night, they go out his door, but James Justice makes a mistake. He calls up his chauffeur, and he says, 'Follow that car. Don't let them out of your sight, and stay at their house all night, and when they leave in the morning, follow them here.' Nancy and Jim look into their rear-view mirror and see a car tailing them, and they say, 'He doesn't trust us? Well, we don't trust him!' And they shake the car. They zigzag around streets, and finally they duck into a driveway, and the chauffeur's car goes right past. 'Oh,' the chauffeur says, 'J.J.'s going to be furious.' He calls and says, 'I've lost them.'

They go into hiding. Next morning, J.J. gets a message by fax: 'Withdraw those two products or your Long Island mansion goes up next Monday at 8pm.' Well, he sends a team of people out to his mansion. They strip the house of everything. They can't find anything that looks like a zip-lock bag with cold cream in it. But sure enough, at 8pm, right on the instant, the whole house goes up—*BOOM!* Nothing but a big hole in the ground.

He gets a message on the fax the next day: 'Withdraw those two products or your Palm Beach mansion goes up next Monday. We'll make that 6am. We didn't realize how difficult it would be for rescue crews at night.' This time, he practically tears the house apart. He plows up the lawn. He chops down a tree that had some tree surgery done on it. He cannot find anything. But sure enough, right on the dot of 6am, *BOOM!* Nothing but a big hole in the ground.

But now it's J.J.'s daughters and wife that persuade him to do something.

They said, 'These crazy people can blow up the whole company. And how do you know they're not right?'

So J.J. puts out a news release: 'Due to charges that these miracle products are carcinogenic, they are being completely withdrawn from the market until we can prove, as we hope we can, that they are safe. Meanwhile, we don't want examples of them anywhere. We'll pay for them to be returned.'

The next day in the office, J.J. is approached by a tall fellow, lean. He looks like General Cedras of Haiti. 'J.J.,' he growls, 'what the hell's going on here? Yesterday, we were a prosperous company. Today, we may go bankrupt. Where's Nancy and Jim?'

'Oh, they're on a sailing vacation. I can't locate them.'

'Argh! Don't tell me that! I've spoken to your secretary.'

Just then, another fax comes in: 'Good! Have the following people for a conference in two months.' The two executives look at the list of names, and these are the most famous scientists in the world. Nobel Prize winners. Thomas Watson, the inventor of the double helix, is there, and all sorts of nuclear scientists and chemists. And then, 'What the heck is going on here?' There's religious people—Cardinal Torricelli from the Vatican, the Dalai Lama from Tibet. And there's a world-famous Tahitian dancer there. And, 'Who's this woman?' She's an old, old woman who's a famous Basque poet. No one who doesn't understand Basque knows what she's writing about—you can't translate poetry—but the Basques all think she's the greatest poet in the world.'

'Oh! This is it. Each one of these people is very famous in their own country, whether they're a scientist or a writer or an artist or a religious person.' There's a Kurd, a chief high priest of the Kurdish people in northern Iraq and eastern Turkey. Two hundred people, and they represent every one of the United Nations and a whole batch of people who are not in the United Nations, like the Polynesians.

The conference finally takes place on a cruise ship. It's the only way they can get away from the media. And Nancy and Jim surface. They'd been in hiding for two months. The boat is about to take off, and everyone is wondering where they are when a little sailboat comes over from Hoboken, and a guard says, 'Nobody can land here!' But she tosses a line and says, 'Tell Mr. Justice that Nancy and Jim are here.'

Then, all of a sudden, the newspapers appear—there's a hundred cameras there, and they're asking, 'What's going on? What's going on?' And the guard quickly clears the way, and with two little suitcases, Nancy and Jim are on board the boat. The boat takes off, and down from a helicopter looking at it, a reporter says, 'Well, this boat that's not allowing anyone from the media on it, there must be some great secret they're discussing.'

And, sure enough, Nancy and Jim tell the two hundred scientists and religious people and artists the terrible secret. The guests say, 'Why on earth do you tell us this secret? Couldn't you have kept it secret?'

'No. We were so stupid as to blow up those buildings. But once we did that, we knew it was only a matter of time before somebody else discovers the secret.'

After a day of discussion, these two hundred people finally come to the conclusion that the only hope for the world is to let the entire world know the secret at the same instant.

So, the boat sails back into New York Harbor and anchors at the United Nations. And with the prestige of this body of people, they get everybody in the world looking at television the same instant. It's midnight in New York, it's noon in Beijing, it's six o'clock in the morning in Europe, six o'clock in the evening in the middle of the Pacific, and so on.

It's agreed that every one of the two hundred people will have forty seconds to speak. The first ones on are Nancy and Jim, and, through the use of pictures, they tell this terrible story. 'You see, mixing these two common products together in a small quantity, and you can see something blown up.'

J.J. is on the air next. He said, 'I was head of the company, earning a million dollars a year. I've retired to be a kind of missionary to persuade business people around the world that if we don't get a world of some sort of peace and justice, then forget it, there won't be any world here at all. It's too easy to destroy each other. I'm appointing as my replacement my biggest rival, Tyler Jones. Tiger Jones, we call him. He wanted to do work for the Pentagon, but I think he's changed his mind.'

And Tiger is on the air for forty seconds, 'Yes,' he said, 'I thought business was all about making money. But I realize if we can't put an end to manufacturing weapons of war, there'll be no world. And all I can say is, it was my two sons who finally taught me this.' His two teenage boys come out and he gives them a hug, and they put their thumbs up.

Well, over the next two hours, all two hundred get forty seconds to speak, and the interesting thing is how many of them are saying, 'Yes, there are things we realize are true now that we weren't willing to realize were true before.' The scientists act a little humble, and so do the religious people and artists and all. They all are saying that the world will either learn to live with our differences or there will be no world. How do we live with our differences? That's the problem.

Eleven hours later, World TV is on again, and this time, the head of every country is on. And this is typical: a man is saying, 'I quit as head of this country eleven hours ago, it's too easy to be assassinated, but I can't get anybody to take my place except old General Lopez. He says it doesn't matter what happens to him, he's eighty-five years old, so, General Lopez, take over.' And General Lopez says, 'Friends, all I can say is, if anyone wants to assassinate me, consider I'm opening up the nation's television and radio to anybody who wants to speak. Just remember, the more signatures you get, the nearer the head of the line you'll be.'

And forty seconds later, another person is speaking: 'I'm turning over this government to the following writer because everybody seems to have faith in this person.' And this writer says something very similar: 'I'm opening up the air. The air has got to be open to everybody, absolutely everybody, even though they may have what some of us think are despicable opinions.'

Two hours later, they're off the air.

And, eleven hours later, now opposition movements are being heard from. And this is typical: 'I didn't expect to see the day when the head of our country, whom most of us think is no better than a common criminal, would let me on the air. But if he means it, we'll shelve our plans to take over the government. I'm not sure how long we could keep it in view of this new invention.'

But eleven hours later, the world is still here, and now other opposition movements are being heard from, and this is typical: 'Please don't believe the man you heard from eleven hours ago. He says he represents *the* opposition, but not on your life. He represents himself and a few hundred men who want to take power, and most of the country doesn't trust them either.'

However, before this two-hour session is over, Nancy and Jim are on the television again. 'Friends, the news fifteen minutes ago is that Peru has just blown up. The Shining Path has blown up most every city, and the government has blown up most every village. You can't live in Peru anymore.' And they show, from the air, pictures of refugees on the roads to Ecuador and Bolivia, trying to get out of Peru.

Well, for forty days and forty nights it goes on, just like Noah and the Ark. And every country has its leading scientists heard from, its leading politicians heard from, its leading artists heard from, people with strange fundamentalist beliefs of this or that. And nearly every single one of them is now saying something a little different than they used to say: 'I realize that if we can blow up every person who believes in abortion, they can blow up every person who believes like me, and, ah, I guess we will have to talk.'

Forty days later, Nancy and Jim are finally on the air again. 'Friends, do you realize what a miracle this is? Not many people thought there would still be a world here in forty days. But with World Television, it seems to work. Except that maybe it would be better if every person was on the air twice, twelve hours later, so some of us won't have to keep getting up in the middle of the night.

'All we have is a few pieces of news. One is that we're hopeful because a team of scientists has found out how to make Wonder Glue out of solar energy. Isn't this wonderful? At last, there's something the hot countries can sell to the cold countries. And this miracle product will now be so cheap that we can use it to make highways by strengthening concrete. You knew didn't you that at one time they thought they might use epoxy to strengthen concrete. But it's too expensive, so it's not used.

'We also have a piece of bad news. It's been found that Acne Off is carcinogenic after all. So maybe the good news and the bad news are tangled up, as usual.

'And we have one other piece of news. Please don't try and locate us. We're going back to being as anonymous as we can. It's not good to be so famous. We're going back to school, to try and learn to be better scientists.

'But,' she says, motioning to her belly, 'down here, new life is starting, because we're that hopeful.' And they both say goodbye in all the languages they can think of: *adios, au revoir, sayonara.*

And that's the end of my story, except that eight months later, when Nancy and Jim are in bed, he's feeling her huge tummy and saying, 'Just a few weeks now,' but in the middle of the night she wakes up with a wail.

'Jim! Oh no! Jim!'

He says, 'What's wrong? Is something wrong with the baby?'

'No. No, Jim, we thought it was the triexeline methylate in Acne Off that triggered the explosion in Wonder Glue. It wasn't that. It was the synthetic hormone. That's the same hormone that is in every woman's body. We're back to square one!' And the two young scientists look at each other with tears streaming down their cheeks.

'Well, we know one thing now, don't we? And if any other person discovers this, we hope they will have the sense to know.'

And that's the moral of my story. Einstein once said about the atom bomb that mankind was not ready for it. If he had known back around World War I where $e=mc^2$ would lead to, I think it's almost certain that he would say, 'No, I will not invent it. But how will I prevent other people from inventing it?'

CHAPTER II SOME PEOPLE

There were certain people that Pete mentioned over and over in his conversations. Some were very heroic, but in some cases, Pete would talk about a very flawed individual who may have done one good thing. Still others were people who said something profound or that amused him. For better or worse, I list just a few of these people here, along with Pete's comments. The fact that three of them share a similar last name is just a coincidence.

ALAN LOMAX

My parents taught classical music: Bach, Beethoven, Brahms, 'the three Bs.' Years later, I told my mother, 'For me, the three Bs are banjos, blues, breakdowns.'

As a teenager, I absorbed whatever the radio had, the pop tunes of the 1930s. I can tell you the hit songs of 1928, '29, '30, '40. Mostly pretty foolish songs, but some of them are damn good. I still sing, '*Blue skies, smiling at me...*' Then as a teenager, my father was doing some research in folk music, and I met a guy named Alan Lomax. His father was a conservative Texan who started collecting cowboy songs. But Alan had been radicalized by the 1930s. He was about four years older than I am, and he was put in charge of the Archive Of Folk Song in the Library Of Congress. And through him, I suddenly realized what tens of thousands of wonderful songs there were that I had never heard before on the radio. I didn't have the faintest idea of the diversity of North American culture. Not only the different immigrant groups from Europe, but the Latinos from the South, and the Native Americans who've been here all the time, and they refused to vanish as people hoped. Well, it was an exciting time for me, the late 1930s, and I started picking a banjo then.

The Lomaxes carried on the tradition of collecting African American work songs. How influential were John and Alan Lomax in charting the history of work songs? Very! Especially Alan. If there was one person you could say was responsible for the revival of interest in folk songs, it was Alan Lomax. You see, most collectors dig up dead bones from one graveyard and bury them in another—that is, their libraries. But Alan said, 'I want to get the American people singing again, and singing the songs which helped build the country, and can help make the country grow better.' And he taught the whole of this country songs like 'The House Of The Rising Sun' and the cowboy songs, '*Come a kayay yippi-yippi-yay.*' 'Home On The Range' is the most famous.

His father just collected them, but it was Alan who found ways to *disseminate* them. He got to the actor Burl Ives and said, 'Burl, quit acting a while and put on concerts. You're a good singer.' And he showed Leadbelly and Josh White that there were audiences. And when he found Woody, he says, 'At last I've found a songwriter just like the old-time songwriters.' He said, 'Woody, don't you ever stop writing songs!' And he said it so firmly, Woody never did.

LEE HAYS

I've often told people that there were two geniuses I knew in my life. One was Woody Guthrie. The other was Lee Hays, who sang bass in The Weavers, and he was also in The Almanac Singers before the war. He was the son of an Arkansas preacher, and he became a socialist as a teenager during the Depression. Once he saw his father filling a bottle with water out of the tap, and this bottle was the one which he baptized people with and said was from the Sea of Galilee. He accused his father of dishonesty, and his father says, 'Well, I just diluted it a little bit, but it was originally from the Sea of Galilee, and when it got a little low, I just added a little to it.'

Lee could make up stories and make up verses. He made up words for 'Kisses Sweeter Than Wine,' although we boiled them down a little bit. He made up the words to 'If I Had A Hammer.' He knew that with a lot of great old gospel songs, just change one word and they have a new verse. So he sent these four verses to me, and he said, 'Pete, do you think you can make up a tune for this?'

Lee Hays could make up stories and make up songs, but he was kind of cantankerous and a little hard to get along with. In the Almanacs as well as The Weavers, he'd say, 'Oh, I don't feel so well, you go on and sing without me.' He probably thought things weren't going right, and he just didn't know how to say it. But the other Almanacs felt he was malingering, and they said, 'Pete, you have to ask Lee to leave us. He doesn't help us at all.' I gave in to them, and so Lee left the Almanacs. We were never quite such a good group after he left, I don't think. Even though Woody Guthrie was with us, we missed Lee's particular brand of humor.

But to the end of his life, Lee had the kind of humor that reaches out. I swear that if there's a human race here in a couple hundred years, it will be the arts, the musical arts, the visual arts, the sports arts, the cooking arts, and perhaps, above all, the humor arts.

Lee Hays came to New York way back in 1940 because he wanted to put out a book of union songs. He'd been a teacher at a little left-wing college called Commonwealth College in Arkansas, where they had this school for black and white. Lee was a teacher there. He came as a student but stayed as a teacher. And when the school was literally run out of business—I think it was burned down by the Ku Klux Klan—Lee came to New York thinking maybe he could get a book published in New York. And I heard about him.

I looked up Lee and found him living with a newspaperman named Millard Lampell. But they were both kind of broke. When we were asked to sing for some left-wing fundraising party—I remember one was in a restaurant in Chinatown—all three of us sang there, and it sounded pretty good! Mill was quick at making up verses right on the spur of the moment.

Pretty soon we had a group, and we called ourselves The Almanac Singers. Lee chose the word. I was reading the book that Woody and I had put out and I came across the word *almanac*, and Lee said, 'Hold on Pete, that might be a good name for us. You know, out in the country, there's two books in a farmhouse. One was the bible to help them get through the next world and the other was the Almanac to help them get through this world.' So, we became The Almanac Singers thanks to Lee.

Lee really had a feeling for words and humor, even late in life, when he was ill with diabetes. He had a little garden, and his neighbor said, 'I'll tend your garden if you'll let me have some of the crop.' And Lee says, 'You know, when I was young, I organized sharecroppers. Now I have sharecroppers!'

He lived with Walter Lowenfels in Philadelphia for a while. Walter was an extraordinary modern poet. When he lived in Paris when he was first married, Walter won a poetry prize he shared with e.e. cummings. Later on, when he saw us singing, he had some words for children, and I put a tune to one of his poems. I still sing it occasionally.

And Lee Hays, he made up a little poem for Toshi:

IN DEAD EARNEST *Pete Seeger, Lee Hays*

If I should die before I wake
All my bone and sinew take
Put me in the compost pile
And decompose me for a while

Worms, water, sun will have their way
Returning me to common clay
All that I am will feed the trees
And little fishes in the seas

When radishes and corn you munch
You may be having me for lunch
And then excrete me with a grin
Chortling, 'There goes Lee again'

'Twill be my happiest destiny
To die and live eternally.

JOHN MUIR

He was born in Scotland, but his father took him to Wisconsin when he was a child. He was a smart kid and was always inventing things. In high school, he actually built a bed that, when an alarm clock went off, dumped whoever was in the bed on the floor.

He went to college thinking that he would spend his life as an inventor, but increasingly he found himself spending all his time outdoors. He didn't like being indoors, and he quit that idea cold turkey. He says, 'I'm going to find something to do where I don't have to be indoors all the time.'

And he walked from Kentucky to Florida in the 1860s. Then he went to California. In California, he just fell in love with the Sierras and hiked along them. He would spread-eagle himself on a big rock because the rock was warmed by the sun, and he could stay there all night long as long as he was hugging this warm rock.

Once, he climbed up a huge Sequoia tree, several hundred feet in the air, just as a huge thunderstorm was approaching, and he tied himself to it so he wouldn't fall out. He just said, 'I wanted to see what happens up in the air during a thunderstorm.' Lightning flashing all around the place. He could have gotten electrocuted, but he survived.

Then he got married and had to run a small business. He made enough to make a living, but he still had time to get out and hike. He became acquainted with other hikers, and in the 1890s the Sierra Club was formed. He was past middle age by then, probably in his fifties. And the Sierra Club grew, and they got Yosemite set aside as a park with Theodore Roosevelt.

But then he lost the battle for Hetch Hetchy, and that just about killed him. He threw in every ounce of his energy. He said, 'Okay, it's not quite as big as Yosemite. We have Yosemite, why do we need another? Of course we need another!' Hetch Hetchy is this beautiful, beautiful canyon about fifty miles north of Yosemite, formed by glaciers, with big cliffs and so on. But Los Angeles and San Francisco said, 'I'm sorry, we *must* have the water.' Muir says, 'But this is going to fill up with silt in a hundred years. You won't have the water then. What are you going to do with Hetch Hetchy then? Are you going to dig it out?' They said, 'Don't worry, that's about a hundred years from now.' And they built Hetch Hetchy Dam and as I say, it just about killed him.

Muir was in his seventies then. He died around World War I. By that time, he was an old man with a long white beard. He and John Burrows liked to have these long white beards.

WANGARI MAATHAI

If there is a human race here in a hundred years, I think one of the people who will go down in history as having saved it is Wangari Maathai. She got a Nobel Prize four for having saved her home country Kenya in East Africa by teaching women how to plant trees and save the ecology of their part of the world.

When she was a very small child, some Catholic nuns spoke to her mother and said, 'We would like to give your child a free education. She can only see you on weekends. Would that be all right?' And the mother must have really trusted them. And a few years later, she was the top student, and the Catholic sisters said, 'We would like to give her a secondary education, but she can only see you on vacations, because it is a little further away and she can't come home,' and the mother again agreed. She and her daughter had continual correspondence. Some year, these letters, if they were saved, could be a fascinating book.

Then, after she had been a top student in what we call high school here, the Catholic sisters says, 'Your daughter is such an absolute genius as a student and we would like to give her five years of college education, but it is in the United States.' She spent five years in the United States, going to a Catholic college in Iowa. Perhaps she telephoned her mother occasionally, but mainly she wrote letters, and she didn't see her home for five years.

When she came back, the political situation was not as good as people in Kenya had hoped. Kenyatta was the man whose guerilla warfare persuaded England to let Kenya become independent and no more part of the British Empire. Toshi and I and our family were there on New Year's night when 1963 changed to 1964, when two thousand people came to a big ceremony out in a huge field and the Duke of Edinburgh and Jomo Kenyatta walked up and saw the British flag come down and the Kenya flag go up. It was a wonderful occasion. Kenyatta lived to 1978, and then the man who took his place somehow managed to get re-elected every year, and I suppose he made a lot of compromises, as any person in power makes. When Wangari got back to her home, she found that foreign businessmen had been allowed to come in and, for a price, cut down millions of trees.

The western part of the country is in the foothills of Mount Kenya, and there were many trees there. Mount Kenya has snow on the top although it is in Africa, and the foothills are not as hot as the eastern part of Kenya, which is more flat down to the ocean. Well, without trees, the land has been eroded, and there was hunger in the villages and sometimes no water in the area, and other times there were floods.

Wangari didn't even try to argue with the government. She went right to the villages and said, 'We are partly to blame because we took money to chop down these trees and now we have to put them back or else we are going to starve.' She taught women how to plant trees, I suppose in tin cans or little jars with the right kind of dark soil in them, and a few years later they had a tree maybe eighteen or twenty inches tall. And now they would have a tree-planting festival, and hundreds of women would go out to a hillside and plant tens of thousands of trees. And then, in future years, they would irrigate and make sure they were growing and so on. Over a period of years, I think they planted thirty million trees. That's what she got the Nobel Prize for.

At one time, she and her organizations tried to stop the building of a skyscraper in a much-loved park in Nairobi, the big city of Kenya. Once again, the dictator had taken money, and they were going to have a statue of the dictator on the skyscraper. It's like putting a skyscraper in the middle of Central Park.

Wangari got a movement going. She was arrested and beaten, but her friends got her out of jail, and she went on. Finally, the dictator decided to resign and have a really fair election, and somebody else was elected.

Wangari managed to survive without being a big person herself. She made sure that other women took the leadership roles and carried on. She traveled around the world, speaking. I met her at Mohonk when Al Gore was showing his movie about global warming. She wrote a book called *Unbowed*, and I recommend it to all sorts of people because it tells her story, especially the story of planting trees in Kenya.

Wood is valuable, and when they cut it down, it didn't grow back. Wangari Maathai knew that if she tried to involve the government they would just brush her off. She had studied biology, and she made use of what she learned. It was not easy.

TOMMY SANDS

Tommy Sands came from a Catholic family, but their home was in the far north of Ireland. They didn't let the difference in their religion matter because his family loved to have singing parties. It was Saturday night and somebody would get a barrel of beer, and there would be twenty or thirty people—as many as the house could hold—and they would sit there singing, hour after hour. And finally, when the beer was all gone, they would bid goodnight. And it didn't matter whether some of them were Catholic or some of them were Protestant. They'd just sing.

Later on, Tommy grew up and became a famous musician. His family was singing in Europe and this country, but Tommy concentrated on singing in Ireland. He says, 'Why can't we do this on a larger scale?' We can sing together, why can't we live together?'

He found out that Stormont Castle in the north had a room that would hold two hundred people. And he got in touch with some very great singers and said, 'Can you come? We're going to sing all night. No politics! Absolutely no politics. We're just going to sing all night.'

Now, he got to the leaders of the gunmen on both sides of the political divide and said, 'We're gonna have a songfest. No politics! Absolutely no politics. But you can hear this person, and you can hear that person, they're all going to be there. We're gonna have a great songfest.'

Stormont Castle was full with two hundred people. Tommy had to leave at one point to buy something, and when he tried to get back in, the policeman says, 'You can't come in. This is a private affair, not open to the public.'

And Tommy says, 'But I'm the guy who organized it.'

'Oh, you're the songman!'

And then the policeman hollers up to the policeman on the other side: 'Let this man in. He's the songman.' And Tommy was so proud of that title that when he wrote his autobiography, it was called *Songman*.

Tommy persuaded the leaders who had been bombing each other and assassinating each other to quit. Tommy Sands may have been bringing Ireland together when music was the only way to do it.

RUTHERFORD B. HAYES

Sometime in the future, you might like to tell the story of Rutherford B. Hayes. I thought he was the worst president we ever had, because he withdrew the soldiers from the North who went to take charge of the South after the Civil War. When the northern soldiers were down there, African Americans could vote, and they elected thousands of people to local offices in the South and elected some to the House Of Representatives, and one was elected to the Senate for six years. Down in the South, they were very angry, but the Northern soldiers were able to see there was going to be a new kind of South. But President Rutherford B. Hayes withdrew the soldiers from the North, and that was the end of what was called 'Reconstruction.'

So, I always thought that Hayes was the worse president, but this is how you can be fooled. The Republicans felt they'd probably lose the next election unless they could find somebody squeaky clean, as they say in politics. During Grant's second term, there'd been one scandal after another. Grant was honest, but the people he was told to appoint were not, and the Republicans felt they would not win the election unless they found somebody squeaky clean.

They found him in a three-term governor of Ohio. And they said, 'Mr. Hayes, would you be willing to run for president?'

And he said, 'For one term only. I love my wife and family and don't want to subject them to that kind of pressure for more than four years, but you can get somebody else to take my place.'

Well, guess what? It was a dead tie when the election was held, and exactly the same number of people in the Electoral College voted for Hayes and for the Democrat, so the election was thrown into the House Of Representatives. And once again it was a dead tie, like 215 votes for Hayes and 215 votes for the Democrat. The Republicans found that one Democrat would switch his vote and vote for Hayes if Hayes would withdraw the northern soldiers.

Rutherford B. Hayes probably figured, 'I could resign right now, but then they'll take the soldiers out of the South anyway.' He wanted African Americans to be able to vote like everybody else, and he thought education would help. He was a lawyer, and he felt this kind of job should be done by talking, not by guns. He had a friend, the governor of Louisiana, and they tried to set up schools, but the Ku Klux Klan was too strong. Anybody who taught at the schools was lynched or made to quit teaching there.

Hayes liked to give speeches, though, and when he was out of office, he would take this new invention, called a railroad, and go give a speech somewhere. Eight years after he was no longer president, the Supreme Court hands down a notorious decision. They said, 'You cannot put a corporation to death. There is no capital punishment for corporations. If a corporation does something illegal, you can fine them, and they have to pay a lot of money.' Before then, a state would hand out a charter to a corporation, and if they didn't like what the corporation was doing, they could take away the charter. But not after 1888. And in a speech somewhere, ex-president Rutherford B. Hayes said, 'Face it. We no longer have a government of the people, by the people, for the people, like Lincoln said at Gettysburg. We have a government of corporations, by corporations, for corporations.'

He said that way back in 1888, and guess what? I read an article in the *New York Times*: Romney, who is running to be the president, comes out and says, 'Corporations are people.'

And there were protestors protesting his speech. The hecklers shouted back, 'No, they're not.'

'Of course they are,' Mr. Romney said, chuckling slightly. 'Everything corporations earn ultimately goes to the people. Where do you think it goes?'

WILLIAM WILBERFORCE

I read about a man named William Wilberforce, who was the son of a banker and was in parliament all his life. And when he was only twenty-four, he got religion, because he met John Newton, who wrote 'Amazing Grace,' and Newton convinced him that slavery was a bad thing and you should speak against it.

And he became a very good speaker. He could speak for two hours, and even people who disagreed with him would come listen. He'd sing songs. He'd tell jokes and stories, and ask questions which they had to answer, and so on. It took him twenty-five years. Every year he'd get a slightly larger majority. But just before Newton died, the majority in parliament voted to stop the slave trade.

And he spoke with the young girl who became Queen Victoria. He got her to believe that slavery itself should be banned throughout the British Empire. And just before he died, after fifty years of making speeches, the British Empire formally abandoned slavery, and the young teenage Queen Victoria signed the paper and so on. And they didn't have a civil war which killed 600,000 people to end slavery.

GEORGE WASHINGTON

Pete often spoke of how during the difficult times that followed the Revolutionary War, officers offered to make George Washington the King of America.

About two hundred officers wrote a letter to him. He read it and he was outraged and had all two hundred of them come to his headquarters in Newburgh. He said, 'I'm shocked at such an idea as you propose.'

They said, 'General, the Continental Congress is not doing its job. They're not collecting taxes. They're printing paper money, which is not worth anything. The country is literally going to Hell, and the British will take over soon if we don't get the country together. So, won't you please take over the reins of government as our king, and we will follow wherever you lead?'

And Washington said, 'I didn't spend eight years fighting royalty to set up a new royalty. I'm absolutely shocked at the suggestion.'

And this story got around the country. It was never printed in newspapers or in history books. It's kind of been slid over as one of the minor things. But it was a strong argument in favor of elected government. Just because a person is a good general, you don't make him the permanent president of the country. That's what usually happens after every revolution. The strong leader is now *the* leader.

And this is why the whole country loved George Washington. Elected government is better than inherited government.

WINSTON CHURCHILL

Winston Churchill had written a sentence with a preposition at the end of it, and one of his young proofreaders had put the preposition back in the middle of the sentence. Churchill now read his speech and crossed it out, and in the margin says, 'This is the sort of impertinence up with which I shall not put.'

JOHN HAYES AT NIAGARA FALLS

When people say, 'It's all up to God, what's going to happen is going to happen,' I tell them a story. This is an absolutely true story about a man named John Hayes. He's retired now, but he was a policeman in Union City, New Jersey, in the year 1960. And one day he said to his wife, 'Honey, let's visit Niagara Falls.'

She said, 'Whatever made you think of that?'

He said, 'I don't know. It just came to me.'

She said, 'That's a nice idea!'

They looked up the calendar, found a weekend they were free, and they drove up to Niagara Falls. They tried to get a room in a hotel, but because of the color of their skin—he's a black man—they were turned down. But across the street was a more expensive hotel, and a man there saw them and said, 'Come over, we have a room for you.' And they got a very good room at a reasonable price.

Later on, they walked out and went over to Goat Island, which is a little island between the big Canadian Falls and the smaller American Falls. At the first bench they sat down, a white person on the other end of the bench got up and moved away.

But now I got to shift gears and tell you the other part of the story.

In Niagara Falls, there was a man about forty years old who had a little motorboat, and he said to a friend of his, 'Would your kids like to go out for a ride?'

And the friend says, 'Sure. Make sure you have life jackets with you.'

He says, 'Oh, yes, I always have life jackets in the boat.'

So, a seven-year-old boy and his sister who was seventeen and this man were out in the Niagara River, and something happened with the motor. It was an outboard motor, and he leaned down to try and repair it, and he just couldn't figure out how to make it work. He straightened up to find out they had passed the point of no return. They had drifted too near the falls. The Coast Guard is supposed to watch out to see this doesn't happen, but somebody wasn't watching.

Well, in the few minutes they had, the man told the girl, 'Swim for it! You might just make it.' And he strapped two life jackets on the boy.

People who saw it said the boat overturned shortly before it came to the break of the falls. The boat and the man and the boy went over the falls. The boy with his two life jackets on bobbed to the surface, and he was picked up by the *Maid Of The Mist*. When he was on the boat, he said, 'Boy, that's noisy! You could get killed doing that.' He didn't know at that time he was the only person in history to go over Niagara Falls with two life jackets and live. The little motorboat was smashed to splinters. The man's body was found five days later, battered, downstream.

The girl was only about twenty feet, I'm told, from the brink of the falls, when John Hayes saw a head in the water, and he said, 'Hey, there's somebody swimming out there!' And he jumped up and ran to the edge of the raging water. She was holding onto a rock but couldn't get to shore. She hadn't enough energy. Holding on to the railing with one hand, he reached out with the other hand and got three fingers. And then he hollered and hollered, and finally another man whose name was Quattrochi, also from New Jersey, grabbed her other hand, and the two men hauled her to safety.

The first words out of her mouth were, 'My brother, my brother!'

And they said, 'Pray for him, lady.' They'd seen the little boat go over the falls. But about thirty seconds later, a shout came up, 'Hey! The *Maid Of The Mist* is pulling somebody out of the water!'

John Hayes is a very religious man, a churchgoer. He's convinced that God told him to go be there. With his policeman's training, he knew what to do. But I tell people, 'If there's a human race here in a hundred years, or two hundred years, it's going to take millions of miracles. Any one of us might be a part of it. No one of these miracles will be necessarily the one thing that will do it. Who thought the Hudson River, which was like an open sewer thirty years ago, would now be swimmable again?'

CHAPTER 12 THE HUDSON RIVER

CLEARWATER

The first time I ever sailed, I was five years old. We'd taken a vacation somewhere in Long Island. They put a life jacket on me and said, 'You sit here. Don't move!'

It wasn't much fun. Other people seemed to be having fun, but I was just sitting there. I never sailed again until I was forty years old.

I always thought sailing was a rich man's sport, but at age forty, I had a job on Cape Cod, and a teenager took me out at midnight in a little beetle cat—that's a boat about ten feet long, with one sail. And he showed me what fun it was, to tack a little bit to the left, and then to the right, and then turn around. It's not how fast you go, it's the fact that you move at all. It's a game with the wind and the waves—something almost spiritual about it.

Back in the Hudson, I bought a little plastic boat, and I was teaching myself how to sail it. My wife said, 'Are you sure it's okay to go out by yourself?' And I said, 'Not only today, but I'm going to stay out all night!'

Out on the river, I saw the whole world slowly grow dark, and the mountains turn to purple, then to black. And the river, which had been golden, changed color gradually. I made up a song about it.

SAILING DOWN MY GOLDEN RIVER *Pete Seeger*

Sailing down my golden river
Sun and water all my own
Yet I was never alone
Sun and water, old life givers
I'll have them where 'ere I roam
And I was not far from home

Sunlight glancing on the water
Life and death are all my own
Yet I was never alone
Life for all my sons and daughters
Golden sparkles in the foam
And I was not far from home

Sailing down this winding highway
Travelers from near and far
And I was never alone
Exploring all the little byways
Sighting all the distant stars
And I was not far from home

Sailing down my golden river
Sun and water all my own
Yet I was never alone
Sun and water, old life givers
I'll have them where ere I roam
And I was not far from home
Yet I was never alone
And I was not far from home

That was actually the second song I wrote about the river. As I looked at the water I was sailing through, I saw lumps of this and that, along with toilet paper. The phrase of John Kenneth Galbraith, the economist, came to mind:

THE HUDSON RIVER 193

'Private affluence—public squalor.' This is America, and I had the money to buy a boat, but I was sailing through toilet waste. I made up my first song about the Hudson:

SAILING UP MY DIRTY STREAM *Pete Seeger*

Sailing up my dirty stream
Still I love it, and I'll keep the dream
That someday, though maybe not this year
My Hudson River will once again run clear

She starts high in the mountains of the north
Crystal clear and icy trickles forth
With just a few floating wrappers of chewing gum
Dropped by some hikers to warn of things to come

At Glens Falls five thousand honest hands
Work at the consolidated paper plant
Five million gallons of waste a day
Why should we do it any other way?

Down in the valley, one million toilet chains
Find my Hudson so convenient place to drain
And each little city says, 'Who me?'
'Do you think that sewage plants come free?'

Out in the ocean, they say the water's clear
But we live on the river here
Half-way between the mountains and the sea
Tacking to and fro this thought returns to me

Sailing up my dirty stream
Still I love it, and I'll keep the dream
That someday, though maybe not this year
My Hudson River and my country will run clear

The idea of a beautiful boat called *Clearwater* started with a book, written a little more than one hundred years ago by a man in the town of Beacon.

I was sailing now, and an artist friend in Cold Spring named Vic Schwarz said, 'Pete, you know they used to have sailboats in the Hudson with a boom seventy feet long?'

I said, 'Oh, don't give me that. Only in America's Cup races is it that big.'

He said, 'No, I got a book on it.'

He gave me a dog-eared, tattered copy of a book written by a man named William Verplank, from an old Dutch family, and his friend Moses Collyer, who had once been captain of a sloop carrying cargo up and down the river. But now this friend was out of a job. Steam had taken over the river, and railroads took most of the passenger business. William Verplank and Moses Collyer wrote this loving book, *Sloops Of The Hudson*, saying, 'These were the most beautiful boats we ever knew, and they'll never be seen again.'

I read the book and couldn't get it out of my mind. I stayed up 'til two o'clock in the morning and wrote Vic a seven-page, single-spaced typewritten letter, saying, 'They built a replica of the *Mayflower*, and Rudy Schaefer the beer millionaire built a replica of the yacht *America*. No one we know has that kind of money, but if we got enough people together, maybe we could raise the money to build a life-size replica of a Hudson River sloop. A mast a hundred feet tall! And on deck, it could be sixty or seventy or eighty feet long!'

I mailed my letter and forgot about it.

Four months later, I met Vic Schwarz on the train platform, and he says, 'Pete, when are we going to get started on that boat?'

I said, 'What boat?'

He said, 'You wrote me a letter!'

'Oh,' I said. 'That's as foolish as saying, *let's build a canoe and paddle to Tahiti.*'

'Well,' he says, 'I've been passing your letter up and down the commuter train, and we've got a couple dozen people who want to get started.'

I scratched my head and said, 'Well, if there's enough nuts, we might do it.'

It was right around that time that the Scenic Hudson organization was getting started, which in a backward kind of way helped to start the *Clearwater*.

If you need to have peak electricity on a hot summer afternoon, it used to make economic sense to have what they call a pump-storage plant. That way, you don't need a lot of big engines for that peak. What you have is one medium-sized engine pumping water up to a little reservoir on the mountain. And then when the power is needed, it's let out with a rush and turns the great big turbines. There's a little pond up near Strom King Mountain, and they wanted to make a bigger pond out of it. They were going to take a big bite out of the mountain right near the town of Cornwall, just before the bend in the river, and they were going to have a pump-storage plant there with big pipes coming down, and there were going to be huge turbines to make electricity for New York City on a hot afternoon.

Some people who lived around there started Scenic Hudson. I remember getting a fundraising letter from Brooks Atkinson, the *New York Times* drama critic, saying, 'The beautiful Hudson is not going to be so beautiful when they finish the Storm King plant.' They had a number of quite well-known people on their committee, including a well-known writer whose name I prefer not to mention. There was a businessman in Cold Spring named Alexander Saunders. He knew Vic Schwartz, and he says, 'Vic, you know Pete Seeger. Do you think he'd be willing to give a fundraising concert for Scenic Hudson?'

Vic asked me and I said, 'Sure,' and so Alexander Saunders went down to a meeting of Scenic Hudson. But when he proposed that I give a concert, this famous writer spoke up and said, 'Don't have anything to do with Seeger! Six years ago, he was sentenced to a year in jail for not cooperating with the House Un-American Activities Committee. If we have anything to do with him, we will be tarred with the same brush!'

Saunders came back and said, 'Vic, I'm sorry. They turned us down. But I'd like to hear some music. Maybe we can raise money for something else.'

And Vic says, 'Well, Pete and I have been talking about raising some money to build a Hudson River sloop.'

'Oh,' says Saunders. 'That sounds interesting.'

Two months later, I was singing on the lawn of the Saunders farm on Old Route 9 in Garrison. It's an old dirt road that was laid out in 1764 by Benjamin Franklin and his daughter, back when Franklin was postmaster general of the colonies, so now they call it Old Albany Post Road. During the intermission, about fifteen or sixteen people met in the Saunders' living room, and we decided we would start an organization called the Hudson River Sloop Restoration, Inc. One of the people there was a lawyer, and he said he could get us the tax-free status.

We started raising money in 1966. That first year, we got all of five thousand dollars. Two years later, we had a fundraising concert on the fields below the castle in Garrison, and I remember someone asking me at the beginning of the day, 'When's that boat going to be built?'

I said, 'Well, we raised five thousand the first year, and ten thousand the second year. However, they say it's going to cost $120,000 to build it.'

Then he says, 'Won't most people lose interest by that time?'

And I said, 'Well, we got to keep trying.'

But that year, a disc jockey from Poughkeepsie came down and gave a real pep talk. He'd say, 'Who's going to contribute five hundred dollars?' and 'Who's going to give a hundred-dollar bill?' And we raised a lot of money.

Then we got our first millionaire, Lila Acheson Wallace, from the family that publishes the *Reader's Digest*. They're very conservative people, and here I was singing songs against the Vietnam War, but she loved the Hudson in her own way, and she said she would give us the last ten thousand dollars. She actually ended up giving twenty thousand dollars.

We had now picked out a naval architect, Cy Hamlin, and a builder up in Maine, a seventy-year-old man named Harvey Gamage who owned a shipyard in the town of South Bristol. Down in New York, they wanted $300,000 to build it, but Harvey said, 'No, I've built many boats like this. I'll do it for $120,000.'

There were some cost overruns. It was $140,000 by the time we paid for it.

I remember Harvey saying to me, 'Well, let's get started.'

I said, 'We only have $30,000, and we've got to raise a lot more.'

And he says, 'You'll find the money comes in quicker once the keel is laid.' Now, that is one of the most important lessons I ever had! Once you're committed to something, you can't back down. Then you've got to go out and raise money.

We laid the keel in October of 1968, and then we went out and raised more money and more money. We got up to about $90,000, and the boat was completed in 1969. But that's when Harvey Gamage says, 'I need the last $50,000. I can't let you take possession of this boat unless I get all my money.' I called up Toshi and said, 'Do you know where we can borrow fifty thousand dollars?' And Toshi got on the phone, and I don't know how, but a week later, she found fifty thousand dollars—a thousand here, and a thousand there—and we were able to give a check to Harvey Gamage, and we sailed away.

We had a hard time finding a captain for the *Clearwater*. Not many people knew how to sail one of these huge old sloops. But down in Florida was a man who said, 'I've had lots of experience on schooners of that type. I'm sure I can handle a sloop.' His name was Alan Anapu. He was the grandson of a Finnish captain of a square rigger, and he just loved to sail. He was about twenty-eight years old, but before he even came north, he said, 'I have to tell you one thing. I'm not going to shave my head just because I got this new job, and I've got curls to my shoulder.'

We said, 'That's okay with us.' But when he arrived, Harvey Gamage and all the workers in the shipyard looked at him and they said, 'This is a captain!?' This was 1969, and long hair was not so common in those days. I had started growing a beard, and once I had to go up to the shop for a wrench, and the man says, 'Get a razor, too!' They thought we were a bunch of New York hippies. They thought this boat would be sunk or sold within a year.

As a kid, I always liked to climb trees. So, when the *Clearwater* came along, I had a lot of fun climbing up the mast. I first had a job putting in the ratlines. These are like rope steps on a ladder that go up the cables on each side of the boat up to the crosstrees on the mast. I had just finished working on these when the topmast was supposed to be attached to the main mast. The rigger's assistant was not there, and the rigger asked the captain, 'Will you go up and guide the topmast through the iron ring that holds it steady up there?' So up goes Alan Anapu, and he was working up there when he said, 'Pete, can you bring me a wrench?' So, I climbed up the ratlines too and brought him a wrench, and there the two of us were, standing way up there, one hundred feet above the deck.

Harvey Gamage was fit to be tied. He didn't have insurance for us. We were up there a half an hour, tinkering around. When we came down, he was furious. He said, 'Don't you ever go up there again until this boat is your boat! My men will do all the jobs up there.'

• • •

The little town of South Bristol, Maine, probably had all of two or three hundred people in it. Before we left, the young minister of the local church came and gave us one hundred dollars—this was a lot of money out of his small salary—and asked if we would sing some songs for the local people. We gathered in front of the post office with one small microphone and about a hundred-fifty or two hundred people gathered around to watch us. They all stayed a safe thirty feet away, except some kids who came up close. Alan sang the 'Sloop John B,' quite a famous song from the West Indies, and we sang some songs about the Hudson River. When we finally left, this young minister said, 'I think you should know that you have been a big education for this town—black and white people trying to save a river and getting this beautiful boat sailed—you have been a very good experience for this whole community.'

And we started sailing—twenty miles to the big city of Portland, Maine. We had a great singing crew. Don McLean, who wrote 'American Pie.' Louis Killen from Newcastle-upon-Tyne in England, who knew some great sailing songs from that part of the world. Gordon Bok—he was not only a great singer and songwriter, but he was the only good sailor on the crew besides the captain.

Louis Killen had sailed on a few big boats but he wasn't a particularly good sailor. I knew port from starboard but not much more. I remember Don McLean slapping the boom, a huge stick of wood, and saying, 'What is this, the bowsprit?' Brother Kirkpatrick and Jimmy Collier from the civil rights movement I don't think had ever been on a sailboat before. And once out in the ocean, I remember going through some big swells. The bowsprit would go thirty feet up in the air, then down dipping into the ocean, then up again thirty feet, and down again, and brother Kirkpatrick was standing there, very silent, holding on to something. I'm sure what was going through his mind was, *How did I ever let Seeger get me out here?*

We sailed down the coast, putting on concerts every night in a different town, and each night raised a little more money, usually about a thousand dollars, and the next day we'd sail another twenty or twenty-five or thirty miles. We had timed it so we could show up for the Newport Folk Festival. I remember a policeman saying when we were onstage, 'Where did you get this million-dollar gang?' because they were all such good singers. And finally, after thirty-five days, we arrived in New York. I think we'd raised over thirty-five thousand dollars to pay off the loans.

Rambling Jack Elliot had not been on the boat five minutes before he was up in the crosstrees. He brought some string with him of some sort, and he tied himself up there and slept up there overnight. Coming through Long Island Sound, we had a strong wind behind us. We were going hull speed—around eleven or twelve knots—and Jack Elliot went up to the bow and started hanging from the cables that go out to the bowsprit. Well, there was Jack, hanging by his hands and letting his feet just touch the tops of the waves like he was walking on water. So, I and another fellow went out there, and we tried doing the same thing. We were nuts! If we had lost our grip and fallen in the water, we could have been killed. The boat would have gone right over us.

Once, about two years later, one of the crewmembers did that exact thing. His name was David O'Reilly, and he was working on the bowsprit, and he slipped and fell in. The motor was on, and the propeller was turning around. It's about three feet long, and if that propeller had hit him, he would have been a dead man. However, he went completely under the boat and bobbed to the surface, fifty feet behind. The captain jumped into the lifeboat. It was released, and *BANG*—the lifeboat dropped into the water, and he rowed down there and extended his hand to David. Forever after, he was called Diving Dave O'Reilly. He eventually became a reporter on the *Philadelphia Bulletin* newspaper, but back then he was one living miracle because he had gone under the boat and had survived.

Alan Anapu was captain for the first year, and a very good captain he was. He never shouted, never got angry, but at times he was quite serious. Once, when we were sailing down the East River, he told us to back the jib. We backed it for thirty seconds, and then we figured, *Why keep on?* and we let go of it. Alan walked up front, and he says, 'When I tell you to back the jib, you keep on backing it. We almost sailed right into the shore!'

The idea I first had about running *Clearwater* was that it was going to be a kind of middle-class cooperative. I thought we'd all be volunteers and have one captain to see that it was safely sailed. We didn't know about the Coast Guard, 'our father which lives in Whitehall Street.' They said, 'You will have not only a trained captain but six trained crew. You can have extra crew if you want, but you will have a minimum of six skilled, permanent crew.'

The Coast Guard had also told our architect that he had to put a V-shaped hull on it. The old sloops had a completely flat hull. They could sit in a mud bank while the tide was low. Our architect said, 'We want to make it just like the old sloops.' And they said, 'The old captains were a little more experienced.' Even so, there were times when boats keeled over. Down near Cold Spring, the Dutch called it the *warigut*, which means the weather hole, and there are more bones of sloops between Storm King and West Point than anywhere else in the river. The wind can come from the mountaintop, and you don't see ripples on the water. All of a sudden, it hits you, and bang goes the boom, and over goes the boat! That's where Ben Hunt was at the tiller in 1865, and there was an unexpected jibe and the mainsheet looped around his neck and took his head off. It dropped thirty feet away.

There's a story about an ocean captain who was needling a river captain and says, 'What would you do if you were a thousand miles out and it was blowing force ten? I bet you'd be scared out of your pants.'

And the river captain says, 'I expect I would be, just as you would be if it was blowing force ten and you're a hundred yards from the rocks.'

• • •

I'm ashamed we had an all-male crew, except for the cook, who was a woman. We've learned since then. It was Pete Wilcox, who came on as a mate first and later became a captain, who knocked some sense into the board of directors' heads. He said, 'Every year, you have to get a new captain. Why? Because it's too much for one person, seven days a week, to be in charge of other people's lives. You got to give him a day off, a week off!' And he started having relief captains. We've had relief captains ever since.

I remember Pete Wilcox coming down the ropes from the top, and three other people sliding down the ropes with him, including the cook. The cook was Kate Cronin, and he says, 'Kate, you could be a captain if you go and get the training you need and get your license. I'll make you my assistant captain.'

In 1972, we sailed the boat to Washington DC, and Don McLean and Jimmy Collier and others put on an hour-long show in the House Office Building for about fifty members of Congress. I had a piece of cardboard cut in a circle, like a plate, and I had it marked with slices of pie on it, which was the federal budget: *Here's how much goes for education, and here's how much goes for paying off past and present wars*—this was 1972, and Vietnam was going on—*and here's how much for housing*. And there was a little thin slice you could hardly see, *Here's what goes to clean up the environment*. I pointed it out, and then I sailed it like a frisbee out over the heads of all there. Well, we got into the newspaper. And Nixon was being chased by lots of people in those days. I guess he figured when you have a lot of wolves chasing you, you toss a bone to one of them to try to get one of them off your tail. That's what he did. So, the Clean Water Amendments of 1972 were passed. And one of the reasons they were passed was because of the *Clearwater* sailing down there.

• • •

Clearwater's only been twice in the ocean. Twice it went to Washington. And both times the captains have come back saying, 'Don't take this boat into the ocean again!' Because the big swells could break it in half. It's a flat riverboat. Its freeboard is only two feet above the water, and with the centerboard up, it only draws seven feet. It can take all sorts of storms on the river, but big swells out on the ocean could break it in two.

I met Captain Travis Jeffrey when he first became a crew member. I'll never forget the joke he used to play on the kids who were putting a net in the water. It's one of the five different things the kids do when they come on the boat. Travis arranged it with another crew member, Al Nejmeh. Al played the part of a stooge. Travis would say, 'Kids, we got to put this net in the water and catch some fish.'

And Al would say, 'Whaddya mean? There's no fish in the water, it's too dirty.'

'Oh, will you please be quiet, I'm trying to show the kids something. Here, you hold one end of the net.'

'Why do I gotta hold it?'

'Well, I've got to see if it's got any holes in it.'

'Well a net's nuttin' but holes,' says Al.

'Oh, will you please shut up, I've got to show the kids something...'

Well, Travis worked it out so that at the end of two minutes, Al was caught in the far end of the net, saying, 'Hey, lemme out!' The kids are all laughing, of course. And it was a very graphic illustration, actually showing how fish get caught in the net.

Later on that same day, Al saw one kid going up in front of the jib horse, and he says, 'It's dangerous up there, come on back this side of the jib horse.'

And the kid said, 'Oh, you don't know nuttin'!' He was so convinced that Al was just one more stupid person on the boat.

Al Nejmeh came from New Jersey, but his parents were Arab. Al became the captain of a huge schooner in Puget Sound called the *Adventuress*, and they do a *Clearwater* job up there, and later he became a professional fireman. In the 1980s, he helped organize the Soviet-American Sail, where people from both countries got to know each other a bit better by sailing together to the Soviet Union and back. Al Nejmeh was a really great guy.

I'm convinced now that the world is going to be saved by millions of small organizations. And one of Clearwater's wise decisions was not trying to start a national organization to save rivers but simply trying to do a good job here on the Hudson. Now there are ten or more schooners around the country doing a *Clearwater* job in their own part of the world: a great big schooner in Puget Sound. Three, I believe, in Lake Michigan. Three more in Chesapeake Bay. One off the coast of Florida in Sarasota. One in Delaware Bay. Three up the New England coast.

And all of them use the *Clearwater* method of teaching. Fifty kids or so pile out of a bus and are immediately divided up into five smaller groups. One group goes to the starboard side and learns to put a net in the water. Another group goes to the tiller, and the captain says, 'Push that stick to starboard, that means over there. Push it to port, that means over here. Now hold her amidships.' And the kids say, 'We're steering the boat!' Another group goes to portside and puts in a net as fine as a lady's stocking. And the kids look as it comes up with some green slime on it. It's put under a microscope. The kids look at it and say, 'Hey, what's those wiggly things?' And the volunteer crew—a few years ago it was my twelve-year-old granddaughter—says, 'That's called plankton. Plankton is for fish what grass is for cows.'

I'm very proud that I planted a seed. But keep in mind, starting something is relatively easy. There was a philosopher who once said, 'Creativity is nice, but maintenance is the essential art of civilization.' Keeping something going—that's the hard part!

If you went swimming in the Hudson forty years ago, you'd be swimming in toilet waste, because every time you flushed a toilet, it went *zupp* right into the river. It had a foul odor and was so dirty that it once caught fire. Now we can swim in the river again. The shad fish have returned. The odor is gone, and people are once again wanting to come to the shore. Real estate values are up in the valley, and some communities are even drinking from the Hudson. There's still things that have to be cleaned up, but we're halfway clean. We still have problems—chemicals in the water and PCBs that shouldn't be there—but we're working on them.

Clearwater teaches us that you don't have to have a lot of money, but you do need to get people together. Getting people together is *the* big job of the next century. We've got to bring people together who have different religions, different languages, different ways of dancing and eating and dressing. But if we do our job right of bringing people together—and *Clearwater* shows us how boats can help bring people together—who knows? Who knows.

THE CLEARWATER PICTURE

There's a beautiful big painting of a sloop that Clearwater used to distribute. It was painted by a famous English marine painter named James Edward Buttersworth, and Cy Hamlin, the naval architect who designed the *Clearwater*, came across a little 35mm photograph of it and used that to design the rigging of the *Clearwater*. It was an 1860s sloop called the *Phillip Paulding*. Buttersworth was a very skilled painter. It shows a lowering sky and the boat zipping through the water.

I found finally where the original painting was. I put a little black-and-white picture in *Yachting Magazine*, asking, 'Does anybody know where this painting is? Does it still exist?' And I told them that 'the *Clearwater* would like to see if we can get permission to reproduce it, and at the moment all we have now is the little 35mm.'

A letter came from Virginia. A woman says, 'My daughter and her husband have it. But it was mine, and I got it from my grandfather, who owned that boat. He came over from Ireland in the 1840s at age fourteen and worked for four dollars a month on the New York waterfront. He probably had a bed somewhere, and an outdoor toilet he could go to, and just barely got enough to live on. However, he worked hard. Age nineteen, he married another Irish girl and the two of them scrimped and saved, and in ten years they'd saved up five hundred dollars. And now he bought a second-hand sloop.'

That would be probably around 1860, I guess. What *Clearwater* cost, a hundred-fifty thousand dollars now would cost a million dollars, he bought for five hundred dollars, a second-hand sloop.

She continued, 'Now he was Captain Michael O'Brien. And he spent his whole life sailing Haverstraw brick to New York City, and anything else. You know, I went out with him when he was an old man and I was eight years old. We sailed his boat to Staten Island, and it sat in the sand at low tide while men with wheelbarrows loaded it with sand from Oakwood Beach, and we sailed it back to New York to help build the IRT subway.'

Most don't think of the subway as having been built by horse and wagon and sailboats. It was the second subway in America. The first was in Boston, which still is more like an underground streetcar, but the IRT was built in 1903.

Somebody saw the ad and probably got in touch with this woman. And our friend Ralph Rinzler went from Washington with a big plate camera, and they photographed the original painting with all its details. And now we had an enlargement made, and a firm in Yonkers printed a thousand copies.

TRAVIS JEFFREY (Clearwater captain) *I was probably still a teenager when I first heard of Pete from the Rainbow Quest TV series that he and Toshi put on. I eventually came to know him when I volunteered for the Clearwater organization. I went up to his house with Charlie King to organize a couple of workshops for one of the festivals they call the Clearwater Revival. He and Toshi* and I hit it off pretty well, and when I began working for the Clearwater, I used to stay there on my days off.

But my best times with Pete were chopping wood. We both had double-bit axes, and we'd go off in the woods and chop wood. And we would talk about things that ordinarily you wouldn't hear him talk about because we were alone. So I came to know him particularly well from chopping wood.

We would chop a tree down together, one of us swinging from the left side, one from the right, and we would switch. Pete always thought it was a good idea to learn both. And one of the reasons for his longevity he attributed to doing physical work. And we trusted each other implicitly. He trusted me with what he said, and with what we did. After all, we were standing about four feet apart, directly facing each other, chopping in the same notch with razor-sharp axes.

While we were chopping, we would sing the old 'Long John' song. And we would make up verses. One time, I forget who hit the particular whack on the tree and it exposed a big hollow, and all these carpenter ants went scurrying out, and so he started to sing, 'Them old ants, done lost their castle, ain't it hard.' But the one I'll never forget was one day when we were just chopping, swapping verses, and he came out with, 'Takes an old fool, to teach a young fool, how to work hard.'

What makes a remarkable person? I don't know, but I know it when I see it. And he and Toshi were remarkable. But rather than count their remarkable qualities, or recount their achievements, mostly I'm just happy to have counted them as my friends during that period.

SARAH UNDERHILL (Clearwater crewmember) *I was part of a culture that came about in the 1960s that became known as the hippie movement. My parents grew up in Berkeley, California, and there was a lot of interest in folk traditions. My mother went to a little prep school in Stockbridge, Massachusetts, and her professors took the kids on trips to see Pete Seeger concerts. After she became a young wife and a mother, she had a guitar and a Joan Baez songbook, so I was soaking this in from a very young age. She had Folkways recordings and Weavers albums, and I loved listening to them.*

So, fast-forward to when I'm coming of age. I was born in 1958, which makes me the tail end of the baby-boom generation. When I was a teenager, my peers who were a few years older seemed to be having the time of their lives protesting, dropping out, joining communes, and saving the world. Come to find out that by the time I graduated, popular culture had moved on. I was crestfallen. I was looking forward to this great experience of being a hippie and saving the world, and instead I was presented with the rat race.

I really didn't want to do it, so I was looking for alternatives, and that's where I found the Clearwater. I was at a survival school on an island off the coast of Maine having all kinds of fun and I heard there was going to be a big anti-nuclear protest at a place called Seabrook, New Hampshire, and the Clearwater was going to be there. I drove myself down there and I found this huge encampment of people and they were dividing up the jobs to be done. I said, 'Well, I want to go down to the beach and pass out flyers to the local people.' I really wanted to see if I could find the Clearwater. I was passing out anti-nuclear flyers when I saw this great big beautiful sailboat sailing by. I got myself on board, and there was Pete Seeger!

Clearwater welcomed me. I volunteered to be an apprentice for the month, and I just stayed. That was forty years ago, and Clearwater has been my main community ever since. I know it's supposed to be the people's boat, but for those who were lucky enough to be on the crew it was a community, a way to learn about living in a group, a way to learn about living outside and using the weather and the natural world, and dealing with the huge environmental forces of the winds and the tides, and dealing with the public and teaching little kids. It was a really great place to grow up, and actually to fall in love, because that's where I met my partner that I was with for thirty years.

Pete and Toshi were a huge part of that. They were mentors and teachers, and they were welcoming and encouraging to everybody. The philosophy that the Seegers had, their worldview, and their ethics, and all the projects that they put their heart and soul into were great teachers for me, and great examples in leadership, and community involvement and activism, and working together to get things done. I love to sing, and the Clearwater provided an outlet to sing in a group with my friends, to learn how to perform, how to be onstage, and basically to be a folksinger, which is one of my great pleasures in life. So, I've got a lot to thank Pete and Toshi for.

Editor's note: since the launching of the boat in 1969, the Hudson River Sloop *Clearwater* has remained a vibrant environmental organization (see the website clearwater.org). The work of Clearwater to clean the Hudson and to educate and inspire the activists of tomorrow, together with that of Scenic Hudson in acquiring land and preserving scenic vistas, has caused some to view the Hudson Valley as the birthplace of the modern environmental movement.

THE BEACON SLOOP CLUB

On the waterfront of the little City of Beacon is a building forty-four feet long. Now, it's about twenty-eight feet wide, but it was once only eleven feet wide. Long ago, it was a diner serving coffee to people waiting for the ferry. Back in the days of horses and carriages, there was quite a fancy restaurant there, and wealthy people would have waiters with finger bowls and so on. But the horse-and-buggy days stopped, and now it was automobiles that filled the ferry, and a few pedestrians wanting to go to Newburgh. I remember it cost a dollar, in those days, for a car. Well, along comes 1964, they build a bridge across the river. The ferry closed. The diner closed.

In 1969, the *Clearwater* had just been built. When we first came to Beacon, we didn't try to stop at the old ferry dock because it was a rotting structure, so we sailed in just to the south, at the property now owned by Scenic Hudson. We had a nice little festival there with about eight hundred people and an electric generator, which ran a sound system. The next year, we had a second festival in the same place. But after each of these festivals, everybody said, 'Well, now I have to get back to my family, my church, my bowling, my beer,' whatever, and we had to start from the bottom a year later, organizing a festival, when the *Clearwater* visited.

After that second year, John Fasulo, a young student just out of high school, says, 'Why don't we have a sloop club, so we know how to put on a festival and can put it on every year with less trouble?' I groaned to think, *Oh meetings! Elections! Minutes! Rules! Arguments!* But he was right. We tried having a meeting place on Main Street, but that cost a hundred dollars a month's rent. But we had one friend on the city council—Joe Gallio was his name, a wonderful man. He was finance commissioner, and he liked what we were trying to do, and he said, 'Oh, you know the old diner down there on the waterfront? It's rotting away. We were going to bulldoze it, but you can go ahead and use it if you want.'

I said, 'Can we have a piece of paper?'

He says, 'No, I can't get that for you.'

His friends probably said, 'Why are you being so nice to that bunch of hippies?'

And he must have said something like, 'Well, we can keep an eye on 'em this way.' Whatever it was, we got use of the old diner.

The floor of the sloop club was so rotten your foot went right through it. We tore out the floor and the counter and gave away the stove and the icebox and poured a cement floor. And I called a meeting. Only three people showed up. Toshi says, 'Don't call it a meeting, call it a pot-luck supper.' Thirty people came! And it happened to be the first Friday of the month, so the Beacon Sloop Club has met on the first Friday of the month for forty years now. We have a pot-luck supper at 6:30 and a meeting at 7:30, and after the meeting a song fest.

John Fasulo was one of our first presidents. Then people were depending on me too much, and I realized nobody really wanted to be president. We tried having a new president every month. I remember a sixteen-year-old was once our president, and somebody proposed something, and the teenager says, 'Okay, let's vote on it.' And somebody said, 'Shouldn't we discuss it first?' And he said, 'No, vote first and discuss later.'

But then a woman—we didn't know she was a life-long Republican—had moved up to Beacon and was trying to figure what kind of a town she was in, and she liked the sloop club, and she looked around and said, 'This club needs a little organization.' Well, by gosh, we all looked at her with smiles and said, 'That's wonderful!' She was our first president who knew how to run an organization. She was president for two years, and then she turned over the job to somebody else, and we've had a new president every two years for over thirty years.

The sloop club had only been going for about eight or ten years when some carpenters in it decided to push out the back wall because we needed a little extra space. They pushed it out about six feet and raised the ceiling a little, and nobody complained, so a few years later we pushed out the south wall about eight feet. There was a tree growing outside the club, but we didn't want to cut the tree down, so we built the new roof right around the tree. It gets all the water it needs because the ground it's planted in is nothing but cinders from old choo-choo trains.

Now we had a club twenty-eight feet wide and we put in a big fireplace with a stone chimney, and at the other end of the club, we have a wood stove and shorter pieces of wood. We always start the fire in the stove first, because if we start it in the big fireplace first there is such a strong draft that it pulls the smoke down when you try to light the stove.

There's no running water at the sloop club, but we made a little addition with a stairway up and put in a composting toilet. We didn't ask permission to do this from the city, although the city is officially the owner of the building as far as we know. I usually say, 'They gave us an inch and we took a yard.'

After seeing the big *Clearwater* operate for about five years, some of us said, 'We need a smaller boat than the *Clearwater*, but the same style, so we can sail into some places that are too shallow for the big boat, or too small, or have too many trees so you can't get the mast into shore.' I agreed. And so I stole the money from my wife. She'd been setting it aside for our children's college education. She said, 'How much is the boat going to cost?' I said, 'I'm told thirty-five thousand dollars.' That was a lot of money back then; it is now. But then it wasn't finished and I had to get more, and then I had to get still more.

Nevertheless, we managed to get it finished, and the *Sloop Woody Guthrie* was launched in 1978, up in Kingston, New York, near where it had been built by the masterful carpenter Jim Kricker and his friends. Some of Woody's family were there, and it was formally christened by Arlo Guthrie. It's been sailing ever since, doing a *Clearwater* job, mostly in the little town of Beacon, opposite Newburgh, New York, doing water testing and bringing people out on the river and teaching them about sailing.

I had hoped at one time there could be small versions of the *Clearwater* all up and down the Hudson. I went around the valley, trying to convince all sorts of groups of people to build their own boat. We even had a captains training program for a time. That's where I first met 'raffish' Rick Nestler, the sloop captain who wrote the great song 'The River That Flows Both Ways.' But, in the end, we found it's far more tricky and more expensive than we thought.

We actually did manage to build two of them. One was made out of ferrocement. It was cast in Maryland and brought to Yonkers to be finished and rigged. We named it the *Sojourner Truth*. But that one didn't last. Some good people down near Hastings sailed it for about fifteen years, but they didn't put a strong enough mooring line on it. One night, a high wind broke the mooring line, and the *Sojourner* smashed into the rocks. Unrepairable.

But the first one is still sailing. We call it a ferry sloop because, in the old days, little towns like Beacon had ferries that were sailboats. And we sail the ferry sloop out of Beacon and take people up and down the Hudson, very careful to stay out of the main shipping lines, where we might bump into steamboats or barges or tugboats. It takes just as much skill to sail a thirty-foot boat safely as it does to sail a seventy-foot boat.

The *Sloop Woody Guthrie* sails Monday to Friday, April to October. If we had enough captains, we could sail on Saturday and Sunday, too, but only rarely do we do it. At the moment, we have five skilled captains, and we take anyone who wants to go out onto the river along with us. The cockpit holds ten.

North of the sloop club is a big peninsula that was once a garbage dump. The city had made it by filling some old barges with rocks and towing them so they formed a big rectangle, and one by one they'd be sunk. But barges rot. Small rocks moved by tides and winter ice filled the area. All kinds of garbage scattered. I can remember, in the 1950s, taking my own garbage there. Although I live just outside the city line, my wife's parents were caretakers of the University Settlement Camp, which is in Beacon, so when I took down their garbage, I took down mine too. This peninsula was filled with cans, broken bottles, corncobs, whatever—and industrial waste also.

In the 1970s, there were some teenagers in the club. Dan Searles was one of them. And these teenagers said, 'That ought to be a park.'

I was cynical. I said, 'Yeah, they will tell us there is no money.'

And they said, 'Well, let's try a petition.'

They were mostly in high school. We took three hundred signatures to city hall. They smiled and said, 'Oh it's a lovely idea, but where is the money?' They were going to throw away the three hundred signatures. We said, 'Give them back to us.' The next year, they got another three hundred signatures, and again only got a negative response. The third year, and again the fourth year, we got another three hundred signatures, from high school students mainly.

Don McClean still lived down in Cold Spring at the time. He'd been active in the early building of the *Clearwater* and was on the first singing crew, and later he sang his famous song 'American Pie' at a Clearwater fundraiser in John Jay High School up in Wappingers. In 1975, Don sang to support the park. Down near the dump, there used to be a huge poplar tree, and it finally blew over or had to be cut down. We were able to make this little platform there, and a few hundred people gathered. But the next year, Don moved to Maine.

It was still a garbage dump when Dan Searles and the other teenagers said, 'The only way we can convince the city that this should be a park—let's hold a festival right here in the dump.'

I said, 'There is only glass under foot.'

Dan said, 'Everybody bring down some rugs.'

And so they cut through the fence and started cleaning up the area as best they could, and we had hundreds of rugs. Some two hundred people were down there, enjoying the festival. I had a friend in Connecticut who brought over a team of tumblers, and they turned somersaults in the air and landed on top of these rugs. They couldn't have done it if we hadn't put them there. That was the third or fourth year, and it might have been one of the things that finally convinced the city.

Not long after that, I was at a meeting at a church in Beacon, and I heard the Citizen's Advisory Committee voting to urge the city council, saying, 'The next money that comes in for community improvement should go for a riverfront park.' Usually it had gone uptown, where white folk lived. The river end of town was mostly black folks. But by gosh—a miracle!

How did it happen? I am not sure. But I rather suspect that some people in the state or the federal or government said, 'That garbage can get in the river. You got to get rid of that.' And the way they got rid of it was to make a park out of it. They spent $800,000 to change a seven-acre garbage dump to a seven-and-a-half-acre park because they had to put rocks and clay over it and around the sides of it, so the poison in the dump wouldn't leach into the river. The clay sheds water like a turtle's back. So, when rain falls on the garbage dump it doesn't flow through the garbage, it flows off the back of the turtle and into the river. I remember because I knew Shabazz Jackson, who had the job of getting great big rip-rap rocks, three and four feet in size, and putting them on the very outside of what is now no longer a tight rectangle but a more-or-less oval pattern where the park juts out into the river.

They were going to put a canal between the park and the railroad, but they were short a couple hundred thousand dollars to do it, and as a result the harbor is now silting up. If they had a canal in there, the tides would run through and help keep the silt from settling there. We may still do that.

• • •

We've been holding festivals in the park now for thirty-five years. Back when we started, what we thought of as a big festival for us would be a few hundred people. However, the Pumpkin Festival last October had two thousand people at it. That is just one of three festivals we run every summertime—the Strawberry Shortcake Festival, the Corn Festival, and the Pumpkin Festival. In 2008, we built a river pool and docked it off the north side of the park, so now kids can safely swim in non-chlorinated river water when the weather gets hot.

A few years ago, the city expanded the park on the south side of the club at the old ferry dock property, and we've started holding some of our festivals there too. In the colder months, we hold events inside the club. We have an annual Holiday Sing each December, and environmental programs, and a monthly gathering of young musicians they call the Something To Say Café. Every Sunday there is a Beacon farmers market at the waterfront, and during the winter months, they have it inside the club, with the fires going strong. But as soon as the weather warms up, we're back outside right on the river.

Here's the song I mentioned Rick Nestler wrote back in the 1970s, although he didn't get around to copyrighting it until 1986. Rick says that back when I was trying to convince people we needed a smaller ferry sloop, he heard me tell a crowd up in Troy, 'I could be happy just spending my days sailing back and forth across the Hudson River.' Rick didn't think 'sailing back and forth across the Hudson River' scanned very well, but he knew that the native Algonquin name for the river, Mahicantuck, loosely translated, meant 'the river that flows both ways.'

The song is a musical history lesson, and it has an awfully good chorus to sing on.

THE RIVER THAT FLOWS BOTH WAYS *Rick Nestler*

Once the Sachems told a story
Of a land, the great spirit blessed
And the people followed the legend
From the great, waters in the west
And they stopped where they found
That the fishing was good
The earth it was fertile
Game ran in the woods

Chorus:
Oh, I could be happy just spending my days
On the river that flows both way-ay-ay-ays.
Yes, I could be happy just spending my days
On the river that flows both way-ay-ay-ays.

First came the trappers—then the traders
Their own—fortune for to find
And the valley—treated them kindly
So the farmers—followed close behind
And the sloops sailed well-laden
'Round the bat-ter-y
With flour from Yonkers—
Furs from Albany

Writers and painters have shown its beauty
From the waters, and on the shore
While musicians, sing its praises
Keeping alive, this old river's lore
And the sun setting golden
O'er the Palisades
The afternoon ends
And daylight fades

Maybe it's that starlight, maybe it's the moonshine
Reflecting on Haverstraw Bay
Maybe it's the fog, rolling down from the highlands
At the break, of a brand-new day
(The crowd that knows the song sings these last four lines)
But apple cider and pumpkins
Strawberries and corn
Make the people of the river
Glad they were born

Oh, I could be happy just spending my days
On the river that flows both way-ay-ay-ays
Yes, I could be happy just spending my days
On the river that flows both ways

Editor's note: if you'd like to hear 'The River That Flows Both Ways,' try looking up Rick Nestler's album *Spending My Days*. He also sings it with school kids on the album *Tomorrow's Children*, credited to Pete Seeger With The Rivertown Kids & Friends.

Captain Dick Manley, Rick Nestler, Leonard Lipton, Donna Patton (who is now Donna Nestler) and others formed the Ferry Sloops Inc. in 1979 and sailed the *Sloop Sojourner Truth* out from Hastings, New York, until the boat met its demise on the rocks in a strong storm in 2002. The Ferry Sloops organization is still active and now sails a white fiberglass boat in the mid-Hudson area.

In the time since Pete dictated this piece, the farmers market outgrew the Beacon Sloop Club and moved to Main Street, and the Something To Say Café ended when the kids who ran it got older and went off to college or took jobs. But the Beacon Sloop Club and its environs remain vibrant, with monthly potlucks and many other events, music jams, and festivals. In 2014, the park north of the club was officially named the Pete & Toshi Seeger Riverfront Park.

RICK NESTLER (Clearwater first mate and river captain) *About nine years after Clearwater got built, Pete said to me, 'You know, Clearwater's a mighty fine boat, but she's a big boat, and she can't get into a lot of the little towns up and down the river like Nyack and Dobbs Ferry. What we need is a bunch of little boats.'*

There used to be boats that sailed back and forth across the river that would act as ferry boats. Newburgh–Beacon is a typical example. Pete contracted the Bearsville boys, Ande Mele, Don Taub, Jim Kricker, and several others to build a prototype out of good Catskill Hoken Pine. They built a beautiful one-third-size Clearwater with local materials. And Pete actually had hopes of having more than one boat, so he bought two sets of rigging.

Then a fellow down in Maryland said he could build the same hull for a lot less money out of ferrocement.' We got a hull built for about five hundred dollars in materials, but it was more flexible and lighter than the wood hull, so Pete went down there and put in bulkheads with plywood and fiberglass to keep it from flexing too much. We had it trucked up to Eddyville, where Pete found out that it would take a lot more than five or six local people to finish it. We then had it transported down to Yonkers, and, by hook and by crook, we fitted it out.

Pete used to say, 'The Sojourner was built in fits and starts. Somebody'd throw a fit and somebody'd start working.' And we were true reuse, recycle people, grabbing parts from wherever we could. Our mast was a utility pole from Con Edison. Clearwater and the other environmental organizations had been beating them up for almost ten years about the Indian Point power plant, but we had a member who was a magazine writer, and he approached them and asked, 'How would you like some positive publicity from an environmental group?' He did a nice story in Westchester Magazine about how even utilities and environmental groups can work together, and we got a utility pole.

We finally got the Sojourner Truth launched and had it towed up to Hastings-on-Hudson, where the boat lived a chunk of its life. In the meantime, Pete had the wooden boat Woody Guthrie sailing in Beacon, and he would get a lot of local Beacon Sloop Club members to sail it.

Just before we started sailing the Sojourner, I had been trying to come up with a song. I was listening to Pete trying to sell the idea of ferry sloops to a crowd up in Troy. We'd sailed up there on the Woody Guthrie and Pete says to the crowd, 'You know, I could be happy just spending my days sailing back and forth across the Hudson River in my little boat right here.' And I thought, Hmmm, 'I could be happy, spending my days' scans pretty well, but 'back and forth across the river in my little boat' doesn't. But I knew the Native American name for the Hudson River was Mahicanituck, and that translates out as 'the river that flows both ways.' So, I had the line 'I could be happy, just spending my days, on the river *that flows both ways,' and I started building around it. It took nine months to finish the song in 1980. Over the years, I've recorded that song four times, and Pete played on every one of them.*

THE SLOOP SINGERS AND THE WALKABOUT CHORUS

The Hudson River Sloop *Clearwater* has always been a singing boat, and Pete was well known for his concerts and festivals up and down the river. But for many years, there were also two additional musical entities that supported *Clearwater*. The first of these, the Hudson River Sloop Singers, was initially comprised of crew members and was later expanded to include other people who had volunteered for *Clearwater* in other capacities. There were some very fine singers and harmonists in the group, and some went on to become nationally known performers such as Guy Davis, who is now a Handy Award-winning blues artist.

For over twenty-five years, the Hudson River Sloop Singers sang at festivals and fundraisers up and down the valley, raising awareness and much-needed funds for Clearwater. In 1987, the Sloop Singers along with Pete released a remarkable album entitled *Broad Old River* containing songs from the Clearwater repertoire. Many enduring friendships and musical collaborations arose from those efforts.

The Sloop Singers officially disbanded in the 1990s, but they reunite each year at the Great Hudson River Revival. The Revival is a five-stage festival with both local and national artists held at Croton Point Park each June. It is not only a fundraising event for the *Clearwater* but also serves as the annual gathering of the larger Clearwater community. The Revival was continuously held each year since 1978 until the pandemic in 2020 and hopefully will happen again in the future.

Clearwater's second performing arm is known as the Walkabout Chorus. In theory, this was to be a people's chorus, meaning anyone who wanted could sing with them as long as they came to the rehearsal. Pete once said, 'There's no such thing as a wrong note, as long as you're singing.' A chorus with no auditions sometimes resulted in unpredictable levels of musicality, but what the singers occasionally lacked in professionalism, they made up in enthusiasm.

The initial idea for Walkabout came when Pete wanted to bring *Clearwater*'s message inland from the river. In 1984, he proposed building a scale model of the *Clearwater* boat that could be hoisted up on a platform and carried in demonstrations and parades while those around it sang.

The six-foot model was built by Andy Mele, who worked on the hull, and the talented artist John Seacamp, who built the rigging, and the Walkabout Chorus was soon bringing it around to events and marches.

There were some very solid musicians who formed the core of Walkabout who kept the music on track, ran rehearsals and chose the song lists. They were also successful in starting the Walkabout Clearwater Coffeehouse. It was sometime in 1989, that one of the Walkabout members, Ron Dressler, approached me with an idea for a monthly coffeehouse to keep the group on track between parades. But, he says, 'not everybody on the executive committee likes me, so if I propose it they might not approve it, so you should propose it at the next meeting.' At the next executive committee meeting, at the waterfront in Yonkers, I volunteered to be a facilitator and brought up the coffeehouse idea, and it passed.

Ron immediately set about gathering volunteers, and he found a four-hundred-seat venue at the Harvey School in Katonah, New York. The first few seasons had some great concerts. We had Pete of course, but also Tom Chapin and the Irish singer Tommy Makem, Sally Rogers, Josh White Jr., Ronnie Gilbert, Vassar Clements, banjoist Tony Trishka, and zydeco great C. J. Chenier, just to name a few.

Now in its thirty-fourth year and at its third location, the Walkabout Coffeehouse continues to provide meaningful music to the community each month from October through May. Every concert starts with a 'teach-about,' where chorus members teach the audience a few songs. This is followed by an introduction by Mike Lavery, a former radio announcer who's been dubbed 'the Mouth Of The Hudson.' Then the featured performer comes to the stage for the rest of the evening. You can find out about their current programs at walkaboutchorus.org.

Looking back on things, one of the ironies is that the Walkabout Chorus—the more 'amateur' of the groups—has outlasted the so-called 'professional' Sloop Singers.

The Sloop Singers and the Walkabout Chorus are just two of the support organizations that have formed around the *Clearwater* over the years. Others include The Riverlovers in the Croton-Ossining area, Ferry Sloops in southern Westchester, New York City Friends Of Clearwater, New Jersey Friends Of Clearwater, and up near Albany, the North River Friends Of Clearwater. Many of these groups have followed the Beacon Sloop Club model of having monthly meetings with a potluck supper followed by singing.

All this musical activity over some fifty years has resulted in the existence of a loosely knit community of like-minded singers and songwriters in and around the Hudson Valley. Many know each other and get together for informal musical gatherings and parties in addition to the official *Clearwater* events. Most know the basic repertoire of river songs and environmental songs, and some also learn and sing each other's songs, such as Rick Nestler's 'The River That Flows Both Ways,' or Bob Killian's 'There'll Come A Day,' or Lorre Wyatt's 'Sailing Up,' or Pete's 'Sailing Down My Golden River.' In some cases, their children have come to know each other and have become singers in their own right.

From 2011 to 2013, Clearwater sponsored a youth singing program featuring some of this next generation called Power Of Song. They appeared at a number of events, including a concert at New York's Symphony Space, and at the Clearwater Revival. My son Jacob was a member.

One day, Dan Einbender, a longtime Sloop Singer, asked Pete if he thought there was now a Hudson River school of music, similar to the well-known Hudson River school of painting back in the nineteenth century. Pete hesitated, not wanting to take credit for anything quite so elevated. But, for better or for worse, I'm glad to have lived in an area with such widespread musical involvement.

GUY DAVIS *I first became aware of Pete Seeger when I went to a summer camp at age eight that was run by his brother John. Pete came and sang songs he had written and songs by some of his closest friends, like Leadbelly and Woody Guthrie, songs of the South, songs of the border. And what we learned from him is something that I do to this day, to get other people to sing along.*

Pete's great gift to this world is not the fact that he was a brilliant musician, subtle, an expert and wonderful singer with a warm voice, and a great storyteller. His greatest gift was that he got people to sing together. Pete's gift was also his great integrity throughout. Pete was very gracious, very humble. I never saw him poking his finger in anybody's chest, telling them what to think. He would discuss what he thought, and you always felt like there was room for you in the room with him.

The first time I actually met Pete, he was standing in my parents' living room. They were friends from way back in the 40s, having to do with the civil rights movement and the workers' rights movement. Then, one day, my dad said that I could go up to Pete's cabin and meet his wife, Toshi. I got into Pete's little red

Volkswagen, and Pete looked over and says, 'Well, Guy, what kind of music do you like?' At that time, I was sort of starting to smell myself like a teenager, and I looked over at him and said, 'James Brown,' and I said it with a tone of voice as if to say, 'Have you ever heard of him, old man?' Well fortunately, Pete did not hold that against me. I got to go up to the log cabin and see him from a more family perspective, and I got to meet Tinya and Mika when they were just girls.

We connected again in 1976, when they held 'Operation Sail' in New York City with these old wooden ships sailing up the Hudson. I stood with a crowd of people over in New Jersey, and of course Pete was the center point there, even though he didn't hold himself like that. That's where I met people like Rick Palieri and Rick Nestler and Danny Einbender. Those are the guys I went on to be Sloop Singers with at the Clearwater Festival. Back then it was called the Great Hudson River Revival and the performers got to mix with the audience, and we'd walk around with guitars and banjos and such and play! Just find a grove of trees and play!

Pete and Toshi, probably in a moment of madness, introduced me to Moe Ash, and I actually have an album on Folkways Records, which is now Smithsonian Folkways. It was a wonderful experience for me.

In the late 1970s, Pete gave me the opportunity to do opening sets for him. I got to meet folks like Fred Hellerman and Malvina Reynolds and Elizabeth Cotton. One day we went up to Boston to raise money for Jacques Cousteau, captain of the Calypso, that ocean-going vessel that sailed about taking measurements dealing with the climate and the environment. I got to meet John Denver in that process. A few weeks later, another fundraiser was in California, and for some reason Pete couldn't go. I got sent out there and I got to open for Don McLean, and Jack Lemon was the master of ceremonies at that event. So this was getting to be quite a life.

I don't know that I was truly worthy of the gifts that Pete gave me in his friendship and in his mentoring me. But I am grateful forever for every moment I had with Pete Seeger.

· · ·

Bruce Taylor and his wife, Connie, are longstanding members of the Walkabout Clearwater Chorus. As a young person, Bruce was drawn to the sound of Pete's booming twelve-string guitar and this led to a life-long relationship as friends, and as Pete Seeger's guitar builder.

BRUCE TAYLOR *I first heard Pete Seeger perform in the mid-1960s, in Burlington, Vermont. It was the first time I had heard a twelve-string guitar, and I was highly intrigued by its unique rich tone with such powerful bass. Soon thereafter, I bought my first twelve-string—a Guild with medium-gauge strings tuned to concert pitch. As I listened to Pete's recordings, I realized that my guitar didn't sound anything like his, and I began to wonder why not.*

A few years passed, and then I got to meet Pete for the first time. I had been told that he would be attending a Clearwater picnic on the Hudson River. I drove over to the picnic wondering how I might find him and if I might get a chance to talk one-on-one. To my shocking surprise, the first person I encountered at the picnic was Pete himself, picking up litter at the entrance gate.

I introduced myself and asked several questions about his guitar. He seemed very impressed by my curiosity, and together we walked to the stage, under which he had placed his guitar and banjo. With guitar in hand, he walked me down to the river and away from the crowd at the picnic. He placed his guitar case on a stone wall, opened the case, and handed me his incredible Stanley Francis twelve-stringer, inviting me to play it. Its heavy strings, low tuning, and incredibly wonderful tone just blew me away!

As I was playing, a young boy came running up saying, 'Mr. Seeger, Mr. Seeger, you've got to come to the stage, the program is about to begin.'

Pete turned to me and said, 'I'll leave the guitar with you and begin the program with the banjo. When you've finished checking it out, please bring it to the stage.' Instant trust!

Stanley Francis, an engineer in Liverpool, England, had custom-made his guitar with a much longer than normal scale length, a concept Pete had originally used on his five-string banjo in 1942, with heavy strings tuned four half-steps below concert pitch—a concept he had learned from Leadbelly.

Several months after this initial meeting, I contacted Pete to ask if he would allow me to make a copy of his guitar. To my delight, he said yes and offered to let me make tracings and take measurements at the subsequent Clearwater revival.

My copy turned out to play wonderfully. Soon after its completion, I managed to show it to Pete at the Beacon Sloop Club. He played it for about two hours, sitting on the floor of the club, and at the end of the evening told me how incredibly impressed he was with my accomplishment.

Two weeks later, he wrote to me to ask if I would be interested in doing some repairs on a few of his instruments, which I happily did. Several years went by, and then he said, 'Bruce, I don't think we can keep the old Stanley going any longer. It's time I asked you to make me a guitar.'

And so our incredible relationship had begun. Over the next few decades, I made him three guitars and did many repairs to several of his guitars and banjos. I also had many opportunities to play music with Pete, sometimes with the Walkabout Clearwater Chorus, and on several incredible occasions one-on-one.

We visited one another dozens of times. On one occasion, my wife, Connie, made one of her delicious apple pies for dessert. The three of us each had a piece, sharing about half the pie. Then we remained at the dinner table, deeply ensconced in a long conversation, during which Pete managed to consume the remaining half of the pie!

There are many reasons why Pete is important, but perhaps most important was his deep, passionate caring for all people everywhere. Pete cared, and he believed we should too. This he communicated throughout his life, through songs, stories, books, articles, and letters. The word is out—time to help spread it.

CHAPTER 13 RECORDING PETE

TAKE IT FROM DR. KING

In 2002, Pete wrote a new song called 'Take It From Dr. King,' which he wanted people to learn. It chronicled the civil rights movement from Rosa Parks onward, and applied its principle of non-violence to the post-9/11 world. The song had unique and sometimes difficult syncopation and Pete wanted it recorded.

Our first attempt failed when we tried recording each verse separately at my home studio and then couldn't get them to fit together. We then tried recording Pete leading it at the People's Music Network where there were some very experienced singers. But when we went over to the studio of Frank Trosterud in Orange County to review the recordings, Pete said he had led it too slowly.

I had met Frank at Imperial Sound & Guitar, a great little music store owned by Bill Imperial that was located in Newburgh at the time and later relocated to New Paltz, New York. Frank and Pete were probably political opposites, but he seemed happy to be working with us, so I made a suggestion: 'Pete, we're in a recording studio right now! And they have a metronome! Let's record it right here, and add the singers in later.' I suppose this was the moment that I became Pete's producer.

Pete made a great recording that day. We added guitar and bass, and the following week, the Vanaver Caravan kids added their voices at the studio of Robert Euvino in Accord, New York. The kids sang their parts with gusto, and one of the parents added some trumpet. But Pete wanted more. For the next several weeks, Pete and I trekked through New Paltz and over the Shawangunk mountains to Accord to work on the song, adding drums and organ and the voices of gospel singer Sharlene Stout and her kids. Then Robert and I worked alone for several sessions, sorting out the final details. When it was ready, we sent it down to Jim Musselman at Appleseed Recordings to include on an album entitled *Seeds*, which was released in 2003. The album contained two discs: one of Pete performing his own songs, and the other containing well-known artists singing their own versions of Pete's songs, including Bruce Springsteen offering up a soulful rendition of 'We Shall Overcome.'

At this point, I thought my involvement with 'Take It From Dr. King' was over, but I was wrong. Appleseed hadn't yet released their CD in January of 2003 when Pete asked for help to release the song in time for Martin Luther King Day. I really didn't know how to 'release' a single song, so I answered, 'Don't you already have people who can do that for you?' But Pete insisted he wanted my help.

I consulted my friend Stephen Kent, a professional publicist whose one-man company Kent Communications handles publicity for many worthy causes. Steve sent me his copy of the Bacon Directory of radio stations, and over the next few weeks, my secretary Gabe Curran and I became radio publicists. We made copies of the CD to distribute with pictures of Martin Luther King Jr. and Rosa Parks on the cover, and a 'one-sheet' with information about the song and a picture of Pete and the Vanaver kids, and we sent them out to 'friendly' radio stations, offering them on-air interviews with Pete if they agreed to play the song. So, on Martin Luther King Day 2003, all over the country, people were hearing 'Take It From Dr. King' for the first time.

SHARLENE STOUT *Pete Seeger was like another father to me. I met him back in 1964, when I was singing at a festival with two other boys and two other girls at St. Andrew's Episcopal Church here in Beacon. I had a good gospel voice, and they used to call me 'Little Mahalia.' When the festival was over, Pete told me he wanted me and the other two young men, Leonard Getter and Jimmy Farley, to travel with him singing. Pete was going to be on a television program called Lamp Unto My Feet and wanted us to sing with him. That was my first adventure. From that point on, we started singing with Pete, doing concerts in different places.*

At some point, I started singing and traveling with Pete all by myself. I guess we were together so much that Toshi started to say, 'Oh, you're Pete's wife now.' She was a lovely, lovely person, always met you with a smile.

I kind of faded away for a while, but then when I came back, Pete was still there. And whenever he was in Beacon, my house was his house. I got married, and my husband loved him. Whenever he'd come past my street, I'd hear a knock, and it's Pete with his banjo, and I'd say, 'Come on in.' He'd say, 'Come on, Sharlene, let's sing!'

He was so wonderful. My house got caught on fire, and I lost someone in the fire, and we were staying at a hotel, and there comes a knock on my door about a week later, and I looked up and it was Pete. It meant so much to me that he would go around trying to find me and my family, to make sure we were okay.

The funniest thing was that my grandchildren couldn't understand why the people at school got so excited when Pete came around the school, because they saw him at the house and he was just regular, plain Uncle Pete. And I had to explain to them who the legendary Pete Seeger was. They just started to understand it now that they're grown.

One time, Pete wanted me to sing with him on 'Take It From Dr. King,' and I remember David came by and picked me up, and we took all four of the children with us to someplace near Kerhonkson. That was the joy of their life, recording and being there with Pete Seeger. And that was how they found out who he really was. He was like a grandfather to them, and I still have great memories of my second father.

PETE SEEGER AT 89

After 'Take It From Dr. King,' Pete came to depend upon me more and more when he wanted something recorded, and one day in 2006, he left a message on my answering machine:

Dave, it's Pete Seeger. And I realize a rather big job is coming up, and you may not have time to do it. I realize I have to put together three CDs out of some two hundred short pieces of tape or something, because I have to record the first verse and chorus of every song in my book. And it's going to amount to about three hours. It's about ten hours or more of work, at least. It has to be done before January 15th. And if you don't have time to do it, maybe I should start finding somebody else who can. It could be an interesting job, though. You'll hear a little bit of two hundred songs. I'll be in the rest of today, Thursday, so anytime you want to call me…

ABOVE The log cabin Pete was building in Beacon in 1949, at the time of the Peekskill Riots, with the help of friends and volunteers from the *People's Songs Bulletin*. *Author's collection.* **LEFT** The fireplace in the cabin, featuring the round river stone that was thrown through the window of Pete's car. *Author's collection.*

RIGHT The Hudson River Sloop Singers at Fulton Ferry, Brooklyn, in the 1980s: Jan Christensen, Rick Nestler, Dan Einbender, Geoff Brown, Eric Russell, Tise Tobin, Peggy Atwood, Pete, Norm Wennet, Rob Dermer, Steve Stanne, Nelson Adler, Roz Schall, Sonny Ochs. *Courtesy of Rick Nestler.* **BELOW** The Singers at the Howland Center, Beacon, 1982: Geoff Brown, Pete, Sonia Malkine, Rita Falbel, Judy Gorman, Rick Nestler, Rik Palieri, Rachel Gatland, Mel Healy, Geoff Kaufman, Chuck Winans, Matt Cartsonis, Jan Christensen. *Courtesy of Rick Nestler.*

TOP LEFT Members of the Hudson River Sloop Singers and guests including Richie Havens at the Clearwater Revival. *Daniel E. Ung, courtesy of Rick Nestler*. **TOP RIGHT** The Singers at the Bardovon in Poughkeepsie, 1989. *Gerry Skrocki*. **MIDDLE LEFT** The Walkabout Clearwater Chorus at the Clearwater revival, 1991. *Courtesy of John Fisher*. **MIDDLE RIGHT** Pete, Stone Soup, and others at Old Whaler's Church, Sag Harbor, c. 1993. *Courtesy of Terry Sullivan*. **ABOVE AND RIGHT** Pete on the rigging of the newly built Hudson River Sloop *Clearwater*, and with Captain Alan Anapu and others at the boat's launch in 1969. *Courtesy of Hudson River Sloop Clearwater, Inc.*

OPPOSITE PAGE TOP What is believed to be Pete's first five-string banjo, a turn-of-the-century S.S. Stewart, and the banjo he made himself by combining a Vega pot with a handmade neck of Arbor Vitae. Each time the head was replaced, Pete re-stencilled the words 'This Machine Surrounds Hate And Forces It To Surrender.' *Author's collection.* **MIDDLE LEFT** David Bernz and Pete Seeger. *Mai Jacobs.* **MIDDLE RIGHT** Toshi in the kitchen. *Author's collection.* **BOTTOM** Two shots of the Walkabout Clearwater Chorus: singing with Pete in 2000, and marching in a parade in 2002. *Courtesy of John Fisher.*

THIS PAGE TOP LEFT The Walkabout Clearwater Chorus aboard the *Clearwater*, 2008. *Courtesy of John Fisher.* **TOP RIGHT** The *Clearwater* docks in Beacon. *Author's collection.* **MIDDLE LEFT** Beacon Sloop Club. *Author's collection.* **MIDDLE RIGHT** When the clubhouse was expanded, they decided not to cut down the spruce tree and instead built around it. *Author's collection.* **BOTTOM LEFT** Pete and Joan Baez at the club. *Author's collection.* **BOTTOM RIGHT** Pete, David, and Dan Einbender relax beside the club's fireplace, which was built by Pete and volunteers after he sent a call out to members to bring rocks down. *Author's collection.*

OPPOSITE PAGE TOP LEFT Pete entertaining at a Corn Festival. **TOP RIGHT** Pete and Martha Sandefer rehearse 'Bach At Treblinka,' as featured on *Pete Seeger At 89*. **SECOND ROW LEFT** Pete, Dan Einbender, and teacher Tery Udell at a recording session with the Rivertown Kids c. 2009. **SECOND ROW RIGHT** Pete and the kids c. 2012. **THIRD ROW LEFT** Pete and Jacob Bernz at the Wappingers Falls peace vigil, 2011. **THIRD ROW RIGHT** Pete and Lorre Wyatt hash out some of their new songs, c. 2011. **BOTTOM LEFT** Pete prepares to play at the Spirit Of Beacon Day celebration in 2012. **BOTTOW RIGHT** Pete performs at a celebration for the building of Clearwater's new maintenance barn in Kingston. *All photographs: author's collection.*

THIS PAGE TOP Michael Scolnick, 'Spook' Handy, Sarah Armour, Jacob Bernz, Pete Seeger, Perry Robinson, Sarah Milonovich, Judith Bernz, and David Bernz celebrate the Grammy win for *Pete Seeger At 89* in the Bernz family backyard. *Michelle Marcus.*
BOTTOM Pete celebrates his ninetieth birthday at the Clearwater Revival, 2009, joined by musicians including Mike Miranda, Jay Unger, David Bernz, Happy Traum, Martha Sandefer, Travis Jeffrey, Al Hemberger, and Tao Rodriguez Seeger. *Jon Bernz.*

TOP LEFT Pete and Toshi in old age. *Author's collection.* **TOP RIGHT** Work O' The Weavers at the Town Crier Cafe, Beacon, November 17, 2013: Mark Murphy, Martha Sandefer, David Bernz, James Durst, and guest percussionist Jeff Haynes. *Courtesy of Russell Cusick.* **ABOVE** Pete enters the stage (helped by Harry Chapin's brother Tom and introduced by David) on that same night to celebrate The Weavers At 65. *Courtesy of Russell Cusick.* **RIGHT** Pete visits David's shop, Jake's Main Street Music, October 2013. *Author's collection.*

Pete was in the process of re-releasing his musical autobiography. *Where Have All The Flowers Gone: A Singalong Memoir*, and he wanted learning CDs included with the book. That message began an almost two-year odyssey to assemble and edit nearly three hundred pieces of music.

Pete asked the Smithsonian for copies of his recordings and three boxes arrived with almost eighty CDs. It was a staggering amount of material Pete had sung into Moe Ash's microphone over the years. Other songs were on commercial labels such as Decca and Columbia. But about seventy pieces of music in the book had never been recorded by Pete or anyone else. We began to record them, mostly with my antiquated home system, but when a song required a woman's voice or a chorus, I was often able to bring Pete to a digital studio or to the Howland Cultural Center in Beacon, where we had a digital team waiting. I also obtained some recordings made by Pete's grandson, Tao Rodríguez, and from singer Randolphe Harris, who apparently had both tried to do some of this work for Pete before.

Next, we needed a person with digital equipment where all the tracks could be assembled in one place and edited with fades and proper equalization. That person turned out to be Jonathan Dickau in Poughkeepsie, New York. I had met Jonathan through Rande Harris when we worked on a CD with clarinetist Perry Robinson in 1998. Jon's basement studio wasn't state-of-the-art, but Jon is a real genius, very musical, and very patient. Week in and week out, I brought recordings over to digitize and de-hiss and add them to the timeline.

Spending so much time in the studio was taking a toll on my family, so I was glad that the project was finally winding down. Or so I thought…

Just as we were getting ready to send the final tracks to W.W. Norton, I got a call from a man named Jim Musselman. He said, 'I just got off the phone with Pete, and he says you've been recording him. Do you think you might have anything we can sell?' Jim was the owner of Pete's putative record company, 'Appleseed Recordings, but Pete hadn't put out a full album in almost a decade. I told Jim about the various recordings we had made, including the less-than-perfect home studio material, and he asked for a sample.

On my next trip to Jonathan's, we started a new timeline on the computer and placed things in an order that seemed to flow well, and we edited in some spoken word to link the tracks. When we had about a half-hour's worth, we sent it down to Jim. He called and said he liked it and that he wanted me to create a full CD. He sent a small budget, and suddenly I was a CD producer.

The standards for commercially sold CDs are higher than for learning CDs, so Jonathan and I worked to improve the tracks, removing extraneous noises and tape hiss, and adding bass and other instruments and some additional singers. We asked the Walkabout Clearwater Chorus to record the three-language version of 'Tzena Tzena' and Robert Boyce's 'Alleluia' round, which we thickened with other instruments and voices. Sarah Milonovich added her violin to both tracks, and Perry Robinson played his clarinet over 'Tzena' to give it a kind of dance-party atmosphere. Pete came to the studio one more time with members of Work O' The Weavers to record 'Little Fat Baby.'

Appleseed Recordings released *Pete Seeger At 89* in the summer of 2008, and I was pleased—and I admit even a bit proud—that I could walk into a Barnes & Noble and go to the music section and find the CD there. That was reward enough for me. But sometime in late fall, while driving along Route 9D, I got a call from Jim Musselman, who said he wanted to be the first to tell me that the CD had just been nominated for a Grammy award for 'Best Folk Album.' I nearly drove off the road.

The following February, much to our surprise and bemusement, Jonathan, Pete, and I all received Grammy awards. Pete never cared very much about awards, and neither did I. My wife Mai and I were not watching the presentations, but suddenly our phone was ringing with congratulations from Jim and from other friends and musicians. A few days later, Pete called to tell me he had just listened to the completed CD all the way through for the first time, and thanked me for putting it together.

We didn't attend the awards ceremony, but when the weather got warm, we held a backyard party and invited many of the participants and other friends. Dave Amram stopped by and jammed with my son Jacob, who was in the process of becoming a great young songwriter. We made music on a makeshift stage in the back of the lawn, and it was a lovely time.

When I tell people this story, I am quick to point out that the Grammy couldn't have been from my production skills, because I was a total novice as a producer, and the material was partly gleaned from cassettes. My family accuses me of false modesty, but I tell people that the CD was listened to by Academy members because of a deep well of goodwill that Pete had rightfully earned from a lifetime of good work.

A MORE PERFECT UNION

Over the years, I helped produce four CDs for Pete, including a joint effort with songwriter Lorre Wyatt. Lorre is best known for writing 'Somos El Barco,' which was recorded by Peter, Paul & Mary, but he also penned the Hudson River anthem 'Sailing Up, Sailing Down,' to the tune of a Jimmy Reed blues. But none of us up and down the valley had seen nor heard from Lorre in many years. It turned out that Lorre had suffered a stroke back in 1996 that took from him the ability to sing or play guitar. Before that, he and Pete had been trying to write songs together. In 2011, after many years of slow recovery, Lorre felt it was time to finish those songs and write some new ones. Pete agreed, and Lorre made several trips up the steep driveway to Pete and Toshi's cabin to hammer out the tunes. Now it was time to record them.

We immediately called upon Jeff Haynes and asked him to engineer and co-produce. Jeff is a world-class percussionist who has played with many renowned musicians, including Pat Matheny, Casandra Wilson, and Brandi Carlisle. He has a great studio attached to his house on the east side of Beacon, and he knew Pete well. Jim Musselman at Appleseed Recordings seemed willing to jump in one more time, and he sent us a small budget.

When it came to recording the songs, the ninety-plus-year-old Pete and the recovering Lorre both seemed to have plenty of energy for respectful disagreement over small word choices or minor nuances of timing. Pete once lovingly said that co-writing songs with Lorre Wyatt was 'like dancing, playing chess, and cooking all at the same time.'

The project became delayed when Lorre lost his voice for several months, so we used the time to put some guest artists on the project. With the help of Jim Musselman's rolodex, these eventually included Steve Earle, Emmylou Harris, Bruce Springsteen, Tom Morello, and Dar Williams. Both Jeff and I were happy to show the embrace of the once politically controversial Pete by these well-known national artists. We had hoped to record Springsteen in Beacon, but no such luck. He recorded his parts at home and sent them to us over the internet.

The CD liner notes describe the material as follows:

> The songs that emerged from these sessions are quite remarkable. They demonstrate a rare combination of optimism and wisdom that can only come from having lived a long life, from having suffered and overcome.

The variety between the songs is both impressive and refreshing. Some are introspective and others outward-looking. Some look to the past while others reference recent events such as Hurricane Katrina or the Deepwater Horizon oil spill. Most often, however, Pete and Lorre use the past as a way of telescoping us towards the future, as we might want to make it. In this collection, you will find humor and resignation, reverence and raucousness, and above all, a sense of the friendship between these two songwriters that extends outward to our shared humanity.

While that description is accurate, it shelters my sadness that the CD could have been better if there had been more time to make some changes and perhaps re-record some tracks at a faster tempo. It had been difficult to reach Pete for input because Toshi was unwell at the time. Despite the ups and downs, the CD contained some worthy songs. 'God's Counting On Me' and the title track, 'A More Perfect Union,' are both good and interesting songs. My personal favorites include 'Over Fields Of Harmony'—the melody of which came to Lorre in a dream—and the environmentally based 'Somebody Else's Eye.'

OVER FIELDS OF HARMONY *Pete Seeger, Lorre Wyatt*

Over fields of harmony
Over fields of harmony
Over fields of harmony, I have flown

Through the fire and the flood
Through the fire and the flood
Through the fire and the flood, I have come

From the whirlwind came the words
From the whirlwind came the words
From the whirlwind came the words, for my songs

All our years become a tale
All our years become a tale
All our years become a tale, that is told

When my days have been consumed
When my days have been consumed
When my days have been consumed, like smoke

I will lay me down to sleep
I will lay me down to sleep
I will lay me down to sleep, in peace

Over fields of harmony
Over fields of harmony
Over fields of harmony, I will fly…

SOMEBODY ELSE'S EYE *Pete Seeger, Lorre Wyatt*

The sun was slowly sinking down, like an eyelid about to close
And weary I lay down to rest, and as I begun to doze
It suddenly occurred to me, like the sunset in the sky
I wonder if we're just a dream in somebody else's eye

Is someone dreaming of a world of rubies and rhapsodies?
Where eagles court the mountain peaks and whales serenade the seas
Where greens of field and forest dance with blues of lake and sky
I wonder how these wonders look to somebody else's eye

So what explains the harm we've done to water and air and land
We held the garden in our grip, and let it slip out of hand
I wonder if we'll change our tune, now that it's do or die
I wonder how the dream turns out, in somebody else's eye

JEFF HAYNES *Before I had moved to Beacon, New York, I only knew of Pete from his songs. One of my favorite bands in the world, Earth, Wind & Fire, did a cover of 'Where Have All The Flowers Gone.' But after we moved, my wife was walking on Main Street, and she recognized Pete and went over and told Pete all about me. That evening, Pete called, and we spoke for about an hour.*

Then I was in the elementary school, and one of the teachers, Susan Wright, asked me to come downstairs and meet Pete, so I grabbed a drum and went downstairs, and that was our first meeting. We played for the children and had a really good time.

Pete asked if he could come over to my house to talk, and we spoke for about two hours. After that, he and I played in the schools a couple of times. Then David Bernz came to me and asked if I could record Pete with a group of kids, and we decided to do it in my home studio, and we put out the CD Tomorrow's Children.

Pete would come over and tell me some of the most amazing stories, and finally it dawned on me to turn the microphones on. Later, when he wasn't coming out of the house because Toshi was ill, I bought a really cool field recorder called a ZOOM, and I would go up to the house and Pete's daughter, Tinya Seeger, would say, 'You want to record Daddy, don't you? Let me try and get everybody out of the house so you can do that.'

I decided to incorporate music with Pete's stories, and we finally put out two audiobooks called The Storm King. David Bernz and I also produced another CD of Pete with Lorre Wyatt. So, I spent several years recording and producing with Pete.

Pete never thought of himself as some kind of superstar. He was a very humanistic person. He didn't want people to get all over him and praise him. He just was Pete. And he just loved his community. He always wanted to involve people with music, and whenever we played, he wanted people to sing. His character was so warm, and he and Toshi always used to tell me that 'the folk process is forever evolving.' I'm just really honored to have met him, and that he shared his time and trusted in me to tell me all those beautiful stories and to just be my friend and teach me a lot about music.

STEVE EARLE *I don't really remember ever not knowing who Pete Seeger was. By the time Pete was on the Smothers Brothers show, which was the first post-blacklisting appearance, I put things together. The Vietnam War was raging, and I started realizing that Pete wasn't just a performer—he was somebody who had paid a lot for what he believed in.*

I started playing coffeehouses when I was fourteen, and I had to do a lot of backtracking, a lot of forensics. I am a folksinger, and the history of where songs come from is important to me. I started understanding who Pete was by backtracking from The Byrds and Bob Dylan.

I didn't meet Pete until the Appleseed compilations were put together. I was asked to sing on 'Walking Down Death Row,' because that's been an important issue for me. Something kind of started then, that Pete remembered who I was when I was around.

I presented Pete with this lifetime union card. I guess they decided that at age ninety-two he didn't have to pay any dues anymore, so I went to the American Federation of Musicians Gala and presented Pete with his lifetime card.

The last time I remember talking to Pete was when we performed together at Odetta's memorial, on the finale. The plan was to sing 'This Little Light Of Mine,' and we'd all just walk off the front of the stage and go down the center at Riverside Church and walk down through the audience and exit at the back of the church. When it came time to do that, everybody else sort of bailed out, and Pete and I were the only two that went down the aisle finishing the song.

I had sung 'Deportee' earlier that night, and when we got to the back of the church Pete started telling me about the song, and as he told me that story I thought, This is folk process that I'm getting, directly from Pete Seeger, and it was a very big deal for me.

Pete had this ability to just be the conscience of us, the way I believe artists should be. And he did it completely naturally, and it never occurred to him to be anything else. There was no calculation, no guile to it. He just came that way. It's a pretty good example for the people who came afterwards.

CHAPTER 14 A FEW DIVERSIONS

Musicians like Pete Seeger and Woody Guthrie had little patience for the rigidity of some Communist Party members way back in the 1940s. There could be endless debate among stalwart members over minute points of theory or policy, and a person could be 'in' one day and 'out' the next just because of some arcane position or statement. There's a story about one particular meeting where someone criticized another person by saying 'he's a diversionist' and Woody stood up and said, 'Doesn't everybody need a little diversion now and then?'

So, in this section, we make a small diversion from the plot, just a few things that should be included to set the record straight.

BOB DYLAN AND THE AXE

In the annals of folk music, few legends have taken on such epic proportions as that of Pete Seeger at the 1965 Newport Folk Festival running around with an axe trying to cut the sound cords on the newly 'gone electric' Bob Dylan. It does make for good theater: an aging Seeger taking on the new folk royalty, brandishing a quintessential woodsman's tool, desperately trying to stem the tide of modernism from taking over his idiom—acoustic vs. electric, folk vs. rock, past vs. present. Gosh, it would make a great movie!

The only problem is, Pete was never really a traditionalist. Pete always experimented and innovated and massaged his music for the multitudes. Early on, The Weavers were criticized for their smoothed-out adaptations of older songs, but that is how they were able to spread folk music to millions on the radio. Even as a soloist, Pete often chose tunings that were easier on the hand and milder on the urban ear than his younger brother Mike, who was a true traditionalist. And Pete had nothing in particular against the electric guitar. In fact, he once opined that 'the electric guitar is the folk instrument of the twentieth century.'

So, what did happen that fateful day on July 25, 1965? I asked Pete about it once, and he told me. The answer was fairly simple: he wanted his father, Charles, to hear the words.

Pete had already worked with Dylan, had gone south with him in the civil rights movement, and had come to respect his artistry and poetry. Now, in the summer of 1965, he brought his musicologist father, Charles Seeger, to hear this great young man at the Newport Folk Festival. Charles was hard of hearing by then—a trait that Pete would also suffer from later on. When Bob came out with a cadre of electric musicians, the electric guitars covered up the words. That may not have mattered to the young ears in the crowd, but for middle-aged Pete and his elderly father, trying to discern Dylan's masterful lyrics above the loud distorted guitars was probably torturous. They were playing 'Maggie's Farm,' Pete said, 'and it's a good song, but we couldn't hear the words.' So Pete made his way to the soundman and told him that the guitars were too loud. Probably with a bit of youthful attitude, the man replied, 'They want it that way!' Frustrated, Pete replied, 'Well, if I had an axe, I'd cut those wires.' And then he walked away.

And that's about it. No epic battle, no madman gallivanting around with an axe. But legends once born take on a life of their own. And although some historians choose to seize on this moment as the end of the folk boom and the start of the rock era, nothing of the sort really happened. Rock started well before Newport, and folk continued well after. And although Dylan branched out and away from folk music, Pete maintained a respect for him throughout his life.

In the 1990s, Pete formed a short-lived organization called The New York City Street Singers. It was an attempt to create a rainbow chorus of choruses. The idea was to have members from different choruses from different cultures throughout the city come together to learn each other's songs and to sing them together in parades. Had it succeeded, it would have been an enduring example of diversity and acceptance. Unfortunately, the makeup of the volunteers didn't match the diversity of the choruses, so the wrong image was being projected.

Some of the choruses were also apprehensive about losing their members to the combined group. But, for a while, The Street Singers managed to hold several successful events, including a large concert in Damrosch Park.

The reason for mentioning it here is that sound travels relatively slowly. In order for singers in a parade to stay in sync with each other, Pete needed many sets of radios and headphone receivers; that way, the song leaders at the front and back of the parade could hear each other in real time. This idea never really worked. New York's cavernous streets and metal structures wreaked havoc with radio reception, and a cacophony usually resulted. But, when the word first went out that Pete needed money for radios and receivers, some of us heard that Bob Dylan, without hesitation, wrote Pete a check for ten thousand dollars. I can't prove it, but I'd like to believe this is true.

HOW TO GET EDITED OUT OF A MOVIE

When The Weavers broke up in 1964, I was only five years old and had never gotten to hear them sing. But in the spring of 1980, The Weavers held a reunion picnic at Lee Hays' home in Croton-on-Hudson, New York, and it had gone so well that they decided to return to Carnegie Hall that November for two nights. This would be their final reunion, and both concerts sold out in less than twenty-four hours. I attended the first night as an audience member and the second as part of Lee's entourage of helpers.

Both the picnic and the Carnegie shows were being filmed for a documentary, and one thing that stood out was a plethora of film crew, cameras, lighting, and boom mics. Before the show, during the concert, and especially at the after-party, they seemed to be just about everywhere, following people around and getting right in their faces as they were conversing. I know these were necessary, but to my twenty-two-year-old self and the rest of us helpers, they seemed downright obnoxious, so, when we saw them coming, we just ducked and went the other way. The inevitable result is that I am not in any of the footage that made it into the movie The Weavers: Wasn't That A Time, although my brother Jon is in there for a few seconds, pushing Lee's wheelchair.

Roll ahead thirty years, give or take, and another film is being made, Pete Seeger: The Power Of Song, and the director sends me an early edit for comment. I told him, 'This film is great, but make sure it has a great arc to the story, like the earlier film.'

He says, 'Well, what do you think the arc should be?'

I told him it should be about a singer who doesn't want to be commercial but does want to be heard, and that this requires him to interact in one way or another with mass distribution. But every time he interacts with the music business, he gets pushed back: The Almanacs get a radio spot during the war, but the next day the newspaper accuses them of being disloyal and they lose their job; The Weavers become the most popular singing group in the country, but then they're blacklisted; Pete gets a recording contract with Columbia Records, but it's during the Vietnam era, and he hears that many of his records are being kept at the warehouse; he appears on the *Smothers Brothers* show, but then the show gets canceled ... but the singer refuses to give up. He sings at every school, church, summer camp, and gathering that he can, day in and day out, year after year, and when you look back on it, you realize that he has been *heard* far more than most any commercial performer—that Pete Seeger is the reason songs like 'If I Had A Hammer' and 'This Land Is Your Land' are on the lips of almost every school child in this country.

The filmmaker and I both looked at each other with a sense of excitement, as if to say, 'Yes, this is the story!'

A short while later, I received a call from Pete's grandson, Kitama Jackson Seeger, who was assisting on the film. He says, 'I want you to know that you were in the movie until the final cut. We had you and Pete singing together in Peekskill but at the last minute, we substituted footage of Pete singing This Land Is Your Land with school kids.'

Some of my friends have occasionally wondered why they don't see me in these films, and I tell them that I seem to have found a way to edit myself out of both of them. The other thing these two great films have in common is that they were both made and directed by my longtime friend, neighbor, and former guitar teacher, Jim Brown, who became a highly acclaimed documentary filmmaker concentrating mainly in the field of folk music and the musicians who create it.

JIM BROWN *The first time I met Pete Seeger, I was about fourteen. I was in a little jug band playing at some left-wing cause and Pete happened to be there. We had amplifiers and Pete had to use our equipment, so in a way, we were on the same bill.*

When I was about fifteen or sixteen, Lee Hays moved to Croton, and he heard us play at a little park on Mount Airy and invited us over. I was working at the time as a gardener, so I became Lee's gardener and his good friend, and that friendship lasted until he died.

Pete was probably his most favorite guest. I remember that when Pete would come, Lee would have me get a lot of vanilla and strawberry ice cream, which were Pete's favorite things, at least in Lee's mind.

A few years later, I was going to school learning to make documentaries, and we had a little show on the 51st State which dealt with some of the very first environmental actions in the Hudson River Valley, and Pete was part of that with the Clearwater. We were also working for the Hudson River Fisherman's Association. Pete and Toshi really got behind us and were champions of what we were doing.

A couple of years later, it seemed that Lee, who had always wanted to write an autobiography, was not going to finish. He and I began to talk about making a documentary film that eventually became The Weavers: Wasn't That A Time? It was somewhat successful, and increasingly after that, I would work with Pete and his manager Harold Leventhal on numerous film projects, and I enjoyed working with Pete immensely.

Pete Seeger: The Power Of Song was something that Harold Leventhal and I talked about from around 1990 on. I had it funded a number of times, but Pete did not like celebrity status and would usually pull out in the end. But when Bush got elected, I was interviewing Pete about Peter, Paul & Mary, and at the end of the interview, I drove him home, and he said, 'I think we should do that film now.'

Pete was one of the most important voices of the twentieth century. He put the earth first, and humanity as a whole before individual wants and needs. He thought that what we did together—not for profit, but to make things better— were some of the most important things we could do. He was the real deal, and he really walked the walk and talked the talk. What made his voice unusual was that he didn't listen to commercial messages that we get bombarded by. Pete rarely listened to the radio or television. He read voraciously. He was very, very smart, and he formed opinions about some of the bigger issues that we face in the world, especially environmental issues. And I think he understood the earth as it holds together, not just the people but the ecosystems and the animals and the sea and the air, and how beautiful and fragile that was. And it was wonderful that he devoted so much great energy inspiring people to really get involved. If there's going to be an end to global warming and a salvation to the problems that we're facing, I think Pete Seeger was the inspiration for some of the solutions.

BRUCE SPRINGSTEEN

The relationship between Pete Seeger and Bruce Springsteen was one of mutual respect—mostly from afar. Bruce is a musical descendant of Woody Guthrie, but over time he became more interested in Pete as well. It probably stemmed from around 1998, when Jim Musselman tapped him to record 'We Shall Overcome' for the Appleseed Recordings CD *Where Have All The Flowers Gone: The Songs Of Pete Seeger, Vol. 1*. It culminated in January 2009 at that magical and very vindicating moment when Pete and Bruce appeared together onstage in Washington DC to sing 'This Land Is Your Land' at the inauguration celebration for Barak Obama, and the entire nation got to witness the once blacklisted performer come home.

I don't intend to chronicle their entire relationship here but to focus on one aspect that says a lot about the integrity of these two strong individuals. The year was 2006, and Springsteen was preparing to release his album *The Seeger Sessions* and go on tour with a big batch of acoustic musicians. In April of that year, Bruce's representatives sent Pete a letter outlining their intentions and offering a license fee for the use of his name. It's not appropriate to disclose the exact figure, but it was a significant sum. Pete always resisted commercializing his name, so he crossed out the amount and sent the letter back with a hand-written 'one dollar.' But Bruce refused to use Pete's name without paying for it.

What followed was a bizarre set of reverse negotiations between Pete and Bruce, one insisting on making payment and the other trying to avoid being paid. Even the lawyers were bemused. I think they eventually settled on having the money put into an escrow account that would be used to support worthy causes.

Toshi had the job of worrying about family finances, but she was proud of what Pete had done and showed me the correspondence. Much of it is confidential and cannot be included here, but I will share most of the contents of one letter Pete wrote to Bruce and his manager that consists mostly of things Pete often said in public. In its scattered and wandering way, it offers great insight into Pete's thinking:

September 14, 2006

Dear Bruce and John,

I write you both because this letter is about finances. I never wanted to be rich, nor be in debt. A few years ago, I was shocked to find that because a few songs of mine had become famous (thanks to PP&M, The Byrds, and others) and because the land we bought fifty-seven years ago for $100 an acre is now worth $100,000 an acre, I am rich, and I really don't know what to do about it. One solution is to give away royalties; as you know, all the royalties from 'We Shall Overcome' go to the We Shall Overcome Fund in Tennessee, and every year Bernice Reagon and the committee give away thousands of dollars for black music in the south. That's where I've told my publisher Michael Smith to send all the royalties for 'We Are Climbing Jacob's Ladder.' I'm deeply proud of the last line: 'brothers...sisters...all.' It was my best songwriting of the year 1973. However, the original PD song was of course one of the truly great nineteenth-century spirituals.

I'm told that in the early days, PD songs were published without any claim for 'adaption and arrangement' but then ASCAP allowed performers to claim ten percent, and in 1940 BMI started and allowed performers to claim one hundred percent and it's been that way ever since. First I knew of it was the mid-sixties. I was at the house of George and Joyce Wein for a committee meeting of the Newport Folk Festival. A phone call came for me from a secretary at Columbia Records: 'Mr. Seeger, I have to know the copyright status of the songs on your new record.'

I gave her the name of the famous old British ballad, 'Barbara Allen,' and I said, 'That's Public Domain.'

'Oh, thank you,' says she with surprise in her voice.

When George Wein asked about the call and I told him, he said, 'Pete, I think you're wrong. Columbia Records didn't write Barbara Allen. You gave them the money as though they did.'

A few years ago, with the late Harold Leventhal and Larry Richmond (TRO) I started The Campaign For Public Domain Reform proposing that when some ancient melody gets new words put to it and it starts bringing in a lot of money, some percentage, five percent? Ninety-five percent? of it should go to the place where the song originated. We rewrote the contract on the children's story Abiyoyo (I put the story together in 1952 but the ancient lullaby was from the Xhosa people in the S.E. corner of South Africa, between Fort Elizabeth and Durban. Mandela is a Xhosa). Last year, $15,000 went to the Ubuntu Fund there for libraries and scholarships.

Two years ago in Westchester County, we had a conference on the idea, but nothing came of it at the time. If my brain does not go too far, after I get this revised version of my songbook out, I hope we can have a second and more productive conference on the subject. I'll let you know if and when.

Bruce, you are truly such an extraordinary singer that it is a great honor you wanted to sing some of these old songs that I recorded years ago. And it was great to hear your new record with two extra songs on it: 'How Can I Keep From Singing' and 'Bring 'Em Home.' You might like to know how I learned the first: Toshi's mother was from old Virginny and had a friend Doris Plenn from North Carolina. But at Christmas in 1955 I remember, by a fireplace, Doris sang me 'How Can I Keep From Singing' and said it was her grandmother's favorite song and her grandmother was against slavery (not easy in North Carolina in 1850). I wrote it down when she sang it to me and printed it in *Sing Out* a year or two later (see enclosed). But I didn't know that Doris made up the third verse back in those McCarthyite days. When Enya recorded it in Ireland eight or ten years ago (the record sold six million!) the British publisher would not give Doris a cent. Doris was quite old then and could have used the money.

I confess that in my conservative old age I wish you had used the original melody.

Oh, a surprising new discovery: Doris didn't know that Anne Warner, who wrote the song in the 1850s, lived all her life with her sister Susan in a little wooden farmhouse on an island in the Hudson across from West Point, only six miles south of my house. The house is kept in repair by a local committee and open to visitors. Susan Warner wrote romantic Christian novels; Anne wrote a famous hymn, 'Yes, Jesus Loves Me,' and didn't die till 1913.

Back sixty-five years ago, both Woody Guthrie and I and probably a million more thought of ourselves as communists or 'fellow travelers.' I drifted out in '49, when we moved up here. Never really liked being a member of a secret organization. But my head was turned around by M.L.

King. And then further turned by reading *Silent Spring* by Rachel Carson. Now I try to persuade scientists that they have a dangerous religious belief: they think that an infinite increase in empirical information is a good thing. Can they prove it? Of course not. First things first: learn how to cure bullies and insane, power-hungry people first. Let's grow not in size but in generosity, in common sense, in ability to talk with people we disagree with. Then perhaps the human race will last longer.

Oh, I'll not burden you longer. You two keep on!

Old Pete

PS Love to your daughter, Bruce, the one who said, 'That sounds like fun.' Love to your family.

· · ·

When *The Seeger Sessions* came out, many of my musical friends lambasted it for having so much bass and drums and so forth. It was a fairly high-energy affair for a folk CD. But I felt differently because, underneath, Bruce had stayed true to the essence of the material. By having the songs clothed in the high-intensity style that his listeners were used to hearing, he succeeded in exposing an entire new generation to the American folk vernacular of, gospel, Irish, New Orleans, Dustbowl, work songs, canal songs, etc. I think Pete felt the same way. He may not have agreed with all of Bruce's choices, but he respected what he had done. At the time, Pete said:

He sent me a copy ten days ago. He is a wonderful singer. He does 'Old Dan Tucker,' I just knew as a banjo tune, but he's got horns and everything else on it. Dan Emmett who wrote this song in 1844 would be delighted, I think. I think I'll have to listen several times to the way he does 'Oh Mary Don't You Weep, Don't You Mourn.' That's usually in major. He speeds it up and does it in minor at the top of his lungs.' I wrote to Bruce and sent a letter to John. I said it's a great record and I was very proud to help inspire it.'

As for the license fee for using Pete's name, I don't know the specifics, but I heard some of it was used to fund Beacon's Calico Ball in the years before it became self-supporting. The Calico Ball is an annual school program run by the Bill and Livia Vanaver and the Vanaver Caravan Dance Company. As guest artists in the Beacon Schools, they teach the kids about the culture and dances of other countries. The finale is a large public performance at the fifteen-hundred-seat high school theater, where students from each grade perform their specific dance with music and colorful costumes from the country of origin. All the result of a standoff between two decent men.

• • •

I didn't reach Bruce Springsteen to get a comment for this book, but I was present in the room at Madison Square Garden, along with many others, when he spoke on the occasion of Pete's ninetieth birthday. Repeating some of his comments on that night should suffice:

> As Pete and I traveled to Washington for President Obama's inaugural celebration, he told me the entire story of 'We Shall Overcome.' How it moved from a labor movement song, and with Pete's inspiration had been adapted by the civil rights movement. And that day, as we sang 'This Land Is Your Land,' I looked at Pete. The first black president of the United States was seated to his right, and I thought of the incredible journey that Pete had taken. You know, my own growing up in the '60s in a town scarred by race rioting made that moment nearly unbelievable…
>
> At rehearsals the day before, I asked him, 'How do you want to approach This Land Is Your Land?' It was to be near the end of the show, and all he said was, 'Well I know I want to sing all the verses. I want to sing all the ones that Woody wrote, especially the two that get left out, about the private property and the relief office.' And I thought, *Of course, that's what Pete's done his whole life. He sings all the verses, all the time. Especially the ones that we'd like to leave out of our history as a people.*
>
> At some point, Pete Seeger decided he'd be a walking, singing, reminder of all of America's history. He'd be a living archive of America's music and conscience. A testament to the power of song and culture, to nudge history along. To push American events toward more humane and justified ends. He would have the audacity and the courage to sing in the voice of the people. And despite Pete's somewhat benign grandfatherly

appearance, he is a creature of stubborn, defiant, and nasty optimism. Inside him, he carries a steely toughness that belies that grandfatherly façade. And it won't let him take a step back from the things he believes in. At ninety, he remains a stealth dagger through the heart of our country's illusions about itself. (*Bruce Springsteen, May 9, 2009*)

JIM MUSSELMAN *I was in Syracuse Law School, and I came upon the case of Seeger vs. United States. I was totally enthralled because of what Pete had done standing up for the First Amendment during the McCarthy era. Pete felt as an American that it was important to stand up and say, 'I can sing in front of who I want to sing, and I can associate with whoever I want to associate with.'*

I had gone to work for Ralph Nader in Washington DC, and I started corresponding with Pete, and working with him on events for Nicaragua and for Chile. Then I became a member of the board of directors of Sing Out magazine and worked with Pete for a long time. Pete once said, 'Make sure your heroes are dead because that way they stay your heroes.'

I also got to see him and Toshi firsthand. Bruce Springsteen had the saying, 'One plus one equals three with relationships.' I saw that with Pete and Toshi because she supported him through everything he was doing.

When the Iraq War broke out, I called Pete up and said, 'We've got to come out and say this war is wrong.' We went to a studio in Woodstock and worked on about four or five songs together, and I was just amazed at how Pete at that age was willing to step up to the plate.

I started Appleseed Records after I was in Belfast, Northern Ireland. Tommy Sands had told me to spend a couple of days in Falls Road, where the Catholic and Protestant neighborhoods were, and to see the similarities between them. I saw these kids growing up in a war zone, and I thought, Ah, Pete Seeger! Let's use music to bring kids together! I came up with the idea to record 'Where Have All the Flowers Gone' with Protestant and Catholic children in Northern Ireland. When Pete listened to the recording, he got tears in his eyes.

But then I thought, Let's record Pete's songs and take them all over the world again. So the idea for Appleseed Records was to use music as a way to build bridges between people, which was Pete Seeger's life and how he had lived it. Harold Leventhal laughed and said, 'You'll never going to be able to pull it off,' and I said, 'They said I couldn't pull off getting airbags in cars.'

So, Appleseed started with the CD The Songs Of Pete Seeger. I got well-known artists to do versions of Pete's songs. It was probably the most comprehensive compilation of any singer with close to three hundred artists participating. Pete probably wrote me hundreds of letters, and the number one thing he wanted was Bob Dylan to be on it. Bruce Springsteen said no twice, and I went back a third time, and then Bruce did 'We Shall Overcome.' Jon Landau, who manages Bruce, actually grew up on Pete, so I think John twisted Bruce's arm.

It was a week before the deadline for the CD, so I sent Bruce about fifteen songs to take a shot at, and that's what later became The Seeger Sessions. Bruce had fun playing the songs and went out himself and bought some of Pete's records and immersed himself in the music, and then he took the songs all over the world. And having Bruce singing songs in front of thirty thousand people that Pete had recorded or brought to the attention of the world for the first time was just wonderful to see.

After 9/11, Tom Brokaw and NBC News did a video of Bruce doing 'We Shall Overcome' with the rescue workers. I played it for Pete, and he said, 'If all I was responsible for in my life was bringing that song to the world, I've had a good life.'

Pete was somebody who showed that one person can make a difference. He loved the concept of seeds, and the seeds that Pete planted all over the world led to major social change—and a heck of a lot of people singing and taking folk music into their own hands. I was just happy to bring Pete's songs to people again and keep the link in the chain alive. I was very proud to work with him and call him a friend.

'MBUBE,' ABYOYO, AND COPYRIGHT REFORM

In the year 2000, the South African journalist Rian Milan wrote an exposé for *Rolling Stone* magazine about how publishers in the United States had exploited the South African song 'Mbube,' also known as 'Wimoweh' or 'The Lion Sleeps Tonight,' making millions in profits without paying the original composer Solomon Linda, who was a black South African. Then, in 2002, the filmmaker Francois Verster released a documentary called *A Lion's Trail*, detailing much of the story. While Pete was generally supportive, he came to feel that he was being lumped in with the rest of the music business establishment, by those with an agenda, as being complicit in the theft.

A number of people are now seeing a movie called *A Lion's Trail*, about the song that The Weavers sang, calling it 'Wimoweh,' but which was originally recorded in South Africa under the name 'Mbube.' It means lion, and they were singing '*The lion is sleeping.*' But the *b* got softer and softer, so it really sounded like '*wimoweh*,' and that's how I taught it to The Weavers.

I heard the record because the Gallo Recording Company in Johannesburg was selling Decca records in South Africa and thought Decca up here might like to sell some of their records. In January 1949, they sent up about seven or eight 78rpm records to Decca. But Decca said, 'Oh, we can't market this kind of stuff.' Alan Lomax, the folklorist, just happened to be working at Decca at the time, and somehow he got them and says, 'Don't throw 'em away. I'd like to listen to these.' I was in bed with a head cold. Alan dropped by and said, 'Decca was going to throw these out, but you might like to listen to them.'

Well, I was fascinated. They were wonderful choral music. As you probably know, South Africa doesn't think a song is a song unless you have not two- or three-part harmony but more like four or five or six or eight parts going all at once.

This particular record, which as far as I could see had just one word in it, which I called '*wimoweh*,' started with the two basses singing, then two tenor voices came in, and then the higher tenors: '*wimoweh a-wimoweh, wimoweh a-wimoweh.*'

They sang about three or four measures, and then in came this wonderful falsetto: '*Eyyyyyy oooeyyyooo eyyyyyyooo…*'

No words. It was a kind of a lonesome falsetto. Then, after doing the falsetto, he just opened his mouth: 'Ahhhh…ahhhh…ahhhh…ahhhh… ahhhh…dah dah dah…'

In those days I could push my voice to get it. However, I lost my voice. Come to think of it, Solomon Linda, the man that first recorded it back in 1939, also lost his voice.

I think I made up the syllables '*Hey up boy, wimoweh, wimoweh,*' and I taught it to The Weavers that way.

In 1950, The Weavers had hits on the radio, recording with Gordon Jenkins and his big orchestra. We sang 'Tzena Tzena' at breakneck speed and it soared up to hit number one, and then some DJs turned it over and discovered 'Goodnight Irene.' We recorded Woody Guthrie's 'So Long It's Been Good To Know Yuh.' And then Decca Records was trying to push Terry Gilkerson and had him lead while we all sang 'On Top Of Old Smokey.' And, soon after, we recorded 'Wimoweh.'

The next year, Al Brackman, who worked for our publisher, Howie Richmond, said, 'Pete, where should we send the royalties for this song? Does it have a composer?'

And I said, 'Well, I guess the guy who wrote it, who recorded it, should probably get it.'

And Al said, 'Well, Gallo Records said we should send it to them. They say they paid him, and the money belongs to them.'

I said, 'Don't send it to Gallo. Solomon Linda will never get a penny.'

He said, 'Well get me the address of Solomon Linda and we'll send the money directly to him.'

Now, my big mistake was not finding out what he meant by *the money*. Eventually, Linda got a copyright for a song called 'Mbube,' but the big money was for a song called 'Wimoweh.' And this money went to The Weavers' manager and to The Weavers. When Toshi found this out, she sent our piece of the royalties to Africa, so Solomon Linda got twenty or twenty-five percent of what he should have gotten from the Weavers recording, and I think he got something for 'Mbube.'

You know how we found Linda? I had a friend who was married to a white South African woman, and I said, 'Do you think you could find a lawyer in Johannesburg who can locate Solomon Linda and get this money to him?' She put me in touch with a lawyer named Harry Bloom who'd been defending Africans in civil rights cases. It took him several months, but he finally found him. Solomon Linda had lost his voice—probably sang 'Wimoweh' too often without a mic. But Gallo, as a favor, had given him a job as a stock clerk for a pound a week or something like that, a very low pay. Just at that same time, a wonderful South African named James Phillips was organizing a union of South African artists to get better contracts from Gallo, and they had a big evening celebration, and the high point of the evening was presenting a check for several thousand dollars to Solomon Linda.

About seven or eight years later, a group called The Tokens had a record where they had added a few notes to the music and ten English words by George Weiss: '*In the jungle, the mighty jungle, the lion sleeps tonight.*' And Al says, 'Pete, we can probably stop them.'

I said, 'Those words are silly. They'll be forgotten.' Well, that shows how stupid I was. That became the big hit. And, of course, with the Disney show *The Lion King*, it made millions.

In 1991, the lawyer for The Tokens and George Weiss sued the Richmond publishers, and the judge agreed: 'Yes, you made up those ten words. If those ten words are used, you get the money. You should send ten percent to Africa, but ninety percent you can keep here.' And, since then, not much money has gone to Solomon Linda's family for 'Wimoweh,' although some has gone to them from the old Weavers record—six figures, I heard.

Now there's been a movie written, *A Lion's Trail*, and they don't give all this detail.

However, I got mad at George Weiss for taking all this money and not sending much to Soloman Linda, and then I realized I'd done the same thing with a little lullaby called 'Abyoyo.'

In 1952, I asked Dr. Alfaeus Hunton, 'Are there any South Africans in New York who can tell me what these songs mean?'

And he said, 'There's hardly anybody allowed out of South Africa, but it so happens that professor Z.K. Matthews is teaching at Union Theological Seminary, and maybe he or his wife can talk.'

Professor Matthews was too busy to see me, but Mrs. Matthews was very nice. And she said, 'Well I've heard your record of what you call Wimoweh, and of course you didn't get the words right, but you got the rhythm and the spirit of it.' She said, though, 'You should learn some of our older songs. The village songs are in danger of dying out in South Africa because people get jobs in the big city, and they leave their home and forget the singing of the old songs. But at the missionary college where my husband used to teach, a group of students put on a whole evening of village songs, and it was so well received that the college took the money to print up a book of South African folk songs with the help of one of the music teachers who wrote out each part. I brought two copies of this book to America. One, I gave to the Schomburg Center in Harlem, and the other I now give to you.'

I took the book and made some copies. I sent copies to the Library

Of Congress; I've given a copy to Bernice Reagon. I gave a copy to the Amendla Chorus in Western Massachusetts, which sings many South African songs.

The book had chapters. A chapter on warrior songs, very fierce songs. A chapter on wedding songs. Seems there's a wonderful custom there when a couple gets married. For twenty-four hours they have what they call a 'wedding competition.' Friends of the groom form a chorus and the friends of the bride form a chorus, and they swap songs all day and all night.

There were some initiation songs. That's when the young men are circumcised and then they have two months of prayers and tests that they must pass, and finally, in the last ceremony, they have a kind of white clay all over their body, and they go down to the river and they wash the clay off their bodies and they come back to the village and are given a new suit of clothes. Now they are Men with a capital *M*. And the whole village sings an initiation song.

One particular initiation song is from the Xhosa people who live in the southeastern part of South Africa, near Durban and Port Elizabeth. The song I'm talking about is 'Someguaza.' Nelson Mandela is a Xhosa, and they sang 'Someguaza' when he was circumcised. Incidentally, I found out later that most of the words are just vocables, but *'somaquaza'* means *'the master of the cutting.'* It's like a European round, except each part is singing something different.

In the same book was a chapter on lullabies. And there was a lullaby which went, *'Abyoyo, Abyoyo, Abyoyo, Abyoyo Abyoyo yo yo yo, yo yo yo …'* At the footnote, it says, 'This lullaby is part of a folk story about a monster who eats people up, and the parents get it dancing, and when it falls down in a fit, it is dispatched by the parents.'

In 1952 when I learned this song, my son was six years old and my older daughter was four years old. I had some work to do, so I thought I'd sing them a lullaby and put them to sleep. But they shouted me down, 'No! We don't want a lullaby. We want a story—a long one.' And, taking my cue from the footnote, I made up a story, just improvised it.

Well, I was going to sing at a children's camp, and so I tried singing it onstage with a microphone and dancing around the stage like Abyoyo did. I've been doing that song now for fifty-two years. It's come out in a book.

And I even made up a second story called 'Abyoyo Returns,' because Lee Hays said, 'It's not fair. You leave Abyoyo out in limbo there. Even monsters have rights.' And so Abyoyo returns, and it's a kind of environmental tale, and Paul Jacobs, who happens to be Dave Bernz's brother-in-law, helped me write it.

Now guess what? I'd collected royalties for 'Abyoyo' all these years and never sent any to Africa. So, I got to my publisher—this is a different publisher, Harold Leventhal, and his publishing company is Sanga Music—and I said, 'Let's find some non-profit place in South Africa to send money.'

First, I was going to send it to Joseph Shabalala's music school. But Joseph Shabalala is Zulu, and the Zulu and the Xhosas are big competitors. So now we've found an organization called Ubuntu, and they're raising money for the education of young children of the Xhosa people. Right now, they're raising money for a library. Later on, it'll be scholarships and so on. And we're already sending them a check for fourteen thousand dollars.

I'm going to get their advice, too, because I want to make up new words to 'Somaguaza,' but my grandson said, 'You've no right, some rich American putting English words to their sacred old initiation song.' But, for example, I had some words. One I call 'The Political Argument': '*Hold fast, don't alter the system.*'

And the second part: '*No, the system has got to go, all the way.*'

And the third part: '*If we change it a bit, perhaps we can live, with the system.*'

You see, '*the system*' is what everybody sings at the same time.

Another was called 'The Family Argument': '*Sometimes, you should listen to Mama.*'

This could be an alto voice that's singing. And then the higher voice: '*She's my mama but sometimes she's wrong, very wrong.*'

And the third part: '*She may be right, she may be wrong, but she's your mama.*'

But then I thought of one that they might not think is disrespectful to their ancient tradition. My grandson is still doubtful. He said, 'Don't make up any new words to that old tune unless you literally have in writing permission from representatives of the Xhosa people saying they would be proud if you sing it.'

I have a birthday song: '*We're here, we're here for someone's birthday.*'
And the higher part: '*For someone's birthday, all of us are here, we are here.*'
And the third part: '*We can sing this song, for someone's birthday.*'
And instead of '*someone's birthday,*' it could be '*Mary's birthday*' or '*Johnny's birthday.*'

I have friends in the People's Music Network like Sol Weber, who loves rounds. He's putting out the book *Rounds Galore*. And Joanne Hammel, who is a great songwriter and a round writer, thinks that we can make up one of these African cyclical songs. Many South African songs in that songbook are, as I say, cyclical songs—a very short song that is repeated over and over and over, like a round, not for two or three minutes but often five or ten minutes or twenty minutes or a half an hour, especially if people are improvising new parts. People who love to harmonize will add parts, high parts, low parts, in-between parts. And who knows, the folk process goes on.

But anyway, we're hoping that Harold Leventhal of Sanga Music and Larry Richmond of the Richmond Organization, who run several different publishing companies—they're hoping that we can start the tradition of sending at least some of the money back to where the original song came from. It might be India or China or Indonesia or anywhere. If there's a beautiful old song, it's technically in the public domain, which means it's up for grabs, and anybody who wants to can change it a little bit and copyright it, saying 'new words and adaptation by so and so,' can collect royalties if the record sells, or if a book sells, or whatever. But we think it should be tradition now, it doesn't even need to be written out in the law, but it would be understood, that some of the money goes back to where the original words came from, or where the original tune came from.

Now, of course, I'm opening a can of worms. There's Christian songs all over the world that have taken their lyrics right out of the four-thousand-year-old bible at various times. And there are many bibles. There's the original Hebrew. You have the translations. You have the Apocrypha, as they say, and Doubting Thomas had his version.

What about the song 'Turn, Turn, Turn'? Should I send some money to London or Oxford, where the King James version was put together, or should I send it to Palestine, where the original words were made up in the year 252 BCE? I checked that date with Julius Lester. They're sure because the style of rhyming in that part of Ecclesiastes was not written by Solomon nor David, but by a man called Koheleth who came through at that time. That was his Hebrew name, meaning 'convoker'—someone who brings people together to talk to them. And I sing this song more than almost any other song in this day and age in the twenty-first century because it's got a very basic truth: what's right at one time could be wrong at another time. What's wrong at one time could be right at another.

Anyway, I'll quit my talking. This has been talking more than I was supposed to. Dave just wanted to know the history of 'Wimoweh,' and I think I told you all that I knew. People interviewed me, but I was very sorry that the movie *A Lion's Trail* by Francois Verster was not a very complete movie. It could have been much better, with humor in it as well as tragedy.

For example, an Englishman from South Africa came to New York about a year after 'Wimoweh' was a hit, and he was hoping he could persuade Decca to issue more South African songs. And I met him, and I said, 'What does *mbube* mean?'

And he said, 'It means *lion*, and what you call *wimoweh* is *mbube*, and it means *the lion is sleeping*.'

I said, 'Do the Africans ever try and put political meanings in their songs?'

He says, 'Oh, they try it all the time, but we weed it out.'

Well, he missed this one, because 'Chaka The Lion' was a great military chief in in about the 1830s. I found out later when I met some South Africans that Solomon Linda, in the very beginning of the recording, sings a short melody, and he was singing, '*You are a lion, but you are sleeping. The spirit of Chaka is in you, but it is sleeping.*' Isn't that great? So, it was a very political song, this great hit song, which Gallo Records just thought was nice music.

Harry Bloom, when he finally found Solomon Linda, had met Hugh Masekela and other musicians. He said, 'You know, I got an idea for an opera, I've got the libretto. Would you like to do the music for it?' It was the biggest hit show in Johannesburg of the twentieth century. It showed for two solid years. And the show then toured in Europe. I saw it in Liverpool. It's a great show, and it was called *King Kong*, about a prizefighter. The music was a variety of South African songs, and Hugh Masekela and some others arranged them, and the female lead was a hitherto unknown young woman, Miriam Makeba. Miriam thought, and she may be right, that 'Mbube' was a very, very old song, and all that Solomon Linda did was make up his version of it, and maybe add that little falsetto part.

I'm told that when he recorded it in 1939, he had not intended to record it, but they'd recorded some six songs that they were supposed to, and the engineer says, 'We have time for another song. Got anything you want to record?' And they put their heads together and decide to record 'Mbube,' and that became the big hit of 1939.

Editor's note: Solomon Linda & The Evening Birds were a popular South African singing group in the 1930s and 1940s, disbanding in 1948. Some say that Linda spent some time as a youth working as a shepherd, guarding sheep from lions, among other things. So, it is possible that 'Mbube' started out as an old shepherd song. Through the years, the song came to occupy an increasingly important place in South African culture in the fight against the unjust system of apartheid. During that struggle, protest songs were sometimes referred to as 'Mbube music.'

In 2004, Solomon's daughters sued Disney for their rightful share of royalties. Their lawyer found an arcane statute still on the books that permitted the court to freeze Disney's assets in the British Empire while the suit was being decided. Subsequent negotiations resulted in a settlement that finally brought significant royalty payments to the Linda family.

GREENWICH VILLAGE AND WASHINGTON SQUARE

In the lexicon of American folk music history, the little area of New York's Greenwich Village takes on mythical proportions. And deservedly so. Many who hearken back to the golden era of the American folk revival conjure up images of 'The Village'—its quaint three-story buildings, the myriad of cafes, and especially the weekly jams beside the big arch in Washington Square Park. One might wonder whether Pete was part of all that, and the answer is yes, but not as much or as consistently as one might imagine. But, like so many things in Pete's life, he was there at the start, or at least near the start.

Any discussion of the Washington Square Park folk scene should rightfully begin with the name George Margolin. Who was George Margolin? Most people wouldn't know. He was never famous, and as far as we know he was never recorded. Folk singing wasn't even his main avocation. But I will tell you what little I know.

George was a friend of my mother, Ruth, so once or twice while I was growing up, George and his wife, Matte, came up to the house in Croton for a visit and a meal. I remember George once strumming a few chords on the guitar, but his hands seemed stiff with age.

One day in my early teens, my mother said, 'Come with me, we have to go down to New York and visit George.' By then, Matte had passed away, and George was ill with bone cancer, puttering around a three-story walk-up near West 10th Street. On the drive down, my mother told me how she and George would go to Washington Square Park to sing at the arch and then go to back his apartment for some hot chocolate. At some point in the conversation, she said, 'George started all of that.' At the time, I really didn't understand the importance of what she was saying.

George's apartment was dim and packed with a lifetime's worth of books and papers and art and pottery and just plain stuff. George moved slowly and deliberately, handing things to my mother, and I realized George was giving things away knowing that he would not be around for very long.

This was the first of several trips down to George's, during which my mother accumulated many gifts. The trips became almost routine—the drive down the Saw Mill Parkway, wending through the city streets, parking in the old garage on West 10th Street that looked out on a club called Your Father's Mustache, and then the trek up the stairs to the crowded little apartment. And then there were no more trips.

Many years later, my friend John Van Valkenburg invited me to a music party in Pound Ridge, New York. He said there would be a lot of good players there, including the banjo player Roger Sprung. In the course of our conversation, he said that Roger had started the jams in Washington Square Park, and I immediately thought of my mother and her story.

It was a good party, as promised, and I did get to play with Roger. During a break, I said to him, 'So, I hear you started the jams in Washington Square.' Roger replied, 'Almost. But there was this one guy who came before me... er, ah, George Margolin!'

In the following years, I have looked up George's name and found some books on folk music history that mention him. There are not a lot of specifics, but the basic story is that sometime around 1947, a little-known printer and painter named George Margolin began bringing his guitar every Sunday to the arch in Washington Square, singing folk songs and labor songs, and crowds gathered. Soon, George Sprung was attending, and he brought his brother Roger, who became a regular. By 1948, the gatherings caught the attention of Pete Seeger and the others at the *People's Songs Bulletin*, and by 1950 they were getting so crowded that Toshi Seeger had to run and get a permit. None of these history books contain a picture of George Margolin, but my mother had some, so I have included one in this book for posterity.

So, yes, Pete was at Washington Square near the beginning. And it's good to acknowledge that the tradition of singing in front of the arch started well before the time for which it is mostly known in the 1960s.

Pete actually lived in the Village off and on during his younger years. He played some of the clubs there and recorded more than one record at the Village Gate. The Weavers started their career with a six-month stay at the Village Vanguard. So, Pete's relationship with Greenwich Village was vibrant. But by the 1960s, Pete's concert schedule and the myriad of causes he was singing for did not permit him to be a regular at Washington Square. By then, the weekly jams—and, in fact, the Village itself—were being populated by a new generation of folksingers. People like Peter, Paul & Mary, Happy and Artie Traum, Barbara Dane, Joan Baez, Bob Dylan, Dave Van Ronk, John Cohen, Richie Havens, Phil Ochs, and a host of others, both amateur and professional, were filling the ranks of a burgeoning folk revival. And many who attended these newly energized gatherings had been inspired to sing by Pete Seeger's visit to their college or summer camp. The wonderful irony is that the blacklist had forced Pete to play these non-traditional venues, which in turn inspired a whole new generation of political singers who marched on Washington, sang us out of the Vietnam War, and took over college campuses around the country—and yes, came every Sunday to a marble arch in Washington Square.

Pete went on to inspire at least two additional generations of young people, including one particular group of very young singers right in his hometown of Beacon, New York…

CHAPTER 15 SOME GOINGS ON

SO OUR VOICES CAN BE HEARD: THE RIVERTOWN KIDS

Pete's work with young people came to an unexpected culmination in 2009, when he recorded the album *Tomorrow's Children—Pete Seeger With The Rivertown Kids & Friends*. Pete's comments on the Rivertown Kids are among his shortest in this book, but they deserve perhaps the longest introduction.

In 2007, the Hudson River Sloop Clearwater organization hired educator/singer Dan Einbender as 'Tideline Education Coordinator' to conduct environmental programs in the Mid-Hudson area. Dan offered his services to the elementary schools in Beacon, New York, and a teacher named Tery Udell responded.

Dan took Ms. Udell's class to the riverfront for programs that involved fishing with nets and examining river water under a microscope. But Dan infused each program with river songs, and it turned out the kids really loved to sing. Ms. Udell realized that something special was happening, so she invited Dan to her classroom. Dan came several times, and soon the kids were singing and writing songs about whatever they were studying. Their repertoire included several songs written by Pete Seeger, so it was only natural that Dan invited Pete to hear them.

That winter, Pete asked the children to join him at the Springfield Baptist Church for their Martin Luther King Day celebration. The Saturday before the event, the kids and their parents gathered at the Beacon Sloop Club to rehearse, and it turned out to be a vintage morning of Pete teaching songs and telling stories. Before long, Pete and Dan were inviting the kids to sing at other events including the Clearwater Spring Splash, the Clearwater Revival, and the inauguration of Steve Gold as mayor of Beacon, and Dan began inviting other musicians such as former *Clearwater* captain Travis Jeffrey and myself to help with the accompaniment.

By the end of the school year, Ms. Udell had incorporated music into many subject areas, including history, poetry, and environmental studies. She dubbed it 'The Rivertown Curriculum,' and each morning, she began class by having the kids sing a song of their own choosing. The children became highly motivated and began learning new songs on their own time and singing in the halls. The kids also became active in their community: they started a recycling program at school, marked local sewers as outflows into the Hudson, and collected food for the local food pantry. They developed a strong sense of identity and began calling themselves 'The Kids From Room 12.'

In September 2008, the new crop of fourth graders arrived expecting to sing. They turned out to be crack learners and were soon singing with Pete and Dan at festivals and events including the 400th Anniversary Hudson River Flotilla, the Beacon Strawberry Festival, and even on the Main Stage at the 2009 Clearwater Revival.

After releasing *Pete Seeger At 89*, Pete lamented that the songs 'Take It From Dr. King' and 'English Is Crazy' had not been included, so he decided to record them with the kids. These recording sessions took place at Jeff Haynes's studio, and the project evolved into recording an entire album with the kids and adult guests.

These events were not without controversy. Pete Seeger remained a lightning rod in America's political storms. Not all parents and school personnel approved of Ms. Udell's new 'curriculum.' Some teachers complained of the noise from the kids singing in the halls. Others complained that Pete's music was 'anti-white.' In the midst of two wars in the Middle East, some parents objected to the words of Pete's song 'Rainbow Race':

Some want to take the easy way
Poison, bombs, they think we need 'em
Don't you know you can't kill all the unbelievers
There's no shortcut to freedom.

One set of parents actually forbade their child to sing if Pete was present. To avoid further controversy, rehearsals for the album were moved to another location after school, and, in response to the complaints, the superintendent imposed new rules forbidding singing in the halls and requiring singing in classrooms to be directly related to the official New York State curriculum. In response to this perceived censorship, the kids wrote one of their best songs:

WE SING OUT (SO OUR VOICES CAN BE HEARD) *The Rivertown Kids*

Well, you're only kids, they say, and you'll run the world someday
In the meantime just relax, don't say a word
We can't vote, but don't you see we can speak out musically
We sing out so our voices can be heard

Chorus:
We sing out so our voices can be heard, can be heard
We sing loud so our voices will be heard

Cars and factories everywhere, fossil fuels pollute the air
And it's making our Earth warmer every day
With the water, wind, and sun, green energy for everyone
And we don't have a moment to delay

And every time it rains, all the waste goes down storm drains
But you know it doesn't really go away
We put trash and gasoline, into rivers, lakes, and streams
And it shouldn't always have to be that way

A factory farm's an unhealthy place, animal cruelty's a disgrace
And you know they use up too much energy
Family farms are the way to go, their food is fresher, this we know
And the money stays in our community

We can help the sick and poor, the world's people deserve more
We sing out for justice and equality

We'll give voices to the meek, help all others hear them speak
And the earth will be the best that it can be

By the end of the 2008–09 school year, Superintendent Ayefsky began to embrace The Kids From Room 12. A watershed moment may have occurred in May 2009, when someone gave her tickets and backstage passes to Pete's ninetieth birthday celebration at Madison Square Garden, where she was able to witness firsthand the love and support Pete received from the musical community. When the next school year began, Ms. Ayefsky requested that each school chorus learn a different Seeger song to perform on Main Street at the Spirit of Beacon Day celebration. The school's music teacher, Susan Wright, also came to value the contribution these children were making to the community, writing an article about them for the summer issue of *Sing Out* magazine.

But one final controversy erupted when Pete and the kids scheduled their album release at the 2010 Clearwater Revival. Clearwater had recently moved their offices to the University Settlement Camp property in Beacon and wanted to remain on good terms with a broad segment of the community. The director at the time, Jeff Rumph, was aware of the divisions, and he became concerned that a group calling itself the Kids From Room 12 would be perceived as being officially endorsed by the entire school district—and, by extension, all the parents.

Shortly before the festival, Will Solomon, one of the festival coordinators, had the unpleasant task of calling Dan and me to let us know that if we used that name, the appearance at the festival would be canceled. Fortunately, Dan had another name in his pocket that he knew would be acceptable to the kids. Just a few phone calls and emails later, the set at the Revival, and the album cover, had been changed to Pete Seeger & The Rivertown Kids.

At the festival that June, over a thousand people crammed around the little Family Stage to see Pete and the Rivertown Kids release their album, with some of the adults who had participated in the recording appearing as special guests. Some said it was the highlight of the festival.

As for Pete's short statement, when asked to say something to sum up his involvement with the Rivertown Kids, he simply said:

The future of the entire human race lies in the hands of children. This was an important collaboration.

In February 2011, *Tomorrow's Children: Pete Seeger With The Rivertown Kids & Friends* received a Grammy Award for 'Best Children's Album' of 2010. The Recording Academy in Los Angeles sent out a special winner's certificate, which was presented to the children at a community-wide celebration.

Over time, the Rivertown Kids shared the stage with many great musicians, including, Odetta, Richie Havens, Dave Amram, Jeff Tweedy of Wilco, and Tom Paxton. In 2011, they provided the chorus behind Pete's spoken word on the Bob Dylan song 'Forever Young' for the album *Chimes Of Freedom: The Songs Of Bob Dylan Honoring 50 Years Of Amnesty International*. Also with Pete, they lent their voices to 'Which Side Are You On?' for Ani DiFranco's 2012 album of the same title.

More important than these accomplishments, these young students discovered how to use their collective voice to write and perform songs about issues that were important to them.

DAN EINBENDER *I was a red diaper baby. My mother, in particular, was involved with the Women's Strike for Peace. I was one of those kids that wasn't allowed to drink milk because it had Strontium-90 in it. The first time I left home on my own, I went to a summer camp on Lake Tiorati, and Pete was a regular visitor. In those days, it was the blacklist, and there was no place Pete could really get commercial work, so he would come to summer camps all up and down the valley. I remember expressing curiosity about this big guitar, and at seven years old, he put it in my hands, and he taught me to play 'Hey Lolli Lolli Lolli' with two very simple, short-form chords. I've taught that same lesson now to hundreds of kids in camps that I've worked at.*

Throughout my life, I wrote Pete letters, and he always answered. Years later, when I met him in the flesh again, I thought I was talking to someone who knew me. I didn't realize that he answered every letter that ever came to him. Toward the end of his life, one of the greatest crosses he had to bear was a promise he had made to himself to answer every piece of mail personally.

When I finally did meet him, I was living in New York City, and I went to a concert around the corner where he was going to play. I got there and watched in shock as he set up chairs for the audience. I'd paid money to see him, and there he was, setting up my chair. At the concert, Pete invited everybody to join him at a festival up in Beacon—a corn festival, which was that Sunday. I took the train up there and walked up to him and said, 'Pete, is there anything I can do to help you?' And I just caught him at a really dark moment. He turned around, and with very sad eyes said, 'I don't know where to begin.'

A couple of weeks later, I left the city and began crewing on the Woody Guthrie boat, and a couple months later, I was cooking on the Clearwater. So Pete led by a kind of example that few souls in history who can match—the things that he's done, and the things that he's chosen not to do.

In 2007, I was working for Clearwater, and my main job was to bring environmental education programming into the Beacon school system. Pete had on his agenda at the time starting a multiracial kid's chorus in town. We went to the schools and did assembly programs, and we invited the kids out to join us in the streets of Beacon on the second Saturday of the month down on the east end of Main Street, where Pete would drive down with his little electric pickup truck. We'd hook up a PA system to it, and he'd lead a singalong. But the kids just didn't come out. We kept on getting more and more adults.

But as part of my job, every class came down to the river to do an introductory program, and one class blew my mind because they loved to sing. I've been singing with kids all my life, and I've never seen a group so homogeneously bent on singing together. They heard a couple of the river songs and learned them really fast. I got invited into their classroom again and again, and finally I said, 'You know what? I'm gonna bring Pete in, because he's gonna love this—here is our chorus, ready-made!'

They were a perfect storm, all races, all fourth-graders. Pete started coming in and telling them stories. The kids got the notion to write their own songs, and Pete encouraged them. The next thing we knew, we were singing with him at concerts.

David Bernz had produced an album for Pete that won a Grammy for 'Best Folk Album' of 2008. In 2009, he calls David, and he says, 'There's a couple of songs I think should be on that album.' And David said, 'Pete, the album won a Grammy, it's already out there, it's too late to put more songs on it.' And Pete says, 'Well, can we record them somewhere?' So David told Pete that we could record them with the kids.

I ran into a local musician, a world-class musician named Jeff Haynes and told him about what we were thinking, and he says, 'Well I got a studio in my garage. You guys can use it for free.' The next thing we knew, we were all in Jeff's studio, and one tune led to another, and before we knew it, we were recording *an entire album for Pete's record company, Appleseed Recordings. We worked our hearts out on it because we did it for Pete. We knew that it was something that was important for him, and the kids adored him, and they would have done anything for him. And they did. We all worked together and made that CD happen, and it was nominated for a Grammy, and it won!*

THE FESTIVALS

Over the decades, there developed in and around Beacon a carousel of festivals and celebrations that mark the seasons. People set their calendars by them and have come to expect them, even to count on them. Many were started or inspired by Pete and Toshi, and others were celebrations that they regularly attended and participated in.

In January each year, the Martin Luther King Day celebration takes place at the Springfield Baptist Church. Pete and other local folk musicians often attended, and later on, Pete brought the Rivertown Kids there to sing with him.

In June, thousands attend the Beacon Sloop Club Strawberry Fest at the riverfront park, where Pete's favorite shortbread recipe is baked by volunteers and then covered with fresh local strawberries and whipped cream made on the spot. Toshi Seeger was often the one ladling out the strawberries, and my son Jesse has volunteered there for many years, helping at the cash box, or cutting the strawberries, or as a general trouble-shooter, which he is very good at.

A week later, Clearwater's Great Hudson River Revival would take place at Croton Point Park in nearby Westchester County. The 'Revival' was a multi-stage festival featuring nationally known performers together with regional and ethnic musicians. It was one of the first festivals in the country to be fully disabled-accessible, and to have sign-language interpreters, and to conduct three-pail separated waste recycling. A festival of that size was only possible due to a dedicated group of volunteers and site crew, and it became the annual community gathering for all those involved with Clearwater and with reviving the Hudson River.

Each August, a corn festival occupies a smaller area of the Beacon waterfront, where a large metal basket on a lever lowers local corn into a cauldron of boiling water while performers sing on a small makeshift stage nearby. Toshi Seeger was often alongside with a generous pot of chili or 'stone soup.'

Each October, the *Clearwater* would dock in Beacon with a harvest of pumpkins on deck in a big wooden crate. This was part of the pumpkin festival, which took place up and down the whole river. *Clearwater* would sail into a town, unload the pumpkins, hold a small festival, and then move on to the next town. Everyone driving on nearby Route 9 could see the boat carrying cargo in the same manner as would have been done in the 1700s. These days, the pumpkins are delivered over land, but the festival remains much the same.

Then, in December, the Beacon Sloop Club has a 'Holiday Sing,' a festive gathering inside the clubhouse itself. Volunteers put up decorations and lights and people bring down sweets to share, and everyone sings holiday songs led by different guest vocalists. Diverse performers such as gospel singers Charlene Stout and Gretchen Reed and the chorus from the Bruderhoff commune have participated, along with local singers and members of the Hudson River Sloop Singers and the Walkabout Clearwater Chorus.

Pete would sing at most of these events, and his appearances often proved to be the high point. When he took the stage, everyone instinctively knew to gather round and sing with him, unabashedly—and, in harmony, if possible.

You never knew who might show up at some of these festivals. Some very interesting people came to the area to visit Pete and Toshi. I remember meeting a very old John Handcox at a Strawberry Festival. John was a labor activist from the 1930s sharecroppers movement and is credited with having written the verses to the civil rights anthem 'We Shall Not Be Moved.' Another time, I looked up and there was Tommy Sands from Ireland. He joined Pete onstage, and they sang for almost an hour. Yet another time, I saw Pete walking with someone whose face looked familiar, and then realized it was Daniel Ortega, the president of Nicaragua.

In between these events were the regular monthly meetings of the Beacon Sloop Club itself, a potluck dinner followed by a meeting and then an open song circle. Pete and Toshi attended almost every meeting if they were in town, and Pete often came early to set the fires and stayed late to clean up and participate in the song circle. He continued doing this right into his nineties.

There is no doubt the activities of Pete and Toshi and the Beacon Sloop Club were an important cultural contribution to the region. But I also believe that bringing so many people together helped reduce tensions between the different religious and ethnic communities living in the area.

Over the past few decades, Beacon has transformed into a musical and cultural mecca. The vacant factory buildings and boarded storefronts have given way to art galleries, restaurants, boutiques, coffee shops, and music venues. Hotels and bed-and-breakfast facilities house weekend tourists from Brooklyn and other parts of New York City and beyond. The east end of Main Street, once so vacant that the city was able to rent it out to a Hollywood studio for Paul Newman's last film, *Nobody's Fool*, is now the focal point for visitors and locals alike as they enjoy views of Mount Beacon, and drink craft beers, and attend concerts at the Howland Cultural Center or the Towne Crier Café. There's a vibrant scene of local musicians and song-writers who play at open-mics and bars and restaurants. The city now sponsors 'Second Saturday,' when there are gallery openings and other events that keep the streets crowded well into the evening. The old harsh neon lighting poles have been replaced with colonial-style streetlamps, and presenters vie with each other for space on public bulletin boards to announce their latest happenings. Real-estate prices have risen along with these changes, but so far at least, Beacon's different populations are still here.

Many have credited Beacon's resurgence with the decision of the Dia Art Foundation to establish a museum at the old Nabisco factory site, or the investments made by certain real-estate developers who purchased and restored some of the older buildings on Main Street. True, Dia Beacon is currently the largest contemporary art museum in the country and features the works of such luminaries as Andy Warhol, Richard Serra, and Dan Flavin. It's also true that real-estate investment did improve the commercial center of the city.

But there had to first be a fertile ground for such investments to have taken place. I have always believed that Beacon's collective soil was enriched by the many festivals and events that Pete and Toshi created and participated in over the years. They helped bring the community together. And, like the allegorical evil giant in Pete's famous children's story 'Abyoyo,' our differences were largely tamed through good food and music.

JOSIAH LONGO *Pete was such a great inspiration to me. I knew Pete all my life for being famous for the things that he does. But when I moved around this area, I started playing at some of the little festivals that Pete did, like the strawberry festival and the pumpkin festival, and the any-other-vegetable-you-can-think-of festival.*

At the time, we were Gandolf Murphy & The Slambovian Circus Of Dreams, a band that no one knew to hire because they couldn't figure out what we were. But Pete always let us do the festivals, and he would say things on the side like, 'Make sure you do singalongs, include other people.' His words like that were very challenging and coincided with the ghost of my father, who always said that music should be people singing along. I grew up in the 60s with The Beatles and learned how to be a very good poser, but I think Pete saw through that and encouraged me toward the real feeling of it all.

Being around Pete made us aware of all the environmental issues and it inspired the consciousness of taking care of Mother Earth. It inspired a lot of songs that the Circus did after we knew Pete. Once you're in, and you can feel the bloodstream of the mother, you really can never get away from trying to take care of her and being grateful for all you get from her. And I think Pete felt that in a very natural way.

I think Pete felt that everybody was family. He engaged everybody to try to be the best they could with singing, and I think that spun off into other parts of his life. If you were around Pete and you suggested doing something, you were doing it within the next thirty seconds at the table with him. So, he made me very aware to not put things off—to just do it right then with what you have.

Something Pete said one time to my wife Tink and myself—we had a very long conversation with him about his ancestry and everything else that happened in the whole universe, and at the end of this very long conversation, Tink said to him, 'So, Pete, what would be your one piece of advice that would be how we should act from this point on?' And Pete said to us, 'You know, every moment is a new opportunity to make everything better. And if you use the moment, you can not only change the future, but you can even change the past if you use that moment well.'

He talked about the eternal present in that moment, and I had just written a song called 'The Eternal Present,' so I was way into having it saturated with the wisdom that Pete insinuated. Because there's always a grid in what Pete says. He can say it in the simplest way, but you feel a logos in it.

Pete was an amazing person. I think he's just an example. You've got to watch out for Pete-worship, or Jesus-worship, or any of the things we always worship. It's more about becoming. So I really hope to become more like a Pete, and then go on to be a better Josiah from it.

THE SONG CIRCLE

One of the things Pete enjoyed most about the Beacon Sloop Club meetings was the song circle at the end. And the more democratic they became, the happier he got.

When we first started singing in the sloop club after our meetings, it was usually a short song-fest. A few people with guitars or banjos sat in a small circle, and a few others sat in front of them, thinking themselves the audience. However, about six years ago, in the summertime, we held our meeting outside, because it was so warm. At the end of the meeting, we were all sitting in a great big elongated irregular circle, and I said, 'Why don't we just sit here and go around the circle?'

All sorts of people who never thought of themselves as singers, but they knew songs, would sing a favorite song, and those of us who had instruments would find what key and start an accompaniment. It was so democratic and so much fun, and really a better song fest that we did the same thing the next month. And when cold weather came, we moved indoors, and we made as big a circle as we could. The inner part of the circle might be anywhere from twelve to twenty feet across, but now it's gotten so crowded we can't always find that much room. But the same principle is there, and whoever is the master of ceremonies or mistress of ceremonies purposely goes from one side of the circle to the other so that no one part of the circle is thought of as 'the center.'

This has resulted in a kind of a song circle which really works! There'll be anywhere from forty to eighty people there, and the MC will take the mic off to the left-hand side and say, 'We haven't heard from you over here yet. Who wants to sing?' Or she might say, 'We have had too many older people sing,' and a younger person will take the mic over on the right-hand side. Or somebody we know is a very good song leader, and the microphone is put right in front of them: 'Your turn now!'

I usually leave after an hour or two, but others stay for three hours or even four hours. And, a couple of months ago, I am told it was five hours. It started at 8:30 and it was after one o'clock in the morning before it stopped.

They are going to have a song circle down in the Meadowlands in New Jersey, near the town of Rutherford, about ten miles south of George

Washington Bridge. During the Depression, the Meadowlands were just big garbage dumps, and there were shacks on top of them where people lived and made their living going through the garbage and seeing if there was something they could sell or use. But in the seventy years since then, they added dirt to some of the swampy areas and put in McMansions. There's now only fifteen percent of the Meadowlands which has not been developed in some way. But a bunch of people in Rutherford wanted to see that those last fifteen percent are not developed. And they had a fundraiser in the Williams Carlos Williams theater, named after the famous poet, and we filled it in November. We got committees going there, and we are pretty sure now that at least fifteen percent of the Meadowlands will be saved from the developers. However, I found out they also had in the front of the theater what had once been a lobby with a flat floor about thirty by forty feet in size. That's about the size of the sloop club, and I said, 'You can have a song circle here,' and sometime next spring they're planning to have a monthly song circle there. They want to organize it right. They are going to contact singers all around, and some people from Beacon might go down and join them.

Meanwhile, we did a fundraiser in Greenwich Village for a very unusual church, or at least they have a very unusual pastor. Down at St. John's Lutheran Church on Christopher Street, the pastor took out the center seats, an area of twenty by twenty-five feet in size. The solid pews are still there on the right and left and in the back. On Thursday nights, they have yoga sessions with everybody sitting cross-legged on the floor, and they also have special programs for poetry, and for children. It's one more example of a church saying, 'Before our church goes out of business, we are going to try and make it a community arts center.' And the minister there is now planning to have a monthly song circle and use people like me and others to go around the circle and see what kind of singing we can get going.

It is an interesting phenomenon. I certainly didn't foresee it myself. All I know is that people who like to sing are getting out and leading songs, and nobody is telling them no. Somebody somewhere says, 'Can you sing a song that maybe we can join in on?' It's happening all over the country now.

• • •

THE VIGIL

At the height of the Iraq war, Chris Ruhe and some others from Beacon started a weekly peace vigil in the nearby town of Wappingers Falls on a busy corner right in the heart of the shopping strip. Chris was a member of the Bahá'í faith and believed deeply in non-violence.

Every Saturday afternoon for a few hours, Chris and others stood holding signs against the war and asking people to honk for peace. The corner was on one of the busiest intersections in the area, with thousands of cars whizzing by on their way to and from the shopping malls and box stores up and down Route 9. Many cars did honk in agreement, although occasionally a car with a different opinion would pass by with a few choice words. After a while, they got permission from the shopping mall that owned that little corner to put a peace pole there which remains today to mark the spot.

Pete came to that vigil almost every weekend, through the hot months and the cold, standing with a quiet dignity and holding up a sign. Other local activists such as Connie Hogarth would also come, and occasionally there would be singing. Once, a soldier from the war joined us.

One Saturday, a group of counter-protesters set up across the road on the northbound side of Route 9. They called themselves the American Eagles, and they began coming every week to counter-protest the vigil—and, in their view, to support the war effort and the soldiers. Although their numbers were never as large as ours, they had a tactic for making themselves look big by using long banners planted with poles to take up lots of physical space. I don't think anyone ever honked for war though, and I never heard any singing over there.

Right around this time, Pete was scheduled to take part in a program at the Howland Cultural Center on the east end of Main Street in Beacon. The Howland Center is a local gem built in the 1870s by the Civil War general Joseph Howland and designed by his famous architect brother-in-law, Richard Morris Hunt. For many years, a lovely woman named Florence Northcut, with the help of others, had been putting on quality music programs and art exhibits for the community there. On this particular day, there was going to be a prominent speaker followed by songs of peace with Pete Seeger and friends. The American Eagles decided to come there to protest. They set up across the street with banners that read 'PETE SEEGER IS A COMMUNIST AND A TRAITOR' and stood there through the whole program.

As it turned out, a bad cold kept Pete in bed that afternoon, but they protested him anyway while the rest of us sang.

• • •

Pete read the following portion of the Declaration Of Independence at Beacon's Fourth Of July Celebration. Notwithstanding his detractors, Pete was, in his own way, very patriotic. But one could imagine that, as he read this, he may have been reminding his detractors that even the founding fathers understood that there comes a time when revolution is necessary.

We hold these truths to be self-evident, that all men are created equal, that they are endowed by their Creator with certain unalienable rights, that among these are life, liberty, and the pursuit of happiness.

That to secure these rights, governments are instituted among men, deriving their just powers from the consent of the governed,

That whenever any form of government becomes destructive of these ends, it is the right of the people to alter or to abolish it, and to institute new government, laying its foundation on such principles and organizing its powers in such form, as to them shall seem most likely to effect their safety and happiness.

THE RIVER POOL AT BEACON

The city of Beacon is beautifully situated, geographically speaking, between the wooded climbs of Mount Beacon and the majestic Hudson River. But for all the natural beauty that abounds there, it lacks one thing: decent public places to swim. For whatever reason, there are no swimming lakes, and until very recently, no public swimming pool.

Right around 1999, Pete had an idea. Now that the Hudson was clean enough to swim in again, why not have a river pool—a floating swimming pool in the river itself, with sides and a bottom like other swimming pools, but porous so the river water could flow through?

Alan Zollner and other members of the Beacon Sloop Club formed a committee and got to work. Money was raised with sponsored swims across the river from the city of Newburgh. They hired a designer and built a prototype that could be used as a children's pool and got permission from the city to place it off the riverfront park.

The children's river pool officially opened to the public on July 10, 2008, with a poolside ceremony of speakers and music. Pete was there along with the architect, Meta Brunzema, who designed the pool, and the activist singers Pat Humphries and Sandy Opatow, who sing together as Emma's Revolution, were also in town for the occasion. These are some of Pete's remarks that day:

Friends, this is really a wonderful day. This river-pool idea has been around for eight or ten years. Actually, a hundred years ago, they had river pools in New York City made of wood. They were about the size of tennis courts and had walls around them and changing rooms. Men and women swam on alternate days. You can read about it in the book by Jacob Reese called *The Battle For The Slums*. He was pushing, as a lot of good people were, to get more recreation for people. They'd get off the boat at Ellis Island, and they were jammed in these horribly crowded little apartments. And so in the summertime, as soon as you could swim, they had about thirty floating swimming pools there.

And a few people in New York said, 'Someday, if the river is cleaned up, we should have floating swimming pools again.' And that's why I met Meta Brunzema. She was born in Sweden and raised in Canada but is an architect in New York. And she found that we were interested in the idea of floating swimming pools in the river. You'd actually swim in the river water. The pool would go up and down with the tide, but it would be anchored in such a way it wouldn't float away even when a high wind came along. And it took us literally about eight years before we got one built. We had to raise a lot more money than we thought we'd have to.

But we invited many of you here today specifically to look and see how the river pool works. This is a children's pool, only twenty-five feet in diameter and less than two feet deep, and small children can safely swim in it. And if all goes well, we hope that in a few years, we'll have an adult pool, which will be more like four and a half feet deep. There'll be a lifeguard there of course. You'll learn more about the details today.

Kingston has a beach, and I think they're going to want to have a children's pool up there. They can tell the family, 'Put your two- and three-

and four-year-olds in the floating pool. There'll be a special lifeguard that has nothing to do but watch them, and you can sit on the bank or sit on the perimeter.' There's a bench running around the edge.

So, we think that many beaches are going to want to get river pools like this.

• • •

PAT HUMPHRIES *I grew up in northeastern Ohio, along the Cuyahoga River, so I've always had a great fondness for rivers.*

I first learned about Pete's music in elementary school because I ordered a record of his kids' songs from the Arrow Book Club. When I was twelve years old, Pete came to the Cuyahoga River Valley to talk about this project that he had going on the Hudson to clean up the river. The Cuyahoga River was in really bad shape at that time. I think that's when I became aware of how Pete's music was changing the world. Somewhere I still have the article that I cut out of the Cleveland paper.

That was just a couple of years after the killings at Kent State, and that's when I really started getting, by way of Neil Young's song 'Ohio,' the connection between music and justice. So reading this article on the heels of that awakening opened my eyes and broadened the scope of what I began to understand about how music really was changing the world, because it was changing me.

Years later, I was living in Cambridge, Massachusetts, and heard about the 'Pumpkin Sail,' and I was invited down to crew on the Clearwater during that week. I came on board in October of 1987, and I was hooked! Two weeks later, I moved to the Hudson Valley, and I worked on the boat throughout the winter doing maintenance, and then sailed as an intern for a couple of months, and worked on Clearwater's on-land program for about six years.

I have so many fond memories of singing and playing music on the boat and along the banks of the river, and swimming in the river. And then working at the Fieldston camp for fourteen years and bringing the kids up to Beacon to pull water chestnuts out of the river. And, of course, coming up to the Strawberry Festival and the Corn Festival, and all the different events here along the river.

SANDY OPATOW *I was raised in Philadelphia. Although there was a river there, we were more pool kids, so I've been enjoying being out here at Beacon Park* *for this dedication of the Riverpool. As we were driving up, Pat was telling me how Pete had this idea about ten years ago, and I thought, If people ever wonder whether one person can make a difference, you can just think of Pete, and having the idea of putting a sloop boat back on the river. And now that has become this long-standing tradition with Clearwater and evolved into all these things including the music festivals. And then here again, with this idea of bringing back river pools. And now you have it.*

TOSHI'S SPEECH

Over the years, Pete said repeatedly that he would never have accomplished what he did without Toshi to help put his many far-fetched ideas into action. While Toshi relished her role as Pete's wife and partner, there were times when it was very hard. There were years when Pete was away most of the time while she was left alone up on the hill to care for the children, carrying buckets of water from the spring before they got the well pump. There were the political attacks, the endless mail, and all the organizing work for the festivals and the sloop club—and, later on, defending Pete from the myriad of requests for appearances and interviews and endorsements. The house seemed an endless stream of visitors, journalists, musicians, and volunteers, all of whom had to be hosted or fed or housed or dealt with in some manner. There was so much food made that some people began to say, 'Toshi doesn't know how to cook for less than twenty.'

Toshi was also a talented artist and producer in her own right, a professional filmmaker, and an accomplished potter. But, to a large extent, she put her own artistic work on hold to be Pete Seeger's wife. All of this prompted Toshi to quip on numerous occasions, 'If only Peter chased women instead of causes, I'd have a reason to leave him.'

Toshi had a wry sense of humor. Someone once related the story of a female reporter who had come to the house to interview Toshi about her life. They spent the afternoon talking, and the reporter dutifully wrote down notes. Then Pete showed up, sat down, and began regaling her with stories, as was his habit. After a while, Toshi leaned over to Pete and said, 'Did you notice she stopped writing?'

The biting humor could be hilarious, but was sometimes a not-so-veiled response to the fact that her life as Pete's wife was very hard work. Not everyone appreciated or understood that. One afternoon while I was over at the house, I spied a daunting pile of correspondence and other papers on the dining table and instinctively took a picture of it. When I showed it to Toshi, she smiled and asked me to make multiple copies to send to her relatives, 'so they'll finally understand.'

Toshi was also a very capable business manager who, along with Harold Leventhal, took care of Pete's books and records and appearances and copyrights. Even though she and Pete were united in their political views, it couldn't have been easy seeing so many royalties being given away to worthy causes, often in other parts of the globe.

Toshi and Pete loved each other deeply, and their marriage was a true partnership. She showed it in many little ways, from making sure he had what he needed when he left the house to combing his hair before he went onstage. But, more than that, she took on the arduous task of organizing so many of Pete's projects down to the minute details.

In 1981, the writer David Dunaway completed a biography of Pete. It was a fairly accurate portrayal, but Pete objected to parts of it, so Dunaway agreed to a revision. When he came to Beacon to do research, I was tasked with getting some people to sit down with him to tell him about Pete and Toshi's involvement here in the Hudson Valley.

We all sat and talked for about an hour as Mr. Dunaway took down notes. Then, as I was walking down the stairs to leave, I turned and said to Mr. Dunaway, as if to put an exclamation point on the conversation, 'You know, Pete might have a broad idea to hold a festival, but Toshi is one of the only people who could tell you just how many rolls of toilet paper ten thousand people will use over two days.' Dunaway didn't even have his notebook open, but somehow, that was the only statement of mine he quoted in the new edition.

Sometime in the 1990s, there was an event held in the town of Garrison to honor Pete and Toshi. This was unusual because the honors usually went to Pete alone. Even more unusual, both Pete and Toshi were slated to speak. Toshi was a fairly private person, and up to that point, I don't think I had ever seen her speak into a microphone. She was scheduled to go first and introduce her husband. Summoning all the irony and wit and work that had shaped her life into one concise statement, she brought the house down.

Almost verbatim, she said:

Hi. My name is Toshi Seeger. Most people have a job where they work eight hours a day, five days a week, forty-eight weeks a year. For the past fifty years, I have had the same job, only my job is twenty-four hours a day, seven days a week, and fifty-two weeks a year.

So, I now give to you Pete Seeger. You know who he is. He's the guy who goes around the country with a banjo singing about worker's rights and women's rights and the eight-hour day.

And then she walked off with a smile.

• • •

Connie Hogarth was a tireless activist who always found the right side—the human side—of an issue. Her eyes had the sparkle of someone who could see over to the other side of the mountain where a better world exists, even while knowing we are only partway up the path.

Connie founded the Westchester People's Action Coalition (WESPAC), which has become a national model for such organizations, and was honored by the creation of the Connie Hogarth School Of Social Justice at Manhattanville College in Purchase, New York. At age ninety-two, she spoke about her relationship with Pete and Toshi.

CONNIE HOGARTH *For seventy years, Pete and Toshi have been part of my life. First, when I joined with my mother for a left-wing group in Newburgh, New York, digging onions and picking apples when farmers were at war, and Pete was there singing. Next was my first vote for Henry Wallace. Pete was touring and supporting Wallace in that presidential election. He didn't win, but that was a seminal period politically for a lot of us. Then in 1974 when we started WESPAC, I went to the 57th Street office of Harold Leventhal to arrange some fundraising concerts with Pete and with Don McLean, and we have been comrades ever since.*

My first husband Burne and I were at the first gathering to raise money to build the Clearwater at the Saunders Farm in Garrison. Then, when WESPAC started to have annual picnics, Pete and Toshi were there almost every year. The second year, Pete brought a kid with a ponytail to sing for this kid's first time. It happened to be Arlo Guthrie.

In 1984, Pete supported me in opposing the Staten Island home porting of nukes, and we managed to pass it. Some objected, but we kept saying, 'Think globally, act locally,' and so Clearwater supported that effort. Pete and Toshi also sat in with us at the Hudson Institute in Peekskill against the Indian Point nuclear power plant. There were only maybe four or five of us. We didn't get arrested, but we made our point.

In 1988, Pete reluctantly joined me for one of the board meetings of Jesse Jackson's rainbow Coalition in Washington DC, but he was glad he did. He met Jesse and the whole gang of people trying to make some inroads.

In 1990, we gave the WESPAC award to Toshi and Pete. This was significant, and I think Pete was happy to accept because it was the first time Toshi had been honored with him. She agreed, very reluctantly, but it was a wonderful event.

In 1998, my husband Art and I moved to Beacon, and we spent time with Pete and Toshi at a number of peace rallies in New York. But very notable for all of us were the two years that Pete, Toshi, Art, and myself, and their grandson Tao, flew together to Fort Benning, Georgia, for the School of America's annual event in mid-December to honor and celebrate those who had been missing in Central America, and Oscar Romero, the treasured archbishop who was killed.

Every birthday since we've been in Beacon, we have shared with Toshi and Pete, and my special birthday cake was an annual treat for both of them. Pete had a love for incredible amounts of ice cream, as did Art, and they had a great time together. And when Art was here in our house, in a hospital bed overlooking the river, Pete came every week to sing for him, and Toshi sat holding Art's hand often until he died in November of 2010.

So, Pete and Toshi were truly our best friends. I know they had best friends all over the world, but for us personally, they were our best friends.

I think he would hate to hear it, but in many ways, Pete was a unique human being. He represented a kind of simplicity and complexity and richness and caring that we desperately need, and all his work, his brilliance, his talent, his music, hopefully will have ongoing significance for generations to come.

• • •

Michael D'Antuono relocated to Beacon around 2013. After a stint as a commercial artist, he left the corporate world to do portraits, but he was soon compelled to create political art. He became a true people's artist, bringing his paintings to where they were most useful. His plan to display a painting of President Obama in a crucifix position in New York's Central Park found him defending himself on Fox News, and his paintings regarding police violence were seen on posters and billboards in Ferguson, Missouri, after the shooting of Michael Brown. His work can be found at artandresponse.com. When he was asked to do a portrait of Pete for local display, I thought it might smooth the way if Pete understood who Michael was, so I drove him up to Pete's cabin for a visit.

MICHAEL D'ANTUONO *Phil Ciganer, owner of the Towne Crier Café in Beacon, asked me to do a painting of Pete for his performance space. At that point, I had stopped doing paintings of musicians and was doing all the activist art, but I started looking up Pete and I thought, Oh, yeah, I really should do a painting of him. The whole time I was working on the painting, I was listening to his music, and listening to stories about him and I was thinking, What I have been painting about the last few years, this guy's been singing about since before I was born.*

Pete just wanted to be a regular guy in town and didn't like adoration, so there was concern that possibly he'd be upset to see a big painting glamorizing him in town. So a friend took me up to his house.

It was amazing because it's exactly what you would expect of where Pete Seeger would live, with the maple trees and the view of the Hudson and the cabin. He was very gracious and told me stories of when he was a young guy, and he would do drawings. He would travel around and do a drawing of somebody's house and knock on their door and say, 'Here, I did a drawing of your house. Would you like this? I'll give it to you and maybe you'll give me some food or something.' And people did. One time, people gave him a chicken. Pete said, 'The thing I learned from that is you got to boil the chicken before you try to pluck it.' Pete was ninety-four at the time, and we had to leave because he was going to go chop wood.

We decided to make posters of the painting and sell them and give some of the proceeds to the Beacon Sloop Club and the Clearwater. I showed Pete a print to review. Pete wasn't concerned about his likeness at all, but he was very concerned about the height of the mountain. He said, 'I know that mountain. That's a thousand feet, you got it two thousand feet.'

I said, 'Okay, I could change that for the posters.'

He said, 'And the train should go around here. There's a train there.'

'I'll put a train in, Pete.'
Then I said to him, 'Pete you know, you're kind of changing my art a lot. What if I changed your songs, like, If I had a wrench...'
Well, he laughed, thank God!

JACOB BERNZ

I am fortunate to have two kind and talented sons, Jesse who excels at computer programming, and Jacob who excels at music and songwriting. Both knew Pete well as they grew up. Pete inspired many young people, but I share the story of Jacob as emblematic.

Being my son on the paternal side and the grandson of the poet Walter Lowenfels on his mother's side, Jacob seemed destined for songwriting, picking up a guitar as soon as he was able and absorbing influences from many places. Pete and other Clearwater friends were regular visitors at the house, and music parties, jams, and river festivals shaped his formative years.

Jacob attended the progressive Randolph School run by his mentor, Eric Tomlins, and a staff of dedicated teachers. But of all his mentors, Pete was perhaps the most influential, taking an early interest in Jacob, sharing his knowledge, and encouraging him to sing. Pete's early favorite was to hear Jacob sing 'Summertime,' and he liked how Jacob could draw out the longer notes.

Jacob started writing his own songs at age ten with help from his teachers at Randolph, and he began listening to singers and songwriters such as Woody Guthrie, Bob Dylan, Joan Baez, John Prine, Townes Van Zandt, Guy Clarke, and, of course, Pete. Before long, he was also gleaning ideas from the work of modern writers like Nick Drake, Josh Ritter, and The Milk Carton Kids.

In 2009, at age seventeen, Jacob and Walker Rumph, the son of Clearwater's director at the time, formed the Something To Say Café. Using the Beacon Sloop Club as a venue, they presented a monthly coffeehouse with a performance from a guest musician followed by a youth open mic. Jacob was also one of the original members of The Power of Song, a group of young singers associated with the Clearwater, bringing music and an environmental message around the Hudson Valley. Pete would often attend rehearsals or sing with them onstage.

In his late teens, Jacob began to record and perform by himself. He was chosen as a finalist in an open-mic contest at the Towne Crier Café, and he began relationships with talented local musicians such as percussionist Jeff Haynes, drummer Lee Falco, and the multi-talented Andy Stack, often including them in his performances. Jacob also occasionally likes to sing and play with his father, which is a special pleasure.

Most importantly, since his teens, Jacob has been pouring out a steady stream of original songs. He seems to have created a genre all his own, synthesizing the new and the old. He writes freely, with little self-editing until later on when it's needed, which leads to creative word combinations and unique phrasing. The songs are personal, poetic, and in his own way socially conscious. In his collection are songs about the Hudson River, about 9/11, about homeless people, about life and love, about challenges and trials and hopes, and about old farms and abandoned factories. The sheer volume of these songs is impressive. There are easily over a thousand, but we don't really know.

Now, at age thirty-two, Jacob remains prolific and is currently working on his sixth album of original material. His parents are very proud of him, and we know that for much of it, we have Pete to thank.

In October of 2013, Jacob and I opened a stringed-instrument shop in Beacon called Jake's Main Street Music. Pete visited the shop and was nice enough to call it 'the best instrument store in the Hudson Valley.' One day in November, Pete showed up in his typical coat and knitted hat and sat down, looking winded. He said he had just walked four blocks but had gotten out of breath.

It was right around that time that he invited Jacob to have dinner with him at the Towne Crier Café. Jacob thought he was going to be attending some sort of meeting, but when he got back, he said that it was just him and Pete. They sat and ate and talked, and I think Pete was happy to share the time with someone who had no agenda, no demands. I don't know what their exact conversation was about, and Jacob didn't know that it would be his last dinner with Pete.

CHAPTER 16 THE LAST HURRAH

THE WEAVERS AT 65

The story of *The Weavers At 65* begins with the Towne Crier Café at forty. The Towne Crier is a music venue owned and run by Phil Ciganer. It first opened its doors in 1972 in the little hamlet of Beekmanville, amid the trees and winding roads of Dutchess County, New York, and is now the longest-running venue of its kind.

Since its inception, the Crier featured a rich mix of acoustic, roots, and ethnic music at a time when many other clubs didn't. The roster of performers appearing there through the years is a veritable who's who of well-respected musicians from Tom Waits to Judy Collins and too many others to list here.

After several years on Beekman Road, Phil moved the café to a slightly larger venue in Pawling, New York, where it remained until 2012. But upon celebrating the forty-year mark, Phil realized he had to either retire or go bigger. That's when some people suggested that he come to Beacon.

The new Towne Crier Café opened in October 2013, the very same month that my son and I opened Main Street Music just a few doors down. Their first event was a free public introductory concert with The Slambovian Circus of Dreams, a creative and raucous band that can perhaps best be described as folk music on steroids. Opening night was a bit of a madhouse, but over the next few weeks, the club began to settle into its new routine.

Just as the new Town Crier was being completed, I suggested to Phil that we have an event to honor The Weavers at their sixty-five-year mark. The Weavers' first concert had been at a fundraiser for the *People's Songs Bulletin* right around Thanksgiving in 1948, so on November 17, 2013, we held 'The Weavers At 65' at the brand-new Towne Crier Café. Tom Chapin came with his top-notch musician friends Michael Mark and John Cobert; I enlisted my group, Work o' The Weavers, to recreate some of the original Weavers arrangements; and Pete agreed to come down and sing a few songs as well.

The concert had some choice moments, including a live telephone interview with Issachar Miron, the composer of The Weavers' first hit, 'Tzena, Tzena,' and a live phone call with original Weaver Ronnie Gilbert, who sang over the phone all the way from California. But the moment I was looking forward to most was putting Pete's very first five-string banjo back in his hands.

As noted earlier in this book, Pete had broken the neck off his first five-string banjo while hopping off a freight train with Woody Guthrie, and we thought we had relocated it with its neck repaired.

I told the story from the stage and asked the crowd if we shouldn't hand Pete the banjo, and there was a great applause. Pete did come up and sling the old S.S. Stewart across his shoulder and played a few notes on it. But the moment was not what I had expected, because as Pete came onstage, I saw that he held two canes, and Tom Chapin was helping him up. Pete was ninety-four years old, but I had never before seen him needing help to get onstage, so that was the moment I realized that something was happening to my friend Pete.

DAVID AMRAM *In 1948, my mother took me to a 'Henry Wallace For President' rally in Philadelphia, Pennsylvania. Henry Wallace played the guitar and sang, and he was charming and very interesting just to see and listen to. Then, I saw this man come out with this strange instrument. I said to my mother, 'What's that?' And she said, 'That's a banjo!'*

He played, and he was terrific. Then when they finished the rally, the banjo player walked out into the audience and was playing his banjo and hanging out with everybody. I said, 'I got to meet that person!' I was seventeen years old. He was Pete Seeger. And I knew him up until the evening he passed away, when I went with Guy Davis Jr. and Pat Humphries to play at their family's request at a little gathering they had in the hospital. And I knew Toshi all that time as well.

He and Toshi were extraordinary people who showed us how we should try to behave with and for others. Pete saw music as a gateway to a higher level for all people in the world to somehow find a way to be together. And, by singing together, by playing together, and being with people who wanted to be together, regardless of their political persuasion—regardless of where they came from, or who they were deemed to be—he showed us the famous prayer of loving thy neighbor as thyself.

Pete was an inspiration to all of us. He was someone who saw the global beauties of folkloric music and all the kinds of music that stem from the root of that precious tree.

· · ·

R.J. Storm played many roles in Pete's life, from instrument maker to doctor, and most importantly just being his good friend. He is a multi-talented individual who apprenticed with Carlos Arcieri in New York to become one of the best violin makers and restorers in the country. After making a violin for Jason Carter of The Del McCoury Band, R.J. built one of Pete Seeger's touring banjos from a piece of dogwood harvested in the woods near Pete's cabin. R.J. is also a trained acupuncturist and a great many other things.

R.J. STORM *Pete was a good man. Not just by word but in deed. Pete never liked contention. He never liked to see other people lose face. He quietly suffered a lot of things. People made a lot of money off him, people argued over him; a lot of people wanted to be like him. He'd sigh, overlook it, complain to his doctor, and plug along.*

I once said, 'Pete, you'll be gone soon. You want to write a letter to anybody, like the people at the sloop club or something? I'll unveil it in a year or two, if you want.'

He thought that was a neat idea, so he wrote a nice letter, sealed it, gave it to me, and says, 'After I kick the bucket, two years, you show this to everybody and read it.'

I said, 'Okay, I'll put it in my vault.'

Months went by. One day, out of the blue, he just says, 'You got that letter I wrote?'

'Do you mean that letter?'

'Yeah.'

'It's down in my vault.'

'Can you get it?'

'Sure.'

'Bring it on up to the house.'

Pete was on the phone when he asked this. One day, he came in for his regular treatment. I said, 'I got the letter.'

He says, 'No, bring it up to the house.'

'Okay.'

So, he got treated. He went back. I brought the letter up to his house. He picked it up. He held it, held it to himself, then tossed it in the woodstove. Burned it up! I said, 'Okay, I guess they're not ready for it.'

I guess, next to his family, I was really blessed to be probably the closest person to him. I spent a lot of time with him. We'd get stuff to eat. Sometimes we'd work in the shop for hours, and I don't think we'd say three words. He liked making bowls and spoons. He liked my little glue spoon. I think the biggest thing he liked to do was just to make a pile of wood chips. Whittling!

Yeah, whittling, that's what he'd say. 'Whittling.'

THE MARTIN LUTHER KING DAY PARADE

One Monday in early January 2014, Pete's daughter Tinya called, asking if I could go that evening to the Springfield Baptist Church to help people rehearse some songs for Martin Luther King Day because Pete wasn't feeling well enough to do it. Springfield Baptist is an African American church that really connects with its community. Pete had a good relationship with Pastor Ronald Perry and gospel singer Sharlene Stout and others at the church and had attended many of their Martin Luther King Day celebrations.

When I got there, I found about forty people waiting to sing together, and some other local musicians at the front of the room. If memory serves, they included Fred Martin, Lydia Adams Davis, and Fred Gillen Jr.

It turns out that Pete had an idea. Pete thought that people today, and especially younger people, should know what it's like to march and sing for something they believed in, so he had proposed starting off that year's Martin Luther King Day festivities with an early morning civil rights march. The proposed route would start at the church at 9am, head east for a few blocks, then go out to Main Street and head west, and eventually turn off Main and return to the church. Pete envisioned everyone singing together by having song leaders at various points in the march leading the same song simultaneously.

There were particular songs that Pete thought should be sung. Many were drawn from his own experience on the famous march from Selma to Montgomery Alabama back in 1965. They included 'If You Miss Me At The Back Of The Bus,' 'Ain't Gonna Let Nobody Turn Me Round,' 'We Shall Not Be Moved,' 'Oh, Wallace,' 'Ain't Scared Of Your Jail,' 'Everybody Says Freedom,' and 'We Shall Overcome.' Most of the songs were very accessible hymns, but 'Oh, Wallace' was hard for some people, because the verse and chorus are technically in different keys and because the word *'all'* in the chorus spreads out over several notes. There are also some complex vamping parts:

I said I read in the papers (dat dat da da dat)
Just the other day (dat dat da da dat)
That the freedom fighters (dat dat da da dat)
Are on their way (dat dat da da dat)
They're coming by bus (dat dat da da dat)
And airplane too (dat dat da da dat)
They'll even walk (dat dat da da dat)
If you ask them to (dat dat da da dat)

Oh, Wallace
You never can jail us a-a-a-a-a-a-all
Oh, Wallace
You know segregation's bound to fall (dat dat da da dat)
(Da da da da da da dat da da da da dat)

Each Monday evening leading up to Martin Luther King Day, we rehearsed in the back room of the church while Pete stayed home, trying to recuperate enough to come to the march. Meanwhile, Bonnie Champion of the Beacon Sloop Club took on the nuts-and-bolts jobs of sending out press releases and obtaining insurance.

But there were some naysayers who thought the march was not such a good idea. After all, this was not a steamy summer in the Deep South of 1965. Here in the northeast in the dead of winter, trying to march and sing and play instruments outdoors on a frosty fifteen-degree January morning might not be an ideal way to show people how to hold a civil rights march. Many doubted whether it could work, or if people would even come.

But Pete had made a career out of unlikely ideas that somehow worked, like piling into an old Buick to cross the country singing for unions, or building a boat to save a river. And somehow people got behind this new idea. Springfield Baptist Church contacted other churches in the area, and they spread the word to their parishioners. *Clearwater* and the Beacon Sloop Club notified their members. It got into the newspapers and into various newsletters, and people shared it through their email lists and personal contacts.

When the morning of January 20 arrived, so many people showed up that they couldn't fit into the church. They filled the street and overflowed onto nearby Willow Street. Were there a thousand, two thousand? Nobody seemed to know. All we knew was that this was big, and they had all come to march and sing, and so we did.

We quickly realized that singing simultaneously was an impossibility with a crowd of that size, but it didn't matter. Song leaders picked songs from the list wherever they were along the route and led the people around them. Different songs and tempos echoed through the streets and people joined in with whatever was in earshot, and it all worked great. So many people had come that by the time the front of the parade re-approached the church, they had to hold us up because there were still people leaving the church, so we kept on marching and singing in place.

I don't recall ever feeling cold that morning, and no one else complained either. And I remember having a realization as we marched along. I looked around and saw all sorts of people—black, white, Hispanic, Asian, men and women, old and young, all putting aside whatever differences they may have had, marching and singing and harmonizing together—and I couldn't help thinking that this was a microcosm of the world Pete Seeger had worked his whole life to create.

Sadly, Pete did not make it to the march. He tried, and he was in his car on the way down, but he got so sick that they had to turn around and bring him back home. But right after the march, R.J. Storm and some others went up to the house and told Pete that his idea had worked. They showed him pictures of the crowd, and he asked what songs were sung and how many times we had sung them, and as the details were described, Pete began smiling ear to ear. Then, Pete looked up and said, 'But I wasn't there, I wasn't there,' and someone said to him, 'Yes, you were there.'

A few days later, Pete entered the hospital. Many of us came down to say goodbye and thank you, and we sang for him and for each other. I remember John Cohen of The New Lost City Ramblers being there with me. Pete couldn't communicate at that point, but we felt he could hear us. Over the next few days, many others such as Judy Collins and Peter Yarrow came and paid their respects and sang to him.

On Monday, January 27, I thought I'd bring my son Jacob down to say goodbye to his mentor, but at the last minute, Jacob decided he wanted to remember Pete as he was. With the evening suddenly open, I decided to go to a local open mic at the Towne Crier Café to try out a new song.

As a late addition to the list, they put me on last, which was somewhere between 8:30 and 9pm. As I got offstage, my phone rang, and I was told that Pete Seeger had just passed.

CODA
BY DAVID BERNZ

Thank you for reading this book. I hope you've gotten to know Pete or to understand him better through these words. But having read so many good things said about him, we should remember that Pete Seeger, like the rest of us, was human and imperfect. He had his dark moments when he was depressed or angry. He made mistakes and was not ashamed to say so. And he'd be the first to admit he didn't have all the answers. He once said:

I can tell you so many mistakes I've made. I could rattle on for hours of mistakes. I can tell you how not to form a chorus. I tried to start one a few years ago. I can tell you how not to build a dugout canoe. I had a whole batch of people trying to build a dugout canoe. Only after it finally rotted away from my mistakes did I learn how I should have made it. And I would say that I've learned that you cannot start a socialist government without finding a way to have some kind of bill of rights for everybody. Because, in small or big ways, the only thing that will save an organization is freedom of speech, and that wonderful little first amendment that's saved our country for two hundred years now.

Much has happened since Pete left us on January 27, 2014: the election of Donald Trump, increasing divisions within our country, the hatred at Charlottesville, the killing of George Floyd and the summer of protests that followed, the COVID-19 pandemic, the 2020 election, the Capitol riots, the invasion of Ukraine...

I sometimes think it's a good thing that Pete didn't live to witness these things. I've heard some people ask, 'What would Pete say?' or 'What would Pete do?' I certainly do not have the answer. But if we learn anything from Pete, it's that people are not just one thing. We're all a jumble of many things good and bad. Even those we strongly disagree with might have some good qualities that we can come to appreciate, and it's important to keep the lines of communication open. Pete strived to find these areas of commonality—whether it was through food, music, art, sports, carpentry, whatever—so that we would come to see others as people and not just as enemies.

Although his passing preceded our current era of extreme divisions, perhaps Pete was prescient when he wrote one of his later songs. As far as I know, it is not in any songbook, and I can think of no better way of ending this book than to share it with you:

SISTER MOON (WALKING HOME) *Pete Seeger*

Sister moon, we see you through the trees
You're watching us while walking home
Papa Sun, another side of Earth
Making all so green, making all so green
Mother Earth, six billion pairs of feet
Seeking a path, seeking a way
Walking home, walking home,
Walking home, walking home

And on the way, we're harmonizing
As each voice finds, a part to sing
High or low, it's not surprising
How good it sounds when voices ring
Ah yes, sometimes there's tangles,
We all see truth, from different angles
Walking home, walking home
Walking home, walking home...

NOTES & SOURCES

ACKNOWLEDGMENTS

Thanks go to many, many people for making this book possible. First and foremost, I thank my family, my wife Mai, and my children Jacob and Jesse, for their love and support and sage advice, and for giving me the time and space to complete it. Thanks to Jawbone Press and editor Tom Seabrook for their openness to this project, for the time and effort they devoted to making this a better book, and for their patience with me. To my agent, Lloyd Jassin, whose professionalism and top reputation in the literary world precede him, for his belief in this book, and for advice and support throughout, even when I tested his limits. To Larry Richmond of TRO/Essex Music Group for permission to print lyrics, for being a keeper of the flame of folk music, and for being an all-around stand-up guy in the world of music publishing. To Michael Pizzuto and the rest of the folks at Concord Publishing for additional lyrics permissions. To Nora Guthrie and Anna Canoni of Woody Guthrie Publications for use of images and lyrics, and for their friendship. To Arlo Guthrie for his generous writing of a foreword and for all those years with Pete onstage and off. To the Hudson River Sloop Clearwater, Inc. for photographs and for all they have done, and continue doing, to keep the Hudson River clean. To my friend Jim Brown for his advice and assistance, and for his fine films in the field of acoustic music. To Lorre Wyatt for lyrics permissions, for writing so many good songs with Pete, and for many kind words. To Richard Lederer for lyrics permission and for having so much fun with the English language. To Judy Leventhal and Caleb Hellerman for photo permissions and more. To John Fisher, Jean Havens, and Steve Siegelbaum of the Walkabout Clearwater Chorus and to Steve Stanne, Karen Brooks, Travis Jeffrey, and Rick and Donna Nestler of the Hudson River Sloop Singers for photos and advice. To all those who contributed to this book in ways large and small, too numerous to mention, including all who granted permissions, contributed photos, lent their advice, or shared stories about their own experiences with Pete. To Tinya Seeger and Mika Seeger for advice, patience, and permissions. Last and certainly not least, to Pete and Toshi Seeger for their exemplary lives, their inspiration, and for the words and music to so many songs that are now preciously woven into the fabric of our lives.

PERMISSIONS

THE BALLAD OF HARRY BRIDGES
Written by Peter Seeger (BMI) / Lee Hays (BMI) / Millard Lampell (ASCAP). Published by Stormking Music Inc c/o Figs D Music (BMI) / Howard Beach Music Inc c/o Kohaw Music Inc. (ASCAP).

BRING ME LI'L WATER, SILVY
Words and music by Huddie Ledbetter, Pete Seeger, Fred Hellerman, Ronnie Gilbert, and Lee Hays. TRO © 1953 (renewed), 1981 (renewed) Folkways Music Publishers, Inc., New York, NY. International copyright secured. Made in USA. All rights reserved including public performance for profit. Used by permission.

DRILL YE TARRIERS DRILL
Words and music by Oscar Brand. TRO © 1964 (renewed) Ludlow Music, Inc., New York, NY. International copyright secured. Made in USA. All rights reserved including public performance for profit. Used by permission.

THE FIRST SETTLERS
Words and music by Pete Seeger and David Bernz. TRO © 2008 Melody Trails, Inc., New York, NY. International copyright secured. Made in USA. All rights reserved including public performance for profit. Used by permission.

GOD'S COUNTING ON ME, GOD'S COUNTING ON YOU
Words and music by Pete Seeger and Lorre Wyatt. © Roots and Branches Music.

IF IT CAN'T BE REDUCED
Words and music by Pete Seeger and Martin Bourque. TRO © 2008 Melody Trails, Inc., New York, NY. International copyright secured. Made in USA. All rights reserved including public performance for profit. Used by permission.

IN DEAD ERNEST
Written by Peter Seeger (BMI) / Lee Hays (BMI). Published by Sanga Music Inc c/o Figs D Music (BMI).

KISSES SWEETER THAN WINE
Words by Ronnie Gilbert, Lee Hays, Fred Hellerman, and Pete Seeger. Music by Huddie Ledbetter. TRO © 1951 (renewed) 1958 (renewed) Folkways Music Publishers, Inc., New York, NY. International copyright secured. Made in USA. All rights reserved including public performance for profit. Used by permission.

THE MIDNIGHT SPECIAL
New words and music arranged by Ronnie Gilbert, Lee Hays, Fred Hellerman, Pete Seeger, and Huddie Ledbetter. TRO © 1950 (renewed) and 1951 (renewed) Folkways Music Publishers, Inc., New York, NY. International copyright secured. Made in USA. All rights reserved including public performance for profit. Used by permission.